AF530805

Professional Portrait Photography

Mike and Pat Q.

AMPHOTO
American Photographic Book Publishing Co., Inc.
Garden City, New York 11530

Library of Congress Cataloging in Publication Data

Mike Q

Professional portrait photography.

Includes index.

1. Photography—Portraits. I. Pat Q., joint author. II. Title.

TR575.M49 778.9'2 79-15327

ISBN 0-8174-2457-1

Manufactured in the United States of America.

Dedication

To two wonderful people who have spent most of their lives giving knowledge and support to thousands of young photographers seeking to improve and develop their skills. To Frankie and Adolph "Papa" Fassbender who are always there to help and advise, we dedicate this book. Their unbelievable knowledge has enriched everyone they touched.

With everlasting love and devotion.

Pat and Mike Q

Acknowledgement

Special thanks to portrait photographers Louis F. Garcia, Joel Gerard, Ann and Jim Monteith, and Ed Noumair whose work had added "class" to our efforts, and to all the cooperative people who permitted us to use their portraits.

Thanks, too, to all the manufacturers listed in the Appendix for their help.

Contents

Introduction

This book develops in a simple and organized manner an understanding of the basics of good portraiture. Understanding these fundamentals can help you develop the insights that are critical to making better portraits. The serious student of photography must constantly avoid the hucksters and equipment manufacturers who promise instant success if you purchase their products, or the prophets who wrote prolifically about portraiture yet are incapable of supporting themselves in the industry. Also to be avoided are the avant gardes who believe that anything that has been done in the past is old hat and must never again be repeated. This set dismisses the work of serious photographers as old-fashioned and stagnant. The good practices in portraiture are never stagnant, and there is nothing wrong with being old-fashioned if you can produce a quality product that people like enough so that they will seek out your services.

Learning the rules means understanding the basic tools of the craft, such as light, emulsions, facial characteristics, basic poses, and human nature. Once you become proficient, only then can you intelligently break the rules and discard the basics with impunity. Attempting to break rules without first understanding them will result only in the occasional, accidental good portrait and many failures. Fine photographs and good portraiture are no accident; they are produced intentionally. Hopefully, the series of building blocks selected here will help you find the most direct route toward developing your own style and individual approach to portraiture.

Each of us learns by emulation. We see a lovely picture and attempt to copy the style, pose, or lighting. Usually our efforts end in frustrating failure and we blame ourselves. But many times the technical information supplied is confusing and inadequate; often the lighting diagrams are poorly illustrated, and frequently the photographer leaves out a few details to protect his "secrets."

Being a talented photographer does not make someone a good teacher. How often have you sat through lectures and demonstrations at the conclusion of which the most that you could say was that the program speaker was entertaining, enthusiastic, and capable. Otherwise, you learned little or nothing. A less exciting program that helped you to develop an understanding and learn techniques which you could put to use in upgrading your own capabilities would be far more functional.

In many schools across America today, students are taught portraiture by instructors with little or mediocre experience in the field. The intelligent student who emulates such an instructor can only succeed in failure. If you intend to seek out knowledge in a given area, it is best to locate the successful people who have already achieved the goals you wish to attain.

There are many fine photographers who have developed their own approaches to teaching. Because the methods set forth in this book have produced an unusually high percentage of successful photographers, one can only conclude that the system has merit, although there are others that are equally successful.

There is an arrangement in some photographic schools whereby aspiring models or pretty young students are selected to pose for the students to give them practical experience in portraiture. Under such conditions, a photographer can easily assemble a portfolio of pretty pictures and assume that he is succeeding in making portraits. But once the shingle is hung out and paying customers start walking through the door, there is usually a rude awakening.

Envision, if you will, a five-foot-tall, 190-pound young lady wearing glasses (that look like they were made from the bottom of Coke bottles) perched on her rather large nose, walking through your portals, smiling to expose some missing teeth, and saying, "I'm getting engaged; I need a portrait for the newspaper." The photographer who has trained solely with pretty models can only experience panic and indecision. The competent photographer should be able to cope with all subjects. Over the years of operating a portrait studio, it will be the exception rather than the rule that you will encounter lovely professional models.

Every person can be photographed well if the photographer has the understanding and insight plus the technical capability to deal with the subject. The concept of the word "photogenic" (meaning how well a person photographs) should be rejected, because each subject can be photographed well if the photographer knows his craft. Whether you plan to do portraiture for fun or for profit, doing it well is a richly rewarding experience.

Chapter 1

What Is a Portrait

DEFINITION

Ask 100 people, "What is a portrait?" and you would probably receive 70 or 80 different answers. Some would maintain that a portrait is any photograph of a person that depicts the individual. Others would give very specialized responses that fit their personal views. For our purposes, a portrait is defined as a pleasing, flattering photograph of an individual or a group which retains likeness so that the people are easily recognizable.

Portraiture is probably the most difficult form of photography because not only must you make an end product that pleases you, it must also please your subject. The more you please the sitter, the more successful your efforts will be. In order to be salable, a portrait must be pleasing and flattering to the sitter. Few people can tolerate pictures of themselves which do not accentuate their better features. It is therefore crucial that a portrait retains likeness. People are never pleased by images that show them in unflattering poses or expressions. Often the photographer is so concerned with the hardware of photography that little or no time is spent in portraying the personality of the subject.

Critics of formal or semiformal portraiture who put unflattering labels on this type of work attack it from a sense of insecurity. It doesn't take much talent, training, or ability to be a critic, and when you meet a person who says that a picture should be totally unretouched, this is probably someone who doesn't know how to retouch. And someone who says that all pictures should be made in natural light, probably has tried to use artificial or electronic lighting and failed in his efforts.

If a customer comes back again and again and brings new members of the family, you must be doing something right. Photographers are individualists. Like other artistic people, each develops personal preferences and concepts of perfection. In a good photographer, these are constantly growing and evolving, and concepts of perfection of two and five years ago are not the same as the concepts of today. There are no rigid conditions under which every photographer can and should work. Individual requirements vary with the type of pictures you wish to make. While this book will suggest some fundamentals, feel free to accept those that fit your concepts and reject those which are contrary to your own feelings. You are an individual, and in the process of developing your photographic capabilities, you can evolve your own approach.

QUALITY, NOT MASS PRODUCTION

This book does not deal with mass-production photography. Rather it is based on the premise that each portrait is special. Although the fundamentals are the same, each subject is handled as an individual and never placed in a mold. Such an approach to each subject or group will make what you do distinctive.

In the past, professional portrait photographers in the United States could operate a business and manage to make a livelihood because they were the only photographer in town. These individuals survived because they had a captive market. They therefore resented the influx of large shopping centers, malls, and department stores with photographic departments that could sell pictures at very low prices and which attracted much of the consumer market by efficient mass-production methods and sales techniques. Many small studios have gone out of business because the quality of their work was no better than that produced by a machine. The defense against cheap, mass-produced photography is learning skills that cannot be duplicated by machines. There is always a market for a superior product, and it is a profitable market.

Many reasons account for the low percentage of successful professional portrait studios. The primary reason for their lack of financial success was not that they were undercapitalized, or underequipped, or that they were incapable of reaching enough of the market and advertising their services. Rather, most of them failed because they were undereducated and could not consistently produce a product that the public wanted to buy. If a photographer can do little more than an automated machine, the mass producer will woo the customers away.

THE COMPETENT PHOTOGRAPHER

Frequently a young photographer who aspires to be a professional is misled by well-meaning friends and relatives who believe that the beginner must give pictures away or merely charge for materials in order to practice and build a reputation. They will encourage you and tell you how wonderful your work is; yet when you deliver the work to them and charge them for it, suddenly they become severe critics, of the same type of work. In a sense, the moment of truth is when you can make pictures for which people are willing to pay substantial fees and still tell you how lovely your photographs are.

It has always been the great American dream of amateur photographers to buy that super camera system with all the electronic gadgetry that will magically transform them into great photographers. But great photographers are not made by their equipment. Surely, it is important to have reliable equipment that will perform with a minimum of care, maintenance, and attention, and there is no question that good equipment is always an intelligent investment. However, pictures are made by photographers, and an extremely competent photographer with poor equipment can easily run circles around the possessor of the shiny super cameras, lenses, and accessories who is not versed in the craft of photography. One advice is to invest in yourself. Knowledge and skills deserve a higher priority than hardware.

THERE IS A MARKET

Many photographers are discouraged from seeking and promoting portraiture because they are intimidated by the large-volume, low-priced pictures advertised with regularity in the local papers, stores, and on TV. A fair segment of the market, particularly in the current economic situation, will seek out and use the inexpensive mass producer. However, there is a market for quality portraiture, and it is extremely profitable. You can get a better share of this market if you understand the negative aspects of mass production and promote the positive advantages of quality portraiture.

Most of the low-priced picture offers are limited to a few, specific days only. If a mother can't take her youngster down to the local shopping center or department store on those fixed dates, she can't avail herself of their "special offer." Nor can she if the baby is teething or the youngster recovering from one of a multitude of children's ailments. On the other hand, the established studio can make the portraits at mother's convenience. This holds true for family groups, engaged girls, communions, weddings, bar mitzvahs, and other occasions when people want photographs made to record a milestone in their family history. The mass producer does not take these things into consideration. Special occasions do not lend themselves to transient department store photographers or studios.

Many people do not like the long lines and prefer to come to a studio that offers them a specific appointment with no waiting. In a studio, the customer has a choice of sizes, finishes, and styles rather than what the mass producer makes available in packages and which, for obvious economic reasons, have to be limited in many ways. The studio can provide additional prints in the future. Not so with many mass producers. Furthermore, the time allotted for a sitting and the personal attention that is required in preparing a family group or a bridal portrait can rarely be matched by the mass producer.

The lighting that often enhances a subject does not necessarily lend itself to automated machine printing. Since the mass producer always attempts to standardize the lighting and posing, the individual photographer can use to advantage the freedom of not putting children or people into a mold. If you make pictures that look no different from those of the mass producer, you lose any logical reason for a consumer to pay you more than your "competitor." Other features that differentiate a quality product from the mass-produced one are clothing consultations, makeup assistance, personal attention, and the convenience of dealing with an established neighborhood studio.

There is now and always will be a market for quality portraiture. With an intelligent and businesslike approach, you can increase your share of that market, not by putting down the economy operation that serves a very useful function in our society, but by building up the positive aspects and meaningfulness of quality, service, and, above all, individuality.

Chapter 2

Types of Portraiture

The small or medium-sized studio finds that it must do a great variety of work in order to make it. Over time, this kind of photography subdivides into categories, most of which deal with special events or times in a subjects' life. Let's take a look at the most typical portraits that are made in studios across the land.

BUSINESS PHOTOGRAPHS

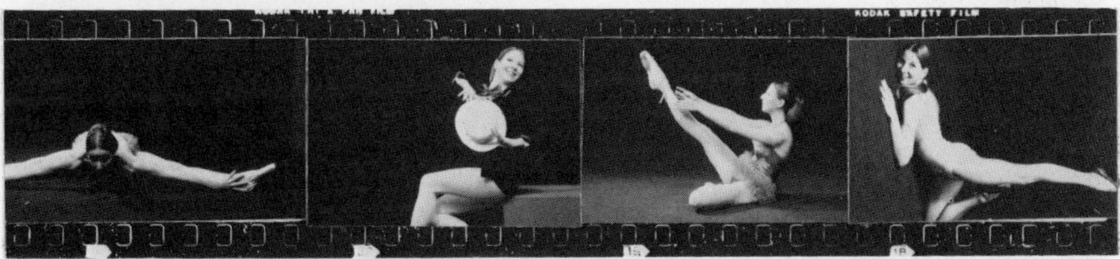

Most people need an occasion, special event, or other reason for having their picture made. Businessmen and politicians usually require a photograph for the local papers or trade magazines after achieving some form of recognition or perhaps a promotion. Appointments for such sittings are generally made by a secretary who has been assigned to find a studio that can do the job in the required period of time. Many of these men, because of business pressures or a dislike for being photographed, delay their appointments until the last minute, requiring the photographer to produce the proper size glossy prints suitable for reproduction on very short notice.

This type of sitting opens the door to additional business. Often these men have not been photographed for 10, 15, or 20 years, and you have an opportunity to sell them photographs for their personal use as well. During their visit to the studio, they are exposed to samples of family portraits, pictures of children, and various pets, and if they are impressed favorably by what they see, they will make appointments to have their family photographed.

The photographer who treats this kind of sitting as a nuisance and does not take the opportunity to explore the other potentials of the customer is missing a great bet. People appreciate any special attention that the photographer offers them. Frequently, clothing suggestions can win a friend and permanent customer for your studio. In addition to the traditional straightforward business-type pose, try to make a series of executive-type portraits that enhance the individual's stature and appearance. This too results in additional sales.

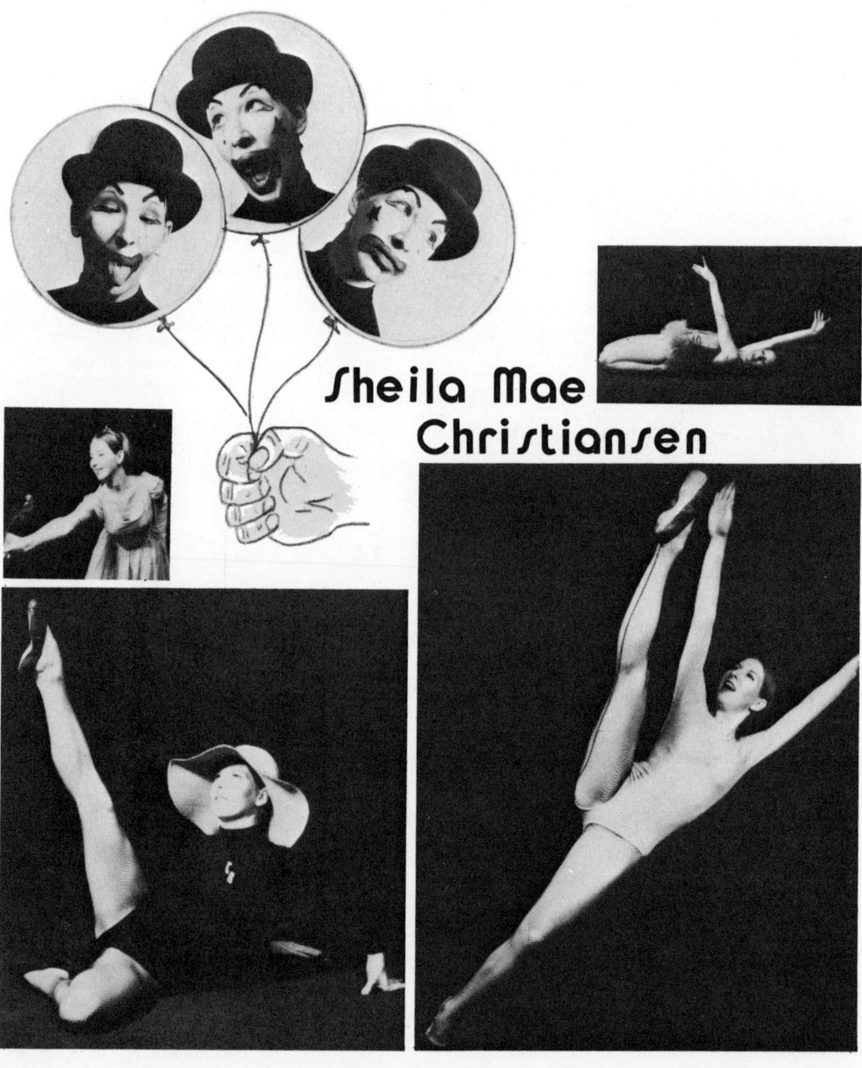

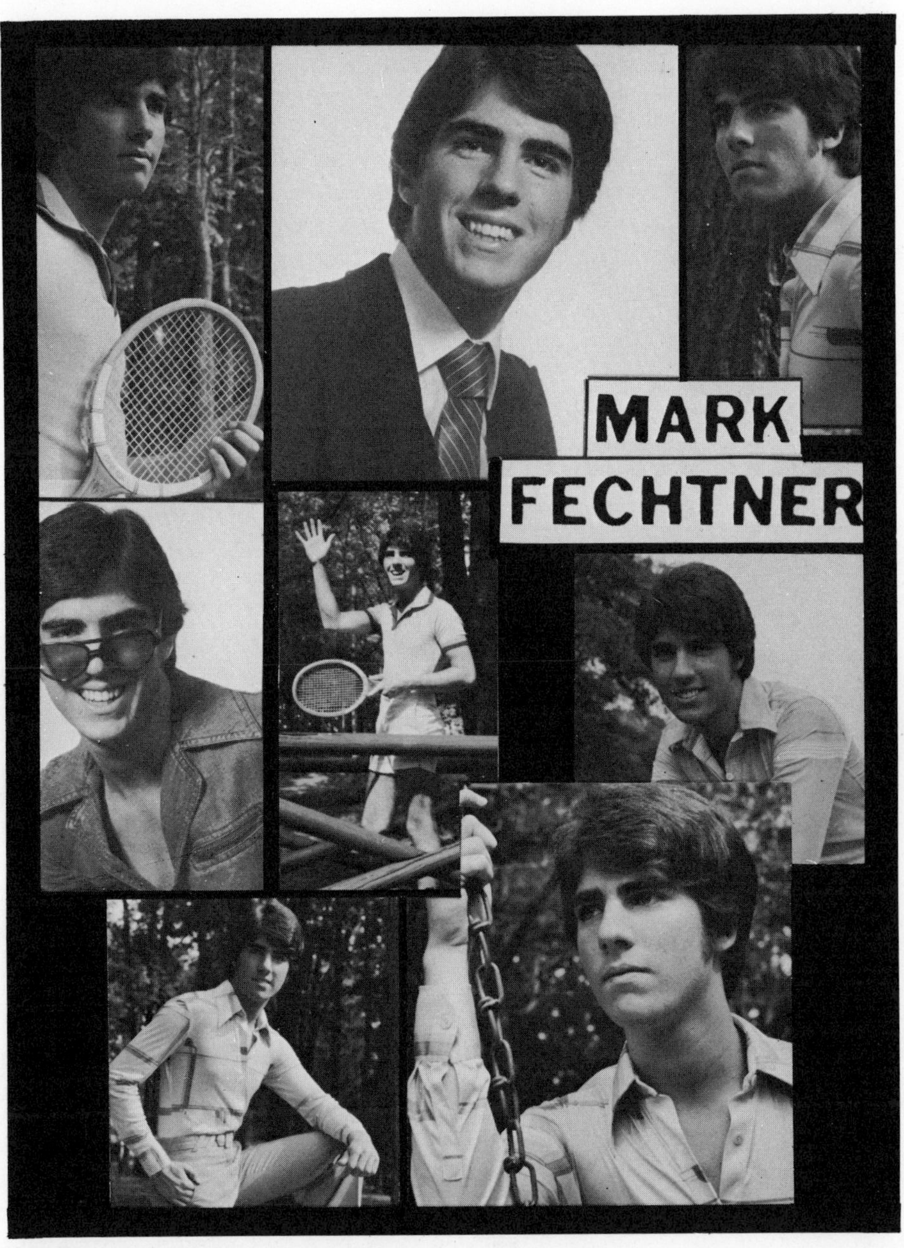

Photographic composites of aspiring models and theatrical hopefuls offer an interesting opportunity to the photographer to work with many types of people. Always try to make composites that are different and which best represent the individual personality. Often this includes outdoor sessions with appropriate props.

IDENTIFICATION PHOTOGRAPHS

Some photographers consider the making of passport, citizenship, and identification photographs as demeaning and beneath their capabilities. Yet such work brings traffic into the studio and exposes the public to the many services which the studio offers. An attractive display of portraits and pictorial photographs can often open the conversation to their particular photographic needs. This frequently results in subsequent appointments for other work.

ENGAGEMENT AND WEDDING PORTRAITS

It is traditional in some parts of this country for a young lady who is betrothed to announce her engagement in the local papers. This requires a glossy portrait of the girl to be submitted along with the details of her engagement. Recently, a number of newspapers have started publishing pictures of the engaged couple, which is an opportunity for the photographer to do a sitting of the couple. Such a momentous occasion in their lives calls for prints for themselves and their families and friends. When the couple comes in, suggest that the sitting include some traditional photographs as well as some love portraits. A love portrait goes beyond the traditional straightforward photograph both in posing and lighting. It is intended to show the feeling between the two people, photographing them as one. Love portraits have gained wide acceptance by young and old. Engagement portraits give the photographer the opportunity to build a relationship with the couple who very shortly will be requiring wedding-day photographs. This very naturally opens the door to the sale of wedding-day portraits or candids. Prior to the wedding, a portrait of the bride in her wedding outfit is usually taken for publication in the local newspaper. This is another opportunity when the photographer can arrange for bridal portraits.

CHILD PORTRAITURE

Over the years, if you have satisfied the bride and groom, the next occasion for photographs comes with the birth of their first child. Photographs of children can be done in many exciting ways, far removed from the staid and traditional dull pictures. The market for child portraiture remains quite large even though there is considerable competition. As children grow and change, many opportunities for interesting and unusual photographs present themselves. Capitalize on a constantly growing list of satisfied customers by contacting people and letting them know about the various services you can perform.

There are many occasions when the religious aspects of family life call for a photographer, for example, Bar Mitzvahs, First Communions, and Confirmations. It is almost a tradition with families that they will return again and again to use your services. People want the memorable moments in their lives recorded, which is probably the primary function of the portrait photographer.

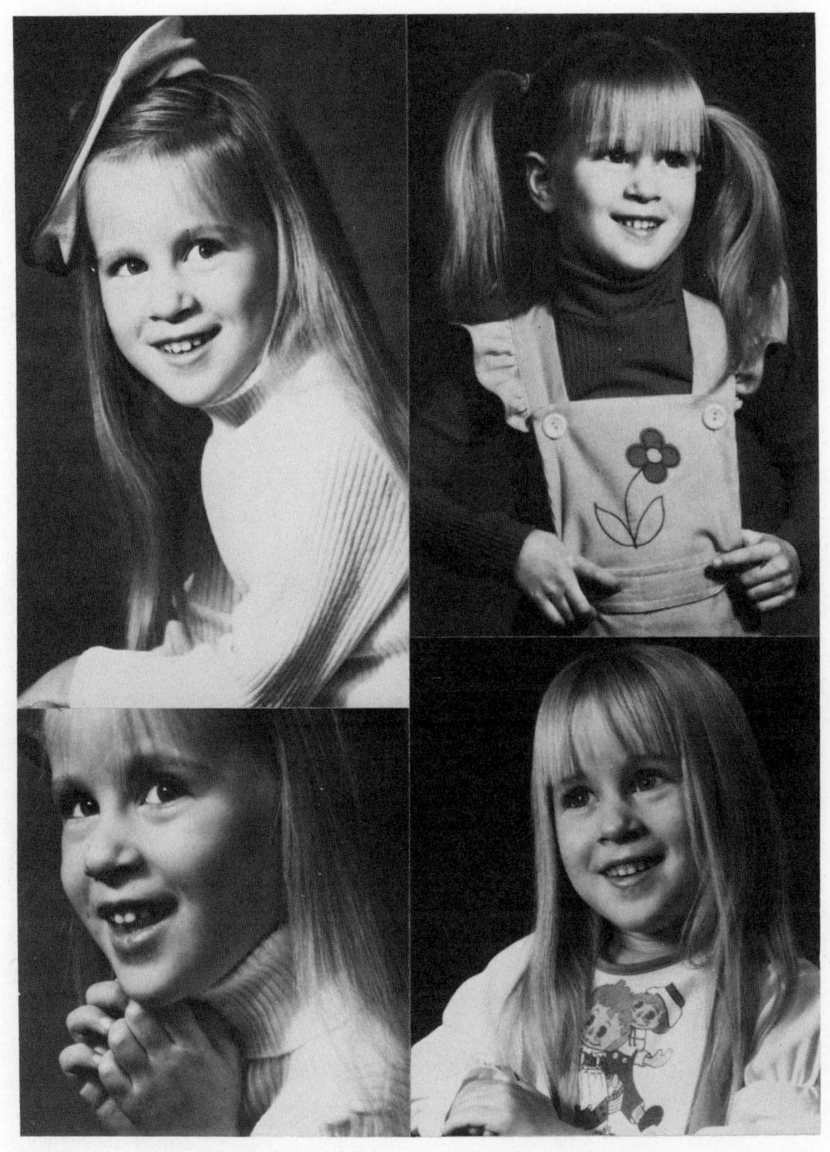

Kristen Aurelio

This montage of a little girl, Kristen Aurelio, was made up from portraits taken at different times and combined for a wall display or as a simple portfolio for a child model.

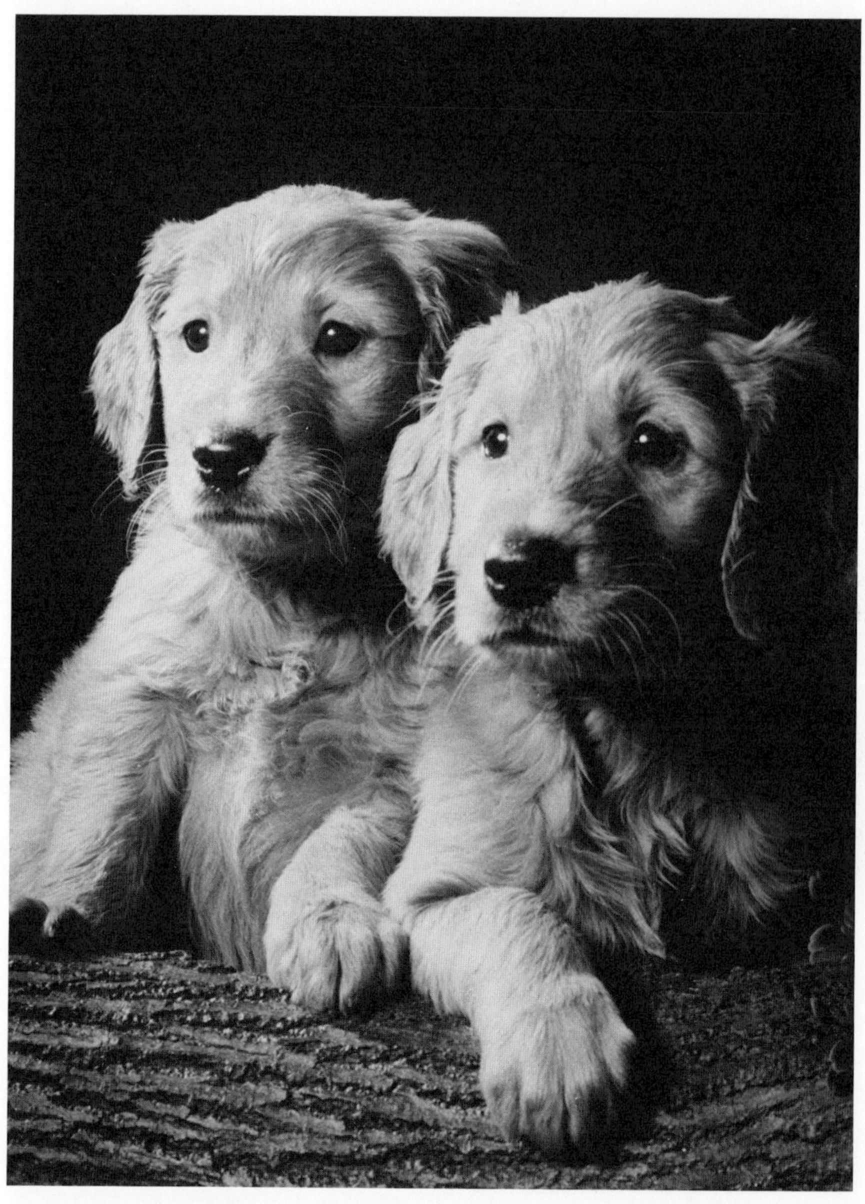

PET PORTRAITS

Another successful service is the photographing of pets. When they see examples of good animal photographs in your studio, clients will frequently tell you about their pet, and this is an excellent time to suggest an appointment to have their pet photographed.

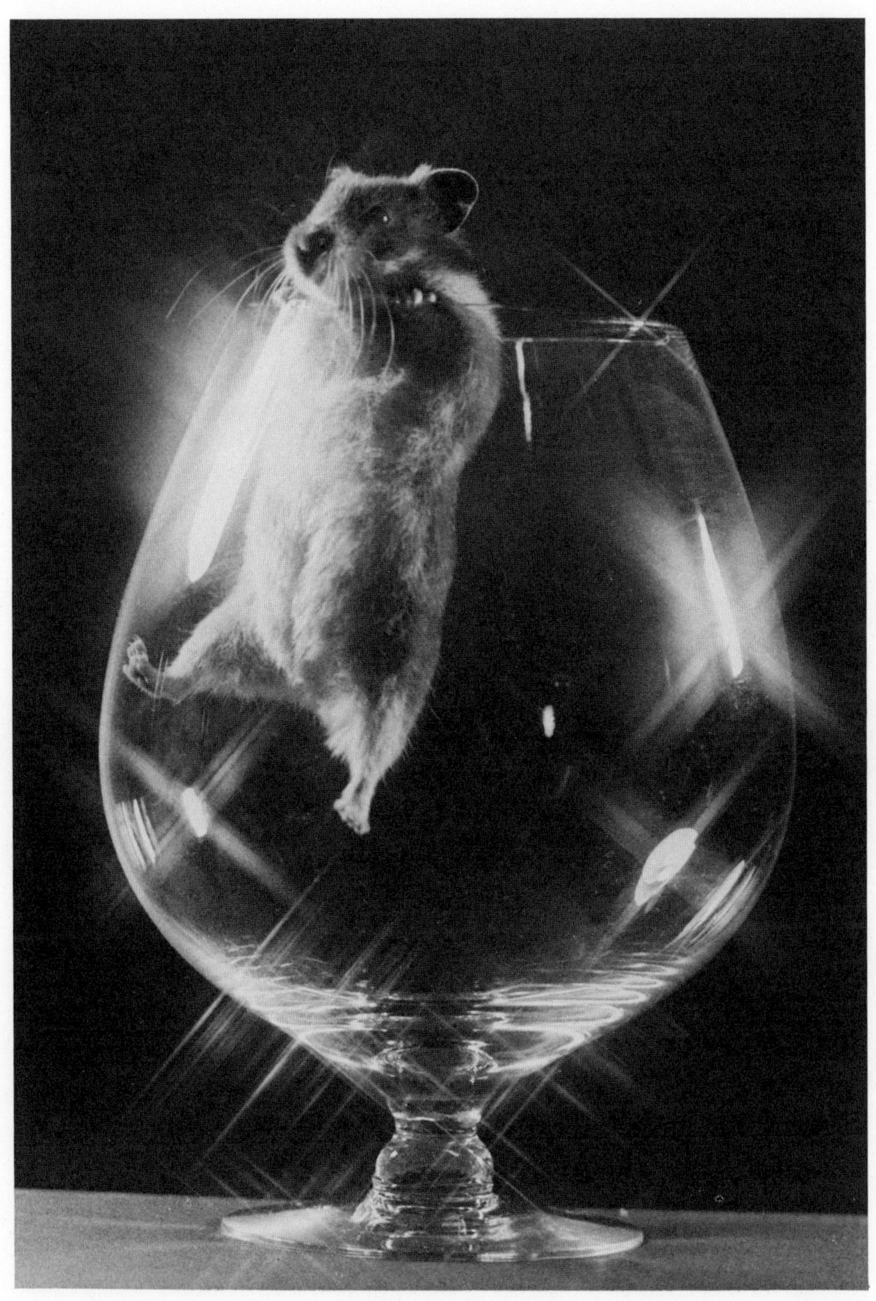

Pets offer interesting assignments that can add spice to the life of any photographer. This endeavor requires a genuine love of animals and a considerable degree of patience.

FAMILY PORTRAITS

There is now a phenomenal growth and interest of the public in family portraits. People are using wall portraits much more than in the last two decades and are displaying them in prominent places in their homes. This has presented an exciting opportunity to master posing and lighting techniques and the arrangement of pleasing groups that result in the sale of wall portraits. Perhaps it is the use of photographs as wall decor that is one of the largest factors in bringing in more family groups into the studio.

During the clothing consultation for sittings, ask whether the sitting is to be formal, semiformal, or informal. Also ask if there are any pets in the family and suggest that they be included in the family portrait. Many people are a little surprised but usually delighted at the suggestion and frequently will bring their pets along for the group portrait.

Chapter 3

Portraiture for Fun or Profit

Whether you hope to become a professional portrait photographer or, as a sincere amateur, want to be able to produce high-quality portraits, you must realize that the equipment, materials, and space required for either a part-time or full-time business are considerably expensive. The aspiring professional must consider the costs as business operational expenses and recognize that rising costs mean rising fees. The amateur can probably absorb the cost of doing a small number of sittings a year, but should his work become very popular with friends and relatives, the cost can become burdensome, and there should be some compensation.

DETERMINING YOUR COSTS

People are often confused about what to charge for their work, and it is almost impossible to determine what an individual should charge. Yet your prices must be based on sound business principles and never on what another competitor charges. They must be determined by your overhead, labor, and profit and return on investment. What your competitors find is a profitable price structure may lead you to financial ruin. Always resist the efforts of photofinishers and custom labs to suggest or determine retail prices. Unless they have a magic crystal ball that can predict your volume, consider your overhead, and predetermine your cost of living, they may be generating many transactions that are profitable for them and disastrous for you. Utilizing their "suggested retail price" can easily place you in the category of photographers who will be out of the business in a very short time.

Overhead Too many photographers assume that if a piece of paper and film cost them $1, then the rest is gravy. They forget the other costs of completing an assignment. They know that their expensive equipment, rent, and utilities must be part of the cost of producing a photograph, yet few realize that such items as travel, insurance, car payments, and the cost of their education must also be included in the pricing. In other words, anything that relates to an expense in performing a service is part of the cost of the product.

Labor Many people don't understand that their time as well as the labor of a wife or friend should be charged on an hourly rate. You must determine the number of hours of labor that go into an assignment, then multiply this by the number of dollars per hour you feel your labor is worth. Add all the other costs and expenses, and you will have determined *your* cost for producing the job.

All child portraits need not show the child smiling. This serious pose makes a charming portrait.
Photo by Gerard Photography, Inc.

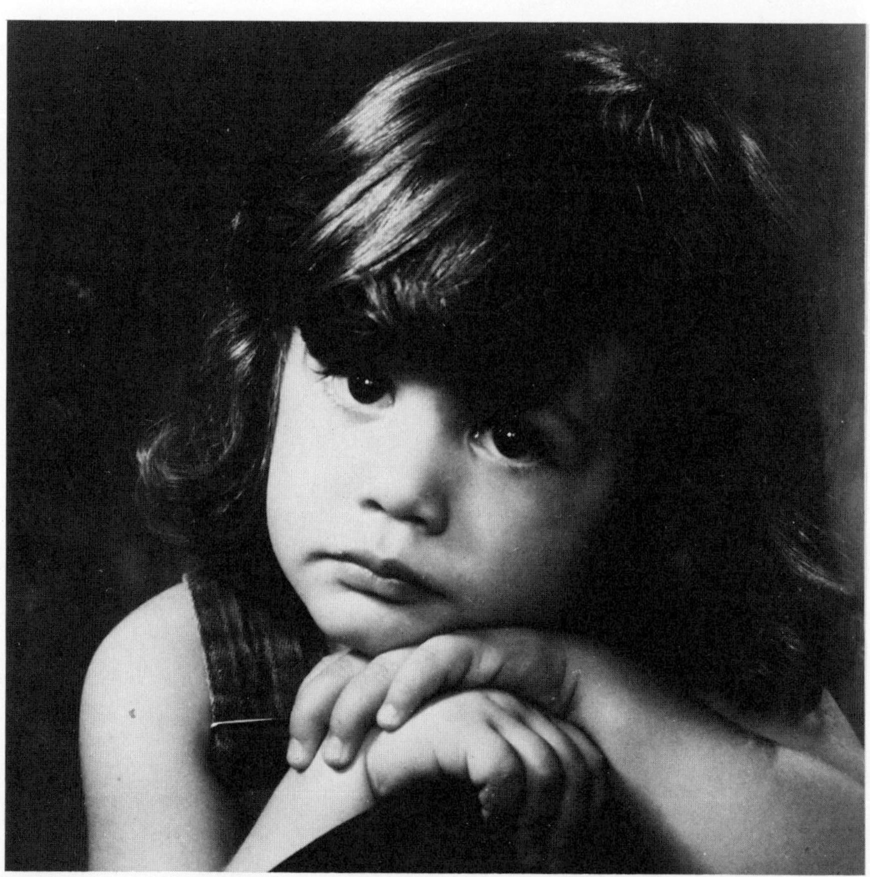

Profit This does not mean salary. Salary is the hourly rate you get paid or pay yourself. Profit is a return on the time and effort of running your own enterprise over and above your salary and other expenses. It is a repayment for your efforts, and no business can endure without showing profit. Many photographers like to think of themselves as artists or craftsmen. This is fine, provided they never lose sight of the fact that a full understanding of the business aspects is essential in order to succeed. Your accountant is probably better qualified to determine what you should charge for your pictures. Getting competent professional advice in these areas can often mean the difference between success and failure. Since you take the risks and gamble your money and time and stand a very good chance of losing both, you should also be entitled to a return on this gamble if your business is successful.

Return on Investment If you were to sell all your photographic equipment and property and invested the money in municipal bonds, you would expect a reliable return of 8-10 percent annually on your investment. It is not unreasonable, therefore, to expect an equivalent return on your photographic investment, paid to you directly through your business.

Marketing The volume of work you produce at a given price must be in direct proportion to your markup. For each $1,000 of gross business you generate, you could earn it in the following ways:

Number of Pictures	Price Per Picture
1000	$1
200	$5
100	$10
50	$20
20	$50
10	$100
5	$200
2	$500
1	$1000

One thousand dollars in gross sales can be represented in many ways. Which is the most profitable, time-consuming, difficult to generate, or satisfying to customer and photographer? By targeting your sales, advertising, and quality toward the most desirable fee per photograph, you can take direct aim at the market you wish to capture.

The company that produces the $1 photograph can certainly make a great deal of money as long as it can bring in several hundred thousand customers, such as the mass-production outfits, because there is a huge market for inexpensive pictures. It should also be obvious that if you can't make better pictures or supply a better service than such companies, then you have little chance of competing or surviving. A simple rule of thumb is to determine whether your prices are in line with the market you serve is this: If nobody complains about your prices as being too high, then they are too low. If 30 percent or more of your customers feel that you are overpriced, then you probably are. If 20–30 percent complain about your prices, your prices are just fine. The average photographer loses almost as many sales because his prices are too low as he does if they are too high.

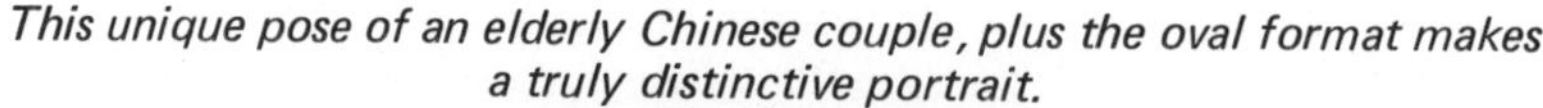

This unique pose of an elderly Chinese couple, plus the oval format makes a truly distinctive portrait.

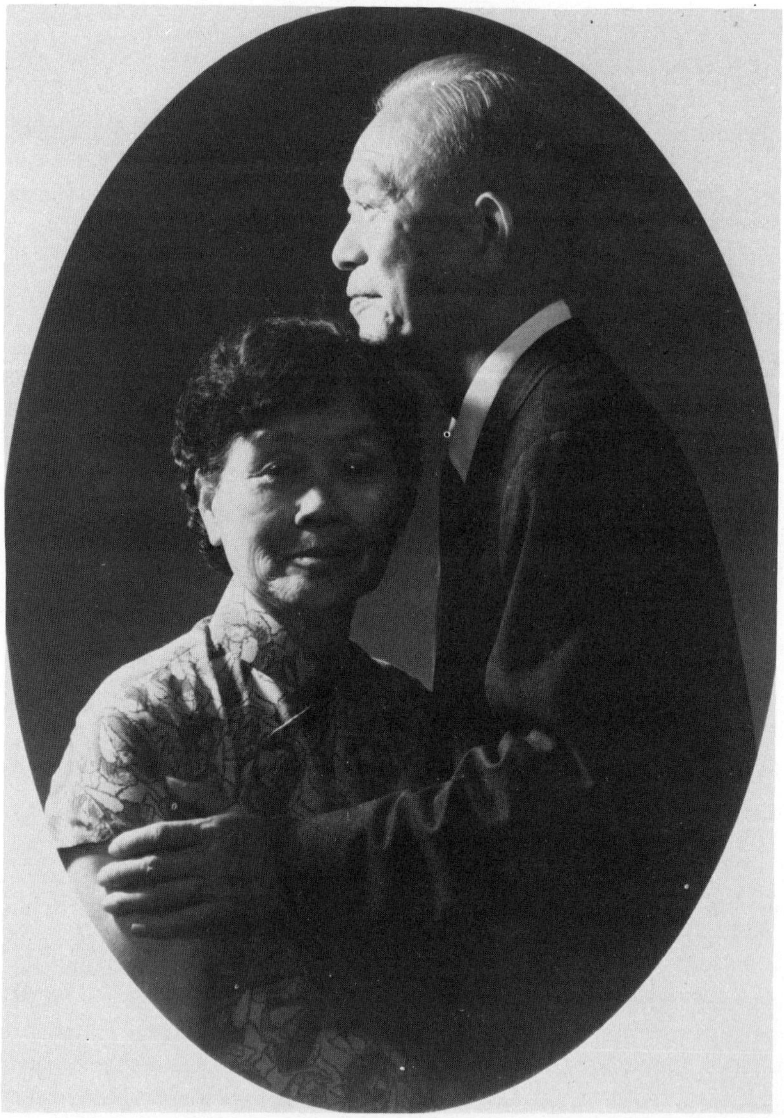

Chapter 4

A Prerequisite: Liking People

Before you rush out and buy lots of nice shiny equipment and print up business cards announcing that you are a portrait photographer, it would be wise for you to do some soul-searching. Ask yourself whether this is really the area for you. A few minutes spent reflecting might save you considerable loss later. What makes portraiture unique as compared to other types of photography is that in each case you are dealing with people. It is therefore essential that you develop a rapport with your subject, and that you like people in general.

Usually the dissatisfaction with a picture stems not from the technical quality of the product but from the fact that there was no relationship between photographer and subject. Having a portrait made is usually an important milestone in a person's life. It is up to the photographer to make it a pleasant, interesting, and relaxed experience. This will reflect in the end product. Sometimes your task is complicated by the fact that the subject has already had one or more bad experiences with an inept photographer, having been treated like a number, marched to an uncomfortable chair, forced into an unnatural position, surrounded by huge, intimidating powerful lights, and then ordered to smile or told to relax. So take the time, either in the initial phone contact or prior to the sitting when clothing, hair, and makeup are discussed, to develop a rapport with each subject.

If it is a child, for example, you can play and joke with the subject so that when you are ready for the session, the child already knows that this is going to be a fun experience. A child can sense when an adult, despite all pretenses, does not really like children. The same is true of pets. If you are a dog lover, you will rarely have difficulty in photographing an animal; but if you are afraid of dogs, rest assured that that animal knows it and will respond in an unhappy way. If each sitting is to be successful, it must be a pleasing experience for the subject. This will directly affect your results and the size of the order you achieve.

In establishing rapport, try to find out the subject's interests. With an engaged girl, it is her guy and plans for the future. With a mother and child, it is some of the wonderful little adventures that she wants to talk about which prove that her youngster is unique and individual. With a businessman, it might be his golf game, tennis, or fishing. Once you get them talking, they relax and don't get the feeling that they are facing a firing squad.

PHOTOGRAPHIC LANGUAGE

Imagine a customer walking into a studio that has lured her with many advertising dollars. She enters a lovely reception room, tastefully decorated with attractive photographs, only to be accosted with such language from a photographer as: "I'll shoot your kid 12 times, blow her up to an 11″ × 14″, and it will only cost you 29 bucks."Sadly enough, the individual who uses these anarchistic terms complains because he gets no respect from the public. The fact is, that this is hardly the way to refer to a product you expect to sell.

Most of these terms originated with the fast-talking, zippy amateur photo magazines. Such talk as "souping" the negative, "cropping" a print, or "burning in" an area, are indicative of a lack of self-esteem in one's own product. Train yourself to use professional terms, as follows:

Instead of	Use
blow up	enlarge or magnify
burn in	print in
crop	compose
shoot	photograph
shots	exposures, photographs, poses
soup	process

Always avoid the word "smile." If you stood in front of a mirror and ordered yourself to smile, that forced, silly-looking grimace staring back at you would convince you that if you want a pleasant expression, get it by saying something pleasant or through better communication with your subject. Also avoid the word "cheese," because it accomplishes little more than "smile." If you approach each sitting as an exciting challenge, your enthusiasm will be transmitted to the subject. After all, everybody likes someone who is interested in them. So if your personality is such that you really don't like people or animals, then perhaps you would be far more successful if you pursued a career in architectural, commercial, industrial, or another type of photography in which you are not "on stage" with every subject you photograph. Unless you truly like people, portraiture is not the field for you.

Chapter 5

Portraiture on a Small Investment

For a beginner to portraiture, there is a considerable amount of confusion about what equipment you might require. True, a super-talented professional with many years of experience could probably take any standard camera equipment and any lighting situation and produce unique and exciting portraits. But for the beginner, this is no way to start. You don't need to invest thousands of dollars in expensive cameras, professional studio stands, and electronic lighting systems in order to produce high-quality portraits. All these conveniences are lovely to possess but have no direct bearing on the quality of the end product. On the other hand, the last thing you want to do is march into a camera store and ask some salesclerk to set you up with portrait equipment. He would probably suggest some reflectors with clamps, short light-duty cords, and photofloods.

Photofloods are the worst kind of illumination for making portraits. (They came into use in the days when films were quite slow and people wanted to take pictures indoors.) Moreover, photofloods (which are nothing more than a conventional tungsten light bulb with a special filament that can be heavily overloaded to produce a great quantity of light) generate a great deal of heat. Not only can you burn yourself handling these bulbs, but you can injure your subject. Because of the heat they generate, the smallest amount of fluid splashed on them while they are in use could cause an implosion which would scatter glass a considerable distance. In addition to being uncomfortable and far too bright for the subject, these bulbs produce light in the wrong end of the color spectrum, and much of the light is low actinic and therefore wasted.

If you persist in using floods, at least move them to the other side midway in the sitting so that your subject will be equally cooked on both sides. Photofloods have a very short lifetime compared to conventional bulbs. Furthermore, there is considerable shift in color temperature of the lamp from the time you start the sitting to the time you end it. In a photo session that lasts for 30–45 minutes, today's films will show a visible change in color when you use photofloods, which makes this type of illumination inefficient for portrait photography. As you will learn later, one of the "secrets" of portrait photography is to have total control over your lighting.

At best, bullet-shaped clamp-on reflectors throw a pattern of light that is considerably greater at the center and less at the edges. Uneven lighting like this can cause all sorts of problems to a photographer. Many of the lights that are fine for making amateur home movies or industrial motion pictures are really not the most desirable for portraits.

MINIMUM EQUIPMENT

Lenses To learn what is the minimum equipment required for taking high-quality portraits, you must first understand something about lenses. The normal focal-length lenses that come with most cameras are usually not suitable for portraits. The reason is that if you wish to work close, these lenses create considerable distortion in objects closer to the lens, and in order to fill the frame with a head and shoulders, you have to distort the individual to an undesirable degree. Depending on the format you use, a lens from 1-1/2 to 3 times the normal focal length is ideal. Longer lenses flatten the perspective too much and also place the photographer too far away from the subject to communicate constantly concerning poses, expressions, and moods.

Tripods and Releases You will also need a tripod, because being able to fix the camera on a solid stand is extremely important in many types of portraiture. In

Whichever tripod you select, a very convenient asset is the ability to quickly adapt from horizontal to vertical format without removing the camera from the tripod.

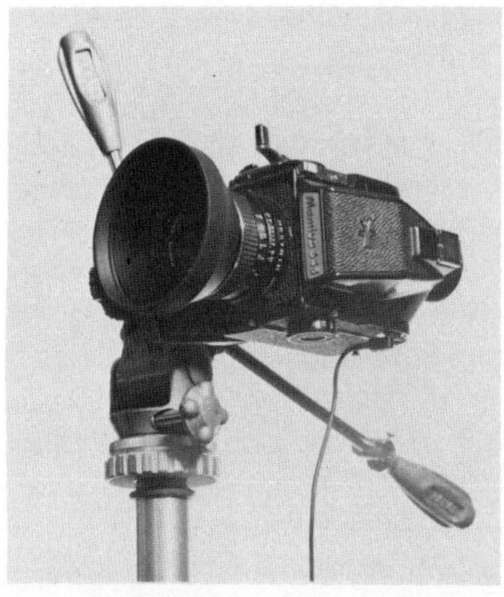

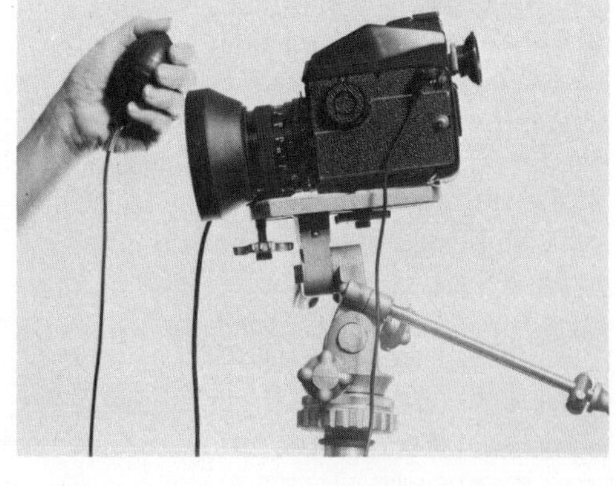

order to be able to move away from the camera, you can use a long cable release or the inexpensive air shutter releases. The latter have a moderate 6- or 8-foot tubing attached which permits you to move away from the camera for the exposure.

Lighting All of us have access to daylight, and with the tremendous popularity of environmental or outdoor portraits today, this is just fine. During the daytime, you can make fine portraits indoors by successfully using window light and simple reflectors. If you prefer to work during evening hours when daylight is not available, then purchase some simple stands that are adjustable for elevation, a relatively flat pan reflector that throws an even, broad, overall illumination without hot spots, and some simple barn doors fitted on these lights so that you can control the light. If you are willing to work at moderately slow shutter speeds, these stands can be fitted with ordinary 150- or 200-watt light bulbs. These will be adequate for single portraits and even for portraits of two people; however, additional lighting will be required for groups. By adding a Soff-Box (see chapter 7), you can take most medium- or large-size portable electronic flashes, fit them to an adjustable stand, add barn doors and modeling light (the latter is essential so that you can see where the light is striking the face), and you have a very handsome lighting system without the expense of buying large, professional studio lights.

The Testrite flat pan reflector with barn doors offers the beginner an inexpensive set of lights with the required controls for portraiture.

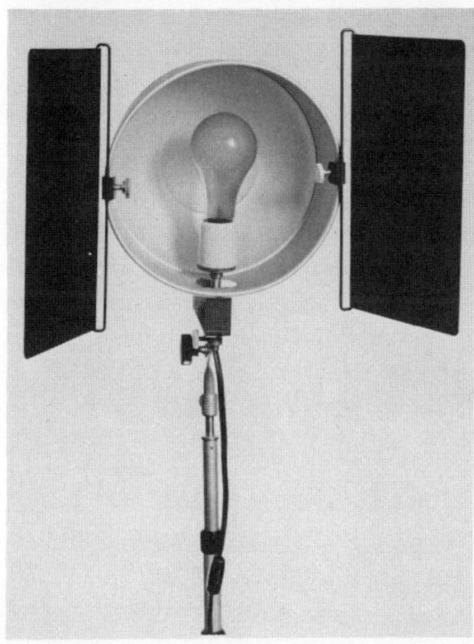

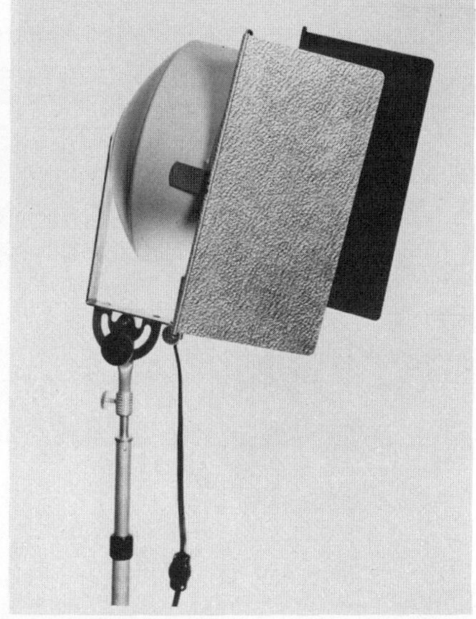

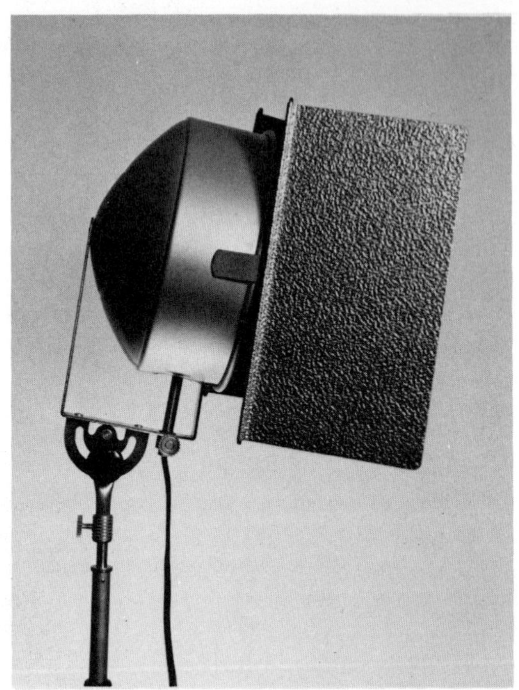

Shallow reflector with barn doors fully open.

Films Given the choice, use slower films rather than the faster emulsions for portraits. With increased film speed, you are able to use faster shutter speeds or smaller lens openings. In portraiture, however, the smaller lens openings are not particularly desirable, and it is advantageous to work with a lens closed down one or two *f*-stops but no more. The price you pay for the high-speed films is usually a sacrifice in grain structure and a contrast that could be extremely objectionable in a portrait.

So you don't have to invest a huge sum in reliable equipment to make portraits. Your prime asset in making good portraits is yourself, your understanding of light, the materials, chemistries, and papers you use, and mastery of the process. Good portraits are not made by accident but by intent. Far more stress should be placed on your knowledge and capabilities because a fine portrait is made with your mind, your eye, and your heart, and the hardware is only an accessory.

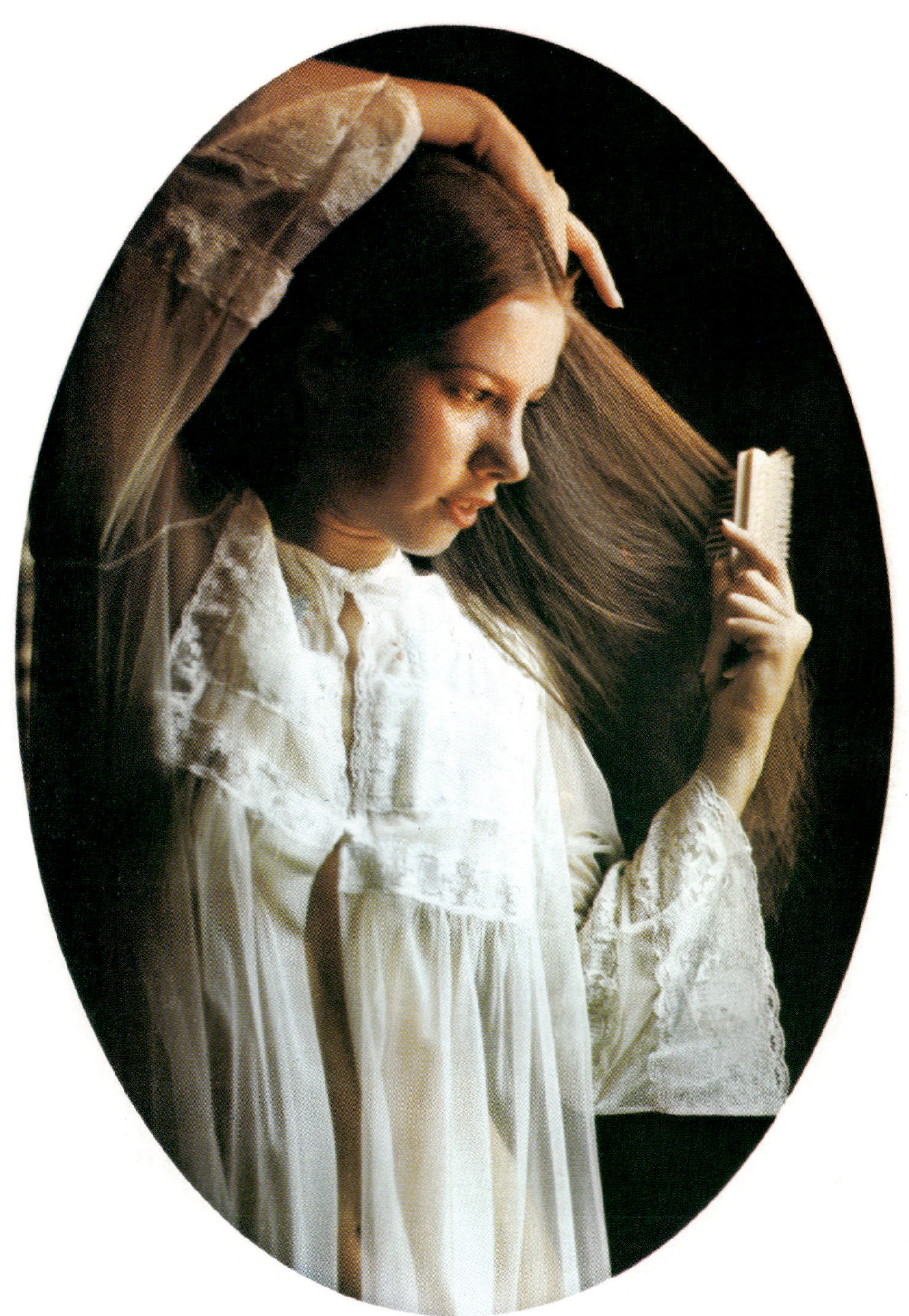

A charming portrait can be made using the right props and window light.

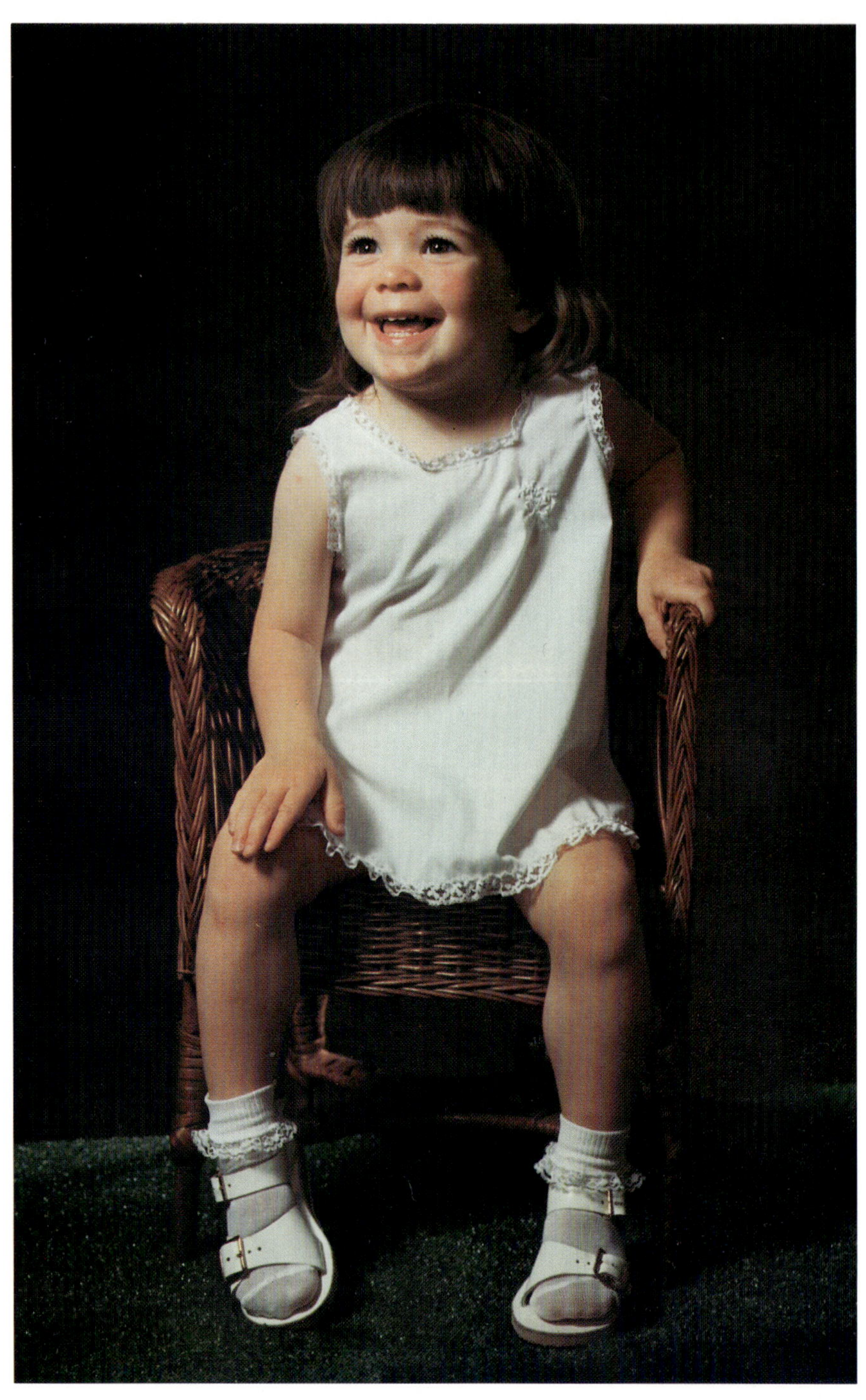

Child portraits present a challenge to any photographer.

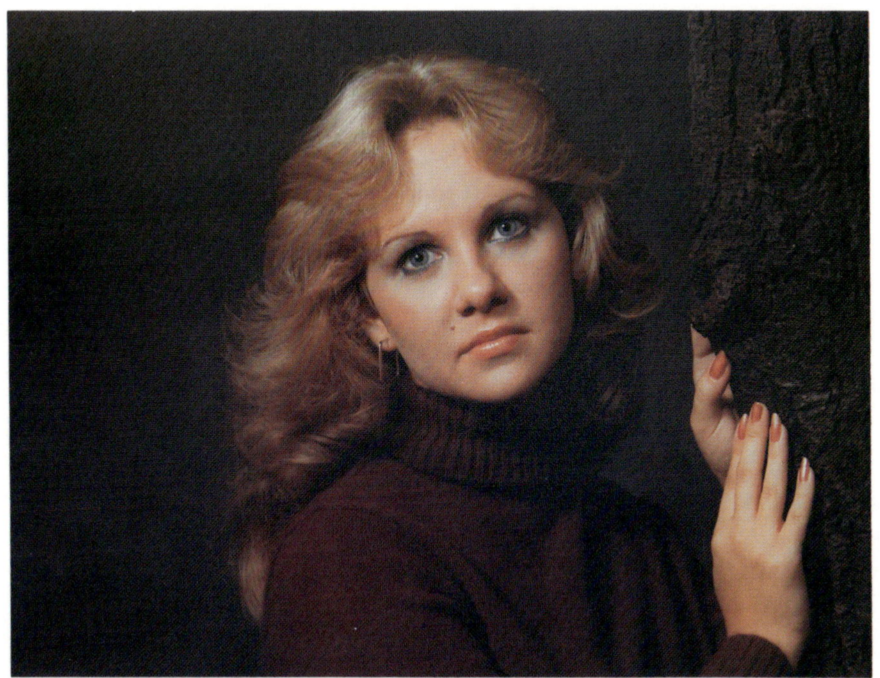

The lighting enhances the young lady's eyes and the modeling of her hands. Photo by Monteith's Countryhouse Studios.

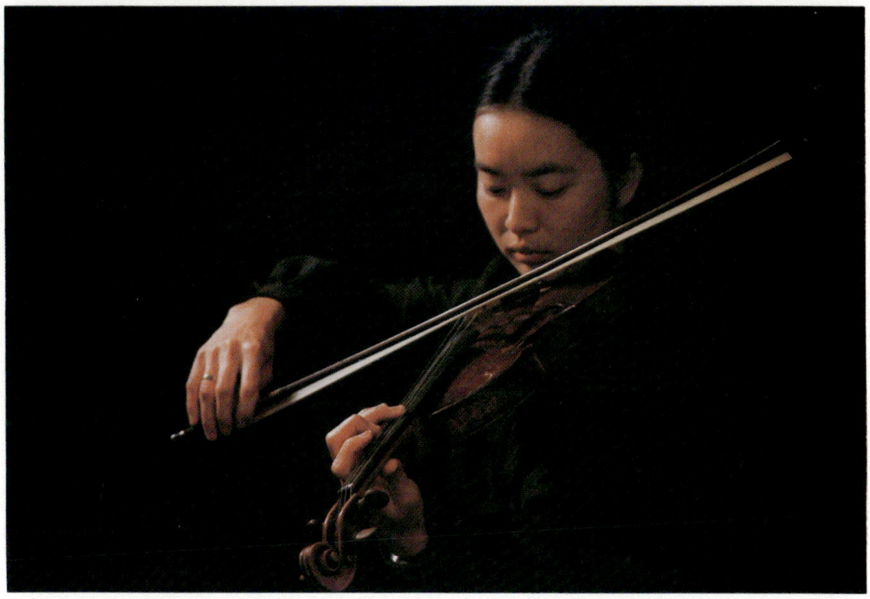

Side lighting models the hands and violin allowing deep shadows to heighten interest.

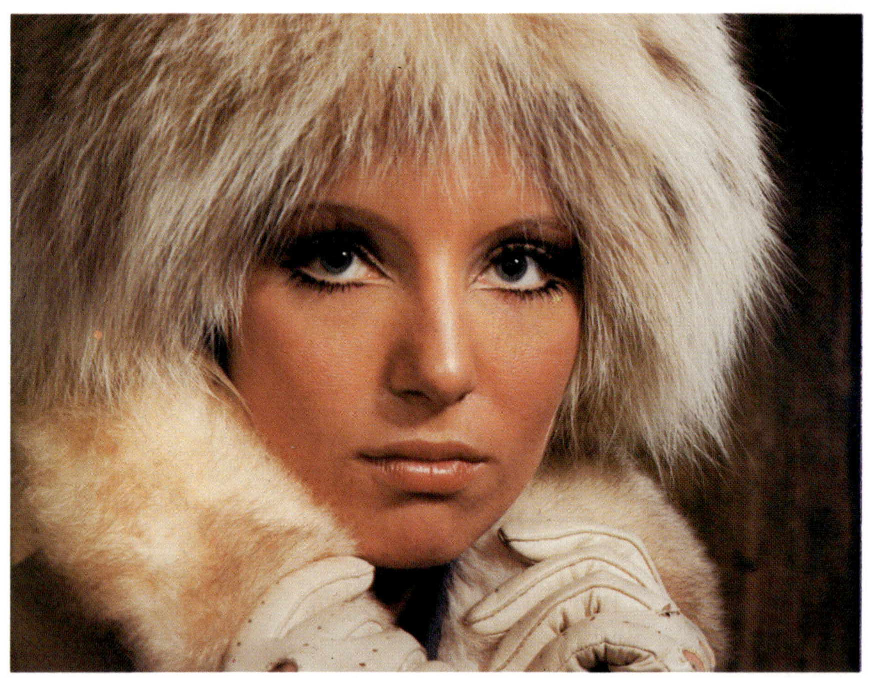

Skin tones and the fine hairs of her fur hat create a sense of intimacy and detail. Photo by Gerard Photography, Inc.

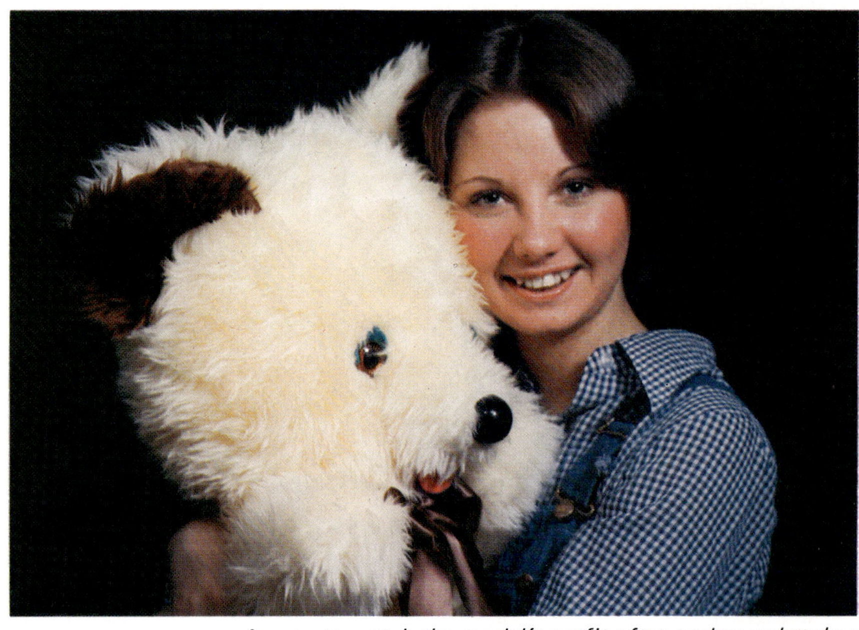

A prop to match the model's outfit often makes or breaks a portrait. Photo by Monteith's Countryhouse Studios.

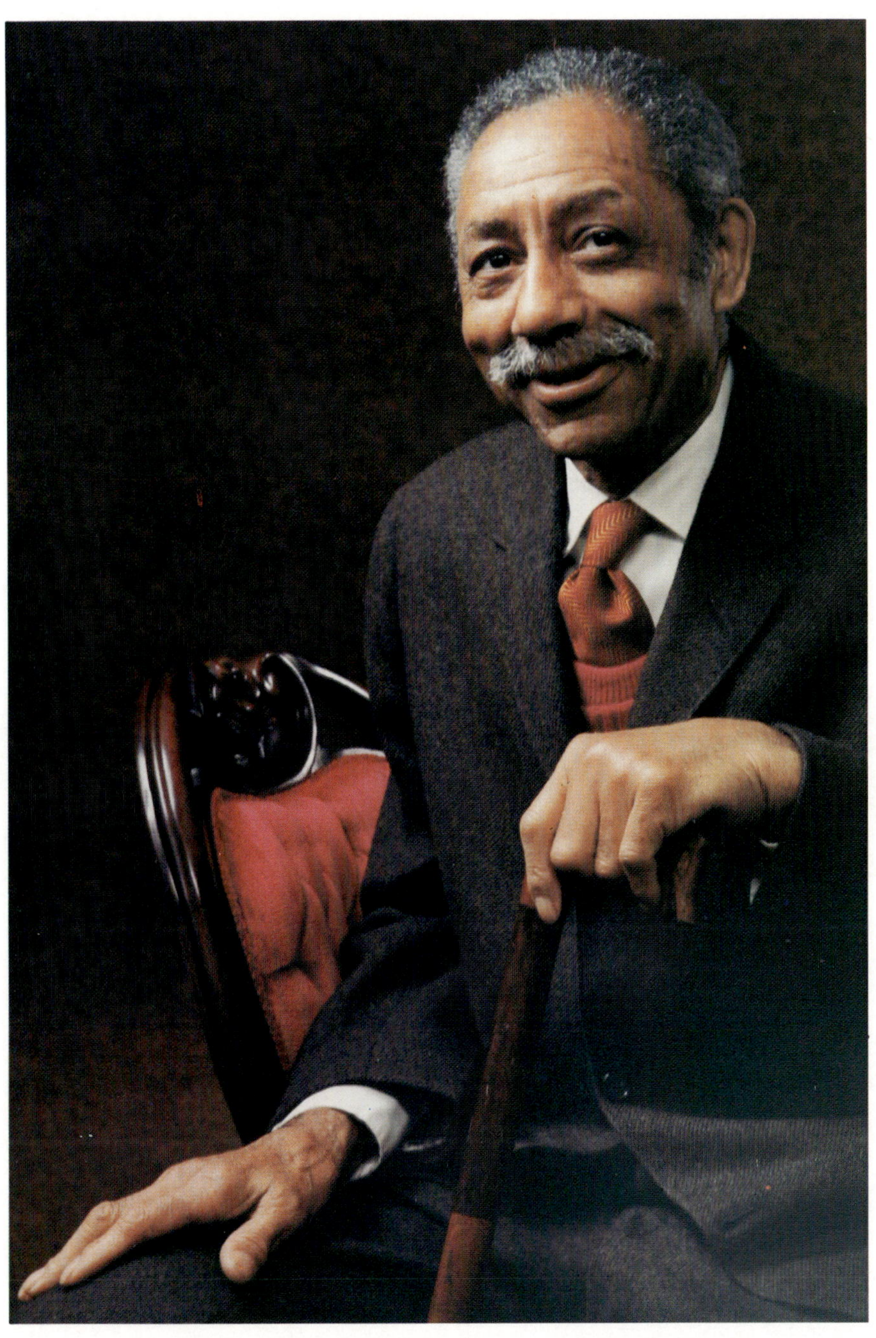

Relaxed and witty, this distinguished gentleman's manner is reinforced by his cane and the beautiful chair. Photo by Noumair Studios.

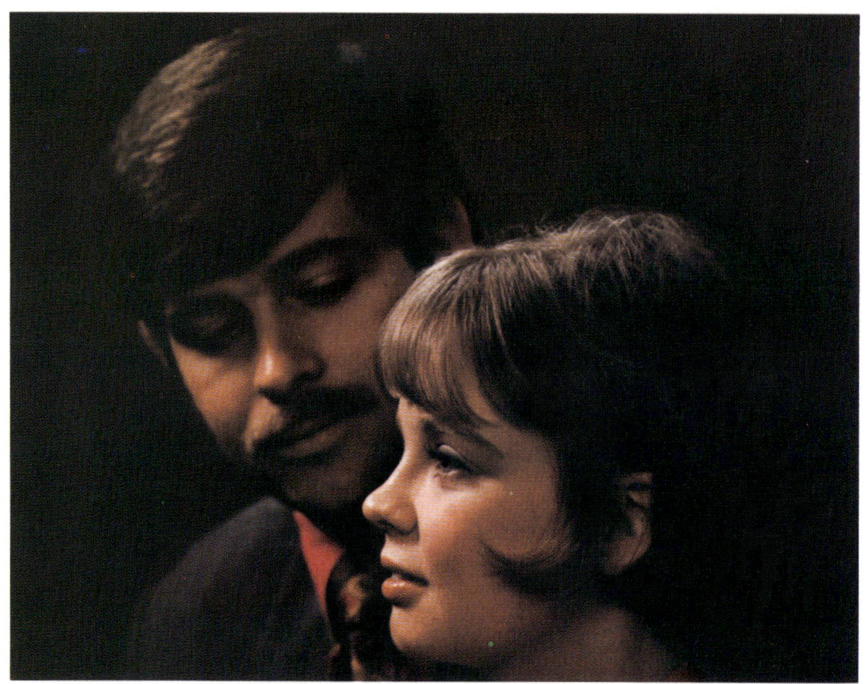

A dual portrait can emphasize one of the models without disparaging the other.
Photo by Al Friedman

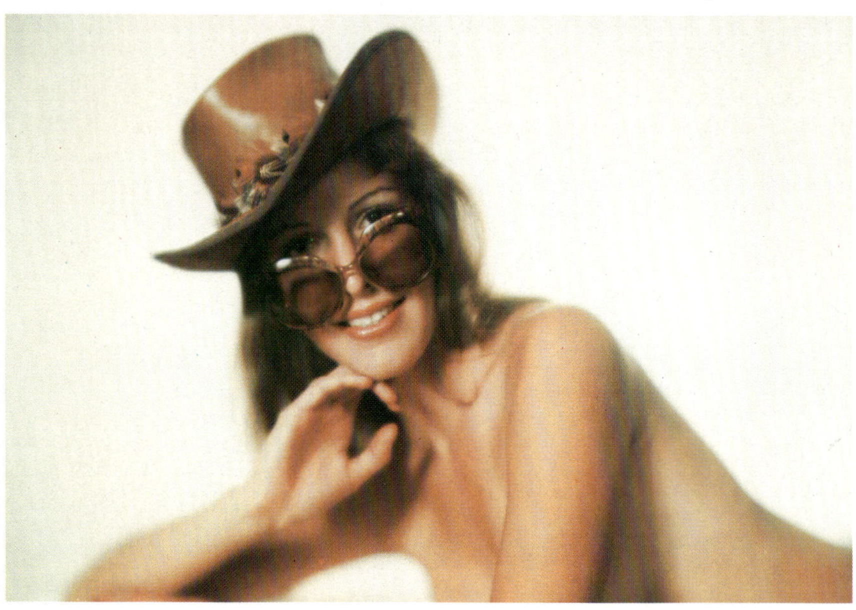

A nude need not be revealing to have charm. Here the props and soft focus help the mood.

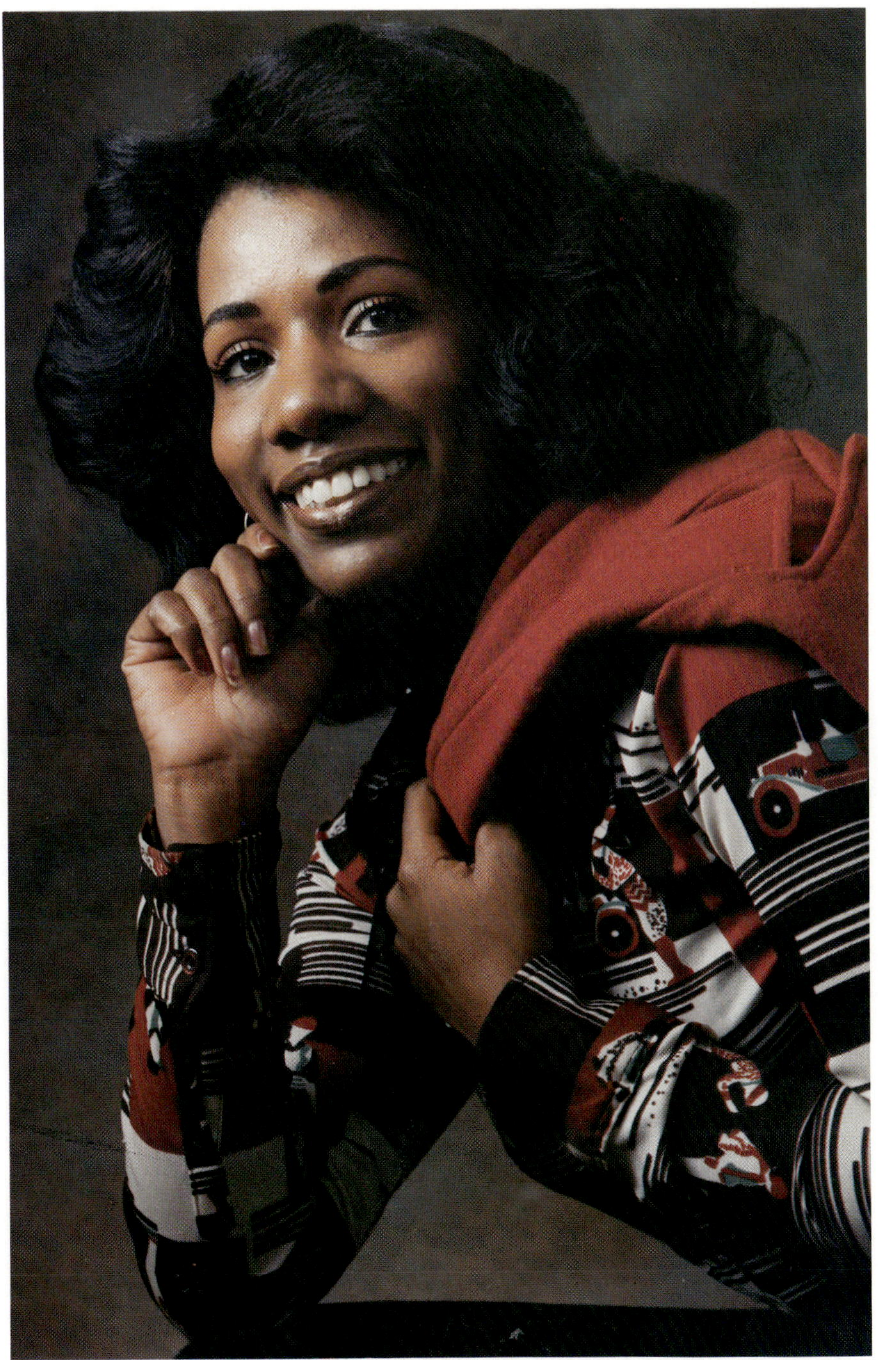

Use of subdued color and highlights add to the charm of the model's smile. Photo by Noumair Studios.

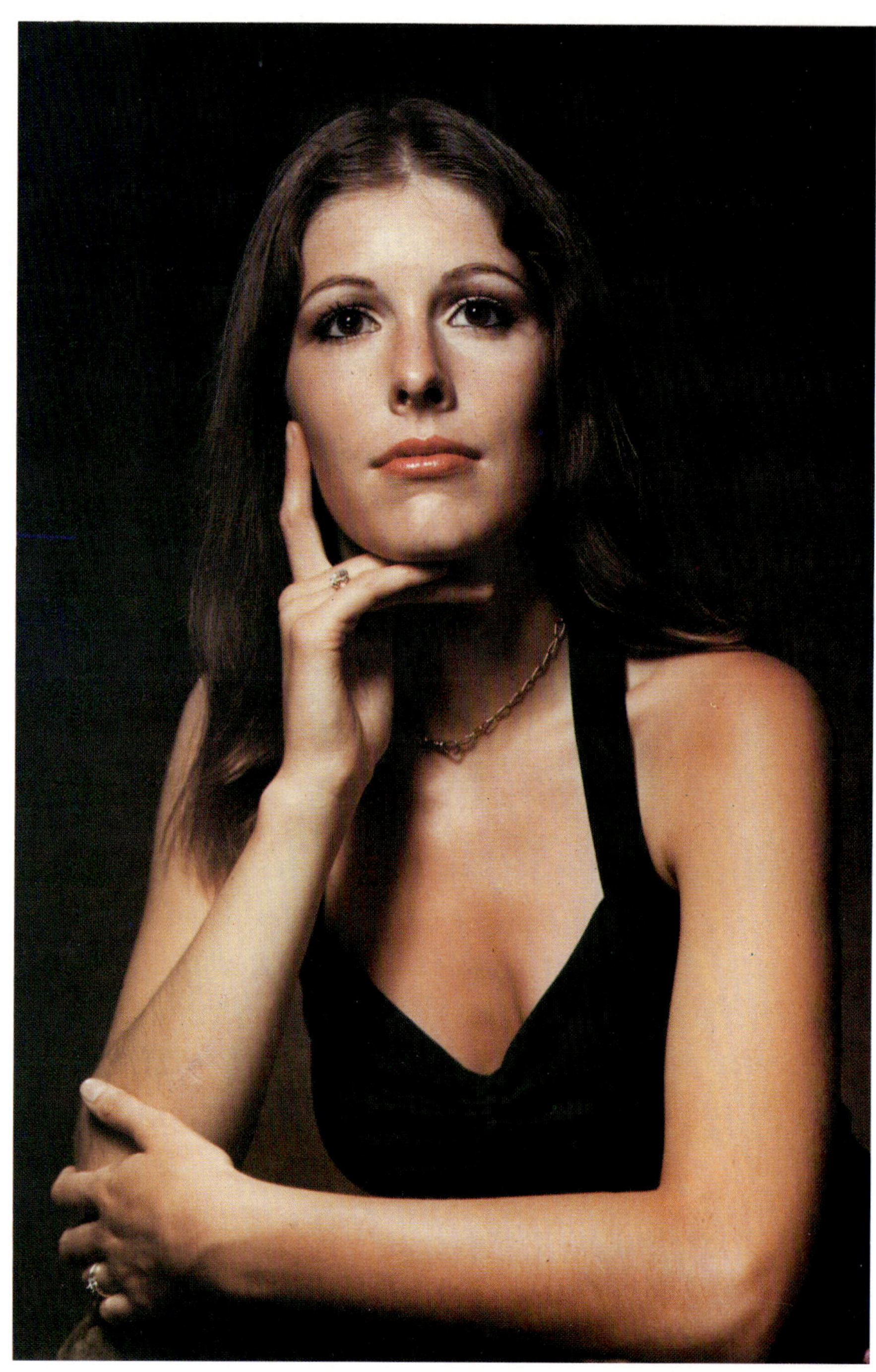

Subtle use of the hands lend feeling to a portrait.

Chapter 6

Camera Equipment

The best advice when it comes to camera equipment is: "Keep it simple." The public is constantly romanced and frequently seduced by the clever people who design, manufacture, and advertise photographic equipment. Each naturally feels his product is superior and spends massive amounts of time and money in selling that product, and loads his equipment with gadgets, some of which are virtually useless while adding to the cost and complexity of the product. A camera is still nothing more than a black box with a lens, shutter, and viewfinder, and those who fall prey to the Madison Avenue sales pitch can easily become collectors of paraphernalia rather than photographers. Super-duper lenses or electronic computer gismos have little to do with making fine photographs. The more complex the equipment, the more prone it is to failure. If you own 47 cameras and 93 lenses, chances are you don't know how to get the best out of any single one. In order to function successfully as a photographer, you must be able to get the most out of your equipment.

FORMAT

Today much consideration is given to format. Modern films have remarkable magnification capability, and spectacular, large exhibition prints can be made from very small negatives, such as 35 mm. From the accompanying chart, you get a proportional idea of how many square inches of film you get with the various format sizes. You may find that the 35 mm is fussy to work with and offers very little capability insofar as controls on the negative. At the same time, the 4″ × 5″ and 5″ × 7″ can be costly if you are exposing color negative material. A reasonable compromise is the 2¼″ × 2¾″ format. This film size has some of the retouching and corrective capabilities which the larger formats offer. It is also the minimum size that you should utilize to produce high-quality portraits. Other advantages of this format are the ease of processing in batches and simplified handling as compared to 4″ × 5″ and 5″ × 7″ materials, and its availability, since many smaller dealers do not stock the larger films unless they are ordered in advance.

Today there is equipment that will make 15 negatives 2¼″ wide × 1⅝″ high; cameras that will make 12 exposures of 2¼″ × 2¼″, or 10 exposures of 2¼″ × 2¾″, and the old standby of 2¼″ × 3¼″, which produces 8 exposures. Cameras which accept 220 film permit twice the number of exposures in each format. However, some emulsions are not available in this size. One of the advantages of operating in a studio is that you can use larger camera equipment that are awkward to carry on outside assignments.

CAMERAS

Many of the better portrait photographers differ in their opinions concerning single-lens reflex (SLR) and twin-lens reflex cameras. The SLR offers positive image placement and a wonderful choice of lenses. When you press the shutter on an SLR, a sequence of functions takes place. Between the release of that shutter and the taking of the picture, a mirror device has to swing out of the way so that the film can be exposed; the lens has to be shut down to the preselected aperture; the shutter has to open and close; then the mirror has to swing back down to its original position and the aperture to open. Moreover, SLRs are also very noisy, which can create problems when you are photographing small children, animals, or a tense subject. The major disadvantage of this equipment, however, is that you have to press the release a fraction of a second before the picture is taken, and the ensuing time lag could cost you an expression that was fleeting. The photographer who uses the SLR must therefore learn to anticipate action by that fraction of a second.

Twin-lens reflex cameras are currently less popular and are not produced by as many manufacturers. However, in a twin-lens reflex, which has a shutter on the taking lens, a press of the shutter releases the catch and the picture is made. The time lag is considerably shorter than with the SLRs. Most good twin-lens cameras have built-in parallax adjustment devices that will work to reasonably close distances, certainly well within the distance for making portraits. In the actual taking of the photographs, you should be aware of the approximate composition of the finished picture and should allow sufficient space to adjust the picture up or down or side to side to improve the composition or fit the requested print size.

LENS CHOICES

Select lenses for the type of work you plan to do. For instance, it is difficult to make a good portrait with an ultra-sharp lens designed for industrial or commercial photography. Such a lens requires a tremendous amount of retouching and possibly subsequent diffusion in the printing process. The three basic lenses are: wide angle, normal, and telephoto. In a small, cramped room, a wide-angle enables you to cover a large area without backing into hallways, while telephotos let you reach out and bring a subject into closer proximity so that you don't have to exceed your range in enlarging and making the final photographs.

Portraiture Lenses Basically, a lens used in portraiture is selected because of its control of perspective. An extremely wide-angle lens will exaggerate the size of anything close to the camera, and although this is perfectly acceptable in commercial illustrations and other areas of photography, it creates a freakish look that is hardly acceptable for a portrait. Extremely long telephotos flatten out the perspective and are therefore not suitable for portraits either. In addition, they place the photographer too far from the subject for effective communication during the sitting and fill the negative with oversized heads. For the 35 mm format, the normal lens is 50 mm, and the 90–100 mm is generally the best focal length for portraiture. In the 2¼″ × 2¼″, the ideal focal length for portraiture is 135–150 mm. For the 4″ × 5″ format, 8½–10-inch lenses are frequently used, and for the 5″ × 7″, 12–16 inches.

In any format you select, it is important to be able to make a head-and-shoulders three-quarter or full-length photograph of your subject without getting too close or too far. Before purchasing any lens, it is always wise to find a friend with a lens of the same focal length that you want to buy, and test it in your working environment to see if it will be suitable for you. Buying the wrong lens can sometimes force you into making pictures that are not precisely what you want. The wrong lens may limit your photography and not permit you the choice of changing vantage point and position at will.

Investment in very fast or super-speed lenses offers no real advantage in portraiture. Use a lens at one or two *f*-stops below the largest opening and avoid stopping down to *f*-16, *f*-22, or beyond in making portraits and group photographs. Although you want the area from the tip of the subject's nose to the back of the cheeks sharp and well defined, you don't want sharp backgrounds that will compete with or fight the subject. An out-of-focus background enhances a portrait. Outdoors, one of the greatest control tools is a wide-open or near-wide-open lens that gives brilliant sharpness to your subject while permitting everything else to fall into a soft, diffused background. This eliminates sharp and distracting lines from trees, leaves, lawns, or structures. The longer focal-length lenses are ideal outdoors because the perspective angle of the lens reduces the amount of background shown behind the subject, thereby eliminating distracting backgrounds.

OTHER EQUIPMENT

Tripods If you are to concentrate on your subject and a certain expression and work patiently to capture that magic moment, the last thing you should be doing is holding the camera. For portraiture, therefore, always affix your camera to a very sturdy tripod. By putting the camera on a tripod and posing the subject, you do not constantly have to refocus each pose. There is ample time to communicate with the subject and, together, create the ideal mood for the portrait. A tripod gives you the freedom to move away from the camera or to move closer and adjust stray hair or clothing so that everything is where it should be. With the camera on a tripod you can focus all your attention on making the picture.

Tripods come in a variety of styles and designs, so take care in selecting one for your work. Most portraits are made at approximately *eye level* to the subject, with slight variations to accommodate for individual facial characteristics (see chapter 16). A tripod that will drop to about 3 feet and extend to about 5½–6 feet is more than adequate for portraiture. You don't need to purchase huge pieces of equipment that offer extreme elevation. However, you may prefer a tripod that has large knobs and controls so that little attention is required in its use and it can quickly be raised or lowered depending on the type of sitting and subject. It is also important that the tripod locks securely so as not to slam the camera. In the case of roll-film cameras, one that permits the loading and unloading of the camera without removal from the tripod is a useful asset. For some reason, the tripod has become a much overlooked piece of equipment. This is understandable in the case of the tourist or snapshooter who doesn't want to be encumbered with the bulk of a solid tripod. For the professional, however, a good tripod is a must.

Shutter Releases A very useful device is an air shutter release, which permits you to move away from the camera position and still make the exposure when you are ready. Some of these releases are sold with 30–50 feet of tubing, though it is hard to visualize moving 50 feet from a subject for a portrait. However, they can be shortened, and with a little experimentation you will find that five or six feet of tubing will permit you a more than adequate range on either side of the camera so that you can move around and direct the subject and still make the exposures when you are ready.

The most important advantage of using an air shutter release is that you can hold the bulb behind your back and make pictures without the subject being aware of when you will do so. This can be a tremendous advantage when photographing nervous people and children, and it puts the equipment (camera, tripod, release, and lights) in the background so that you can work directly with your subject. This very inexpensive piece of equipment is one of the handiest devices that you can buy.

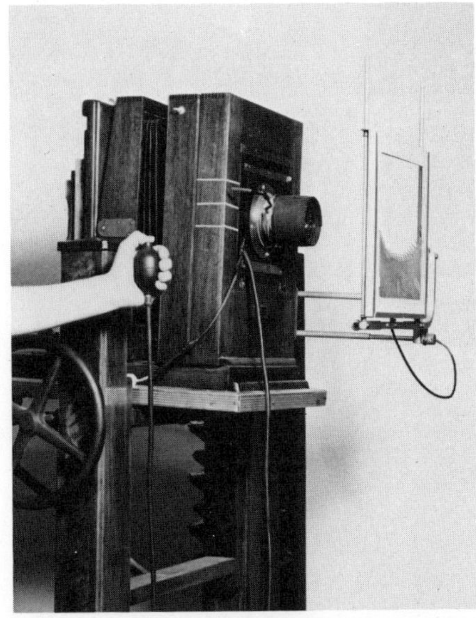

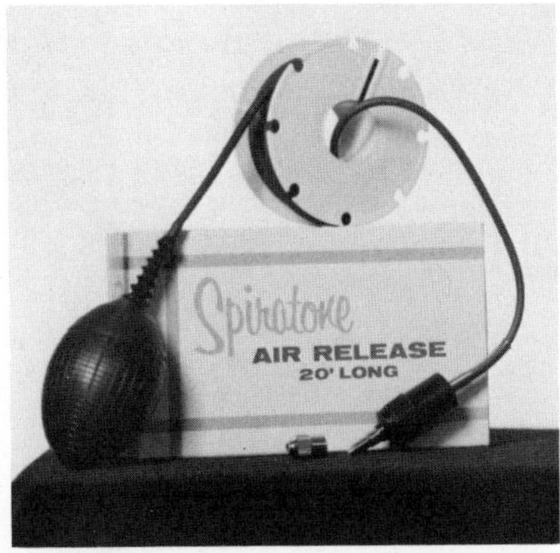

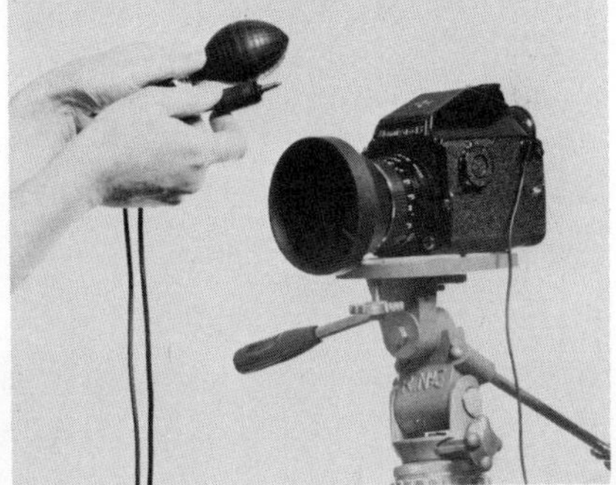

The original and modern versions of air shutter releases used for positive control of exposure.

Lens Shades Once you remove your lights from the camera position and start to exercise lighting controls that shape the face three-dimensionally, there will be occasions when, because of a particular pose or lighting, you will have to move the lights to the side of, and sometimes behind, the subject. If you were to attempt to make photographs without a suitable lens shade, you would lose many exposures due to lens flare. Even when lens flare is not very obvious, a small amount of it will degrade the photographic image, making the blacks in the picture appear gray. Whether you use a professional mat box or a homemade sunshade, be careful that it does not extend too far and cut off a segment of the image.

Vignetters These devices are utilized to throw selected areas out of focus and thereby concentrate attention on the subject. There are a number of mechanical devices that can be attached to a camera or tripod and are adjustable insofar as distance from the lens and height in front of the lens to produce partial diffusion

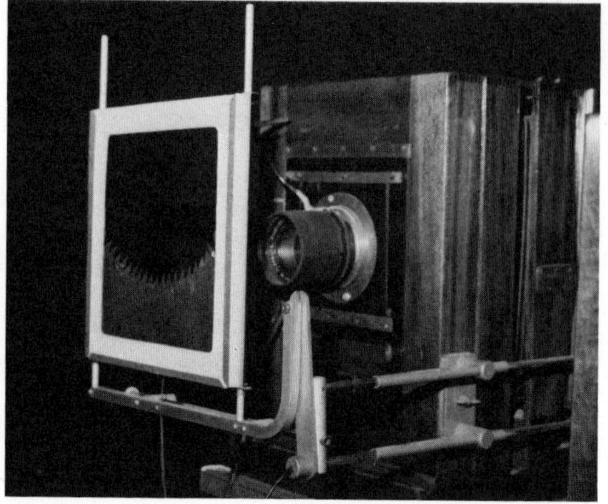

An example of a professional, large-camera vignetter permanently mounted to the side of the camera and offering complete up-and-down, side-to-side, and backward-forward adjustments from the back of the camera ground glass viewing position. Manufactured by Photogenic.

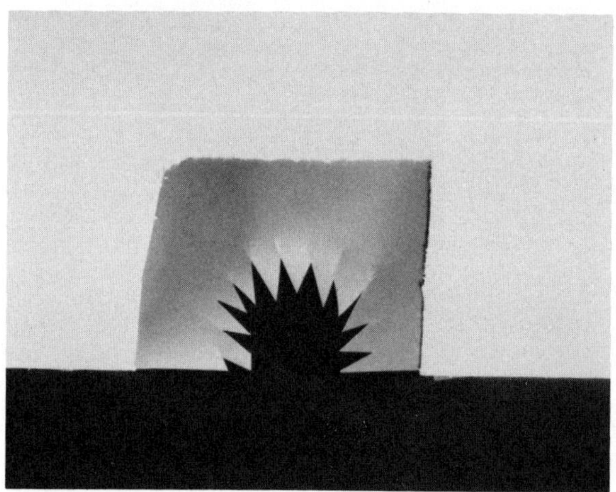

A tape-mounted homemade matte acetate vignetter for manual use with small cameras.

effects. Very often a vignetter can simplify a fussy scene and produce a more interesting and exciting image. It is another tool of the craft permitting control. In an SLR, the use of a vignetter is simplified because there is no guesswork and you can see precisely the effect you will get when the lens is stopped down to your taking aperture. A little experience with vignetters will quickly teach you when they are advantageous and when they become superfluous.

You can improvise in vignetters with some simple homemade devices, including sheets of matte acetate or ordinary Kleenex tissue. For a dark

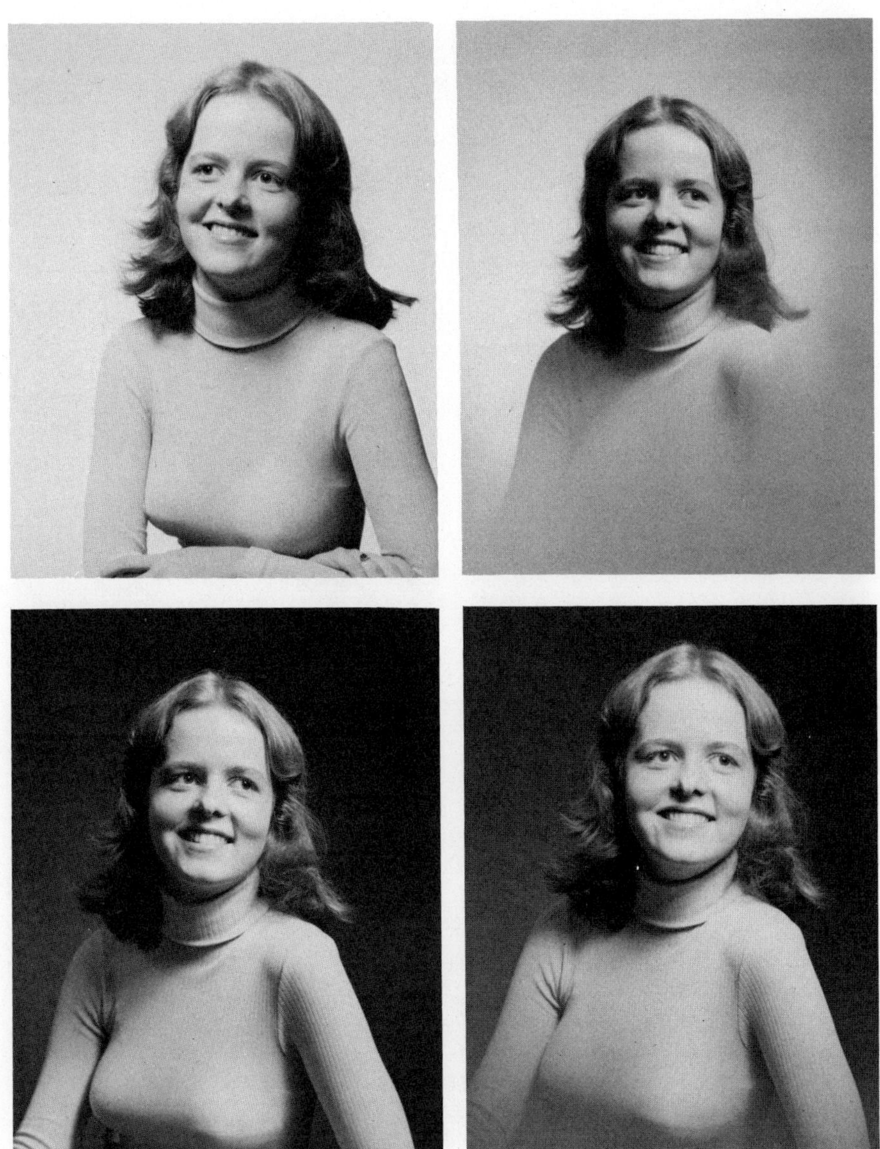

Photographs (top) taken against a light background with and without a vignetter. Photographs (bottom) taken with no vignetter (left), and slight vignetting (right).

vignetter, simply place a black glove over your hand. Even a skylight or UV filter on the camera lens can be turned into a vignetter by painting clear nail polish around the outer edges of the filter. Never put nail polish or similar material on your lens as you may ruin it permanently. For a temporary or quick effect, smear

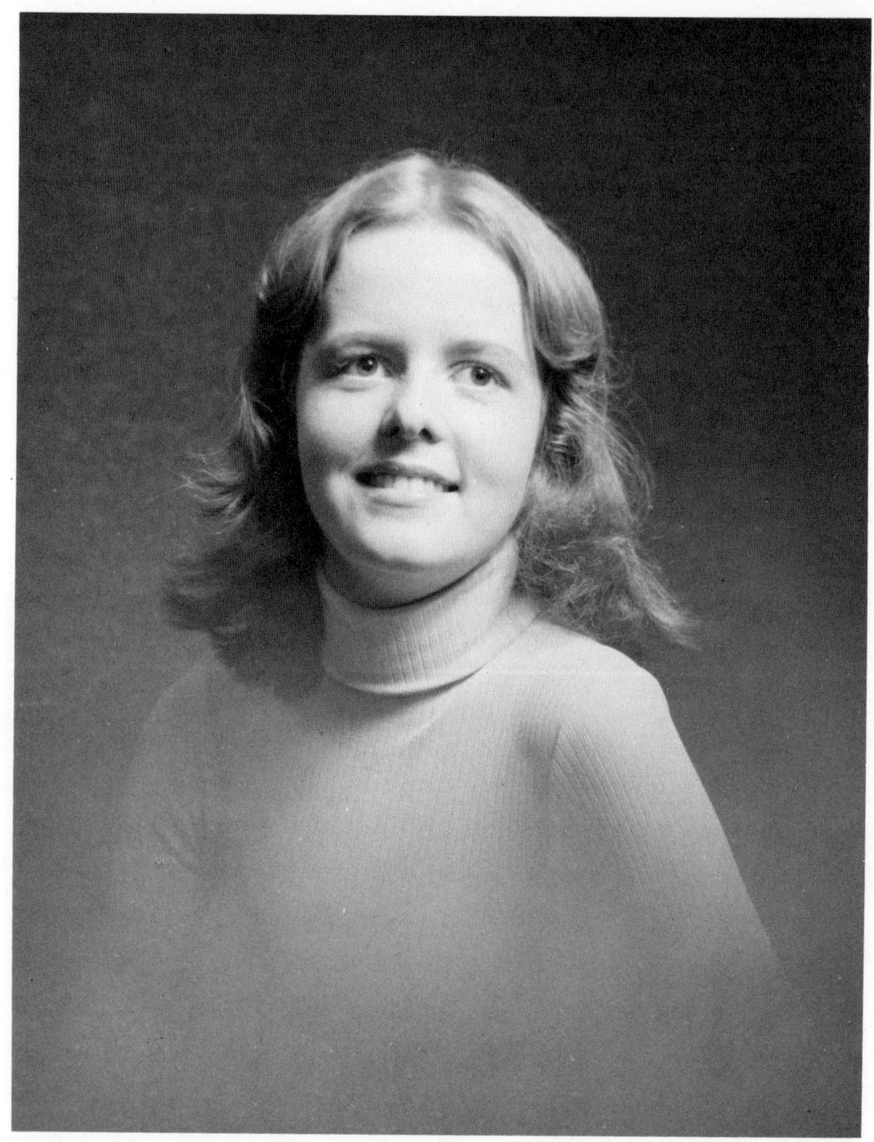

Photograph taken with considerable vignetting.

Vaseline or any clear material on the filter. If the result is not satisfactory on your first try, wipe it off and try again. If you own one of the special-effects matte boxes, you can prepare a series of vignetters in advance and drop them into the box in the appropriate position to achieve the desired effects. These boxes are useful for many other functions, including multiple-exposure effects.

DIFFUSION DEVICES

There is a lot of misunderstanding about diffusion devices, because of a lack of knowledge of the basic principle. The fact is that there is a tremendous difference in the effects achieved with in-camera diffusion and that achieved during printing of the finished photograph. If you diffuse in camera, the bright areas, or highlights, of the original scene will spread into the dark areas, or shadows. This type of diffusion causes a halo which degrades the shadow areas but leaves the highlights with much of their original sparkle. On the other hand, if you diffuse during the printing stage (either black-and-white or color), the bright areas in the negative, which represent the shadows, will diffuse out into the highlights and degrade them in the finished print. When the highlights are thus degraded, they look dirty. So although you can achieve the same degree of diffusion, the two types of diffusion appear radically different in the end product. In addition, in-camera diffusion is permanent and cannot be adjusted or removed later, while diffusion in the printing stage can be repeated until you achieve your objective.

Soft-Focus Lenses It is not true that in-camera diffusion can create the same effect as the old portrait lenses of the past. A diffused image produced by a soft-focus lens has an unusual quality that is a combination of diffusion and sharpness. Soft-focus lenses are difficult to use, and few small- and medium-format cameras manufactured today will accommodate this type of lens. If you

Years ago, when Eastman Kodak manufactured enlargers, it produced an optical disc for moderate or extreme diffusion. These make wonderful camera diffusers.

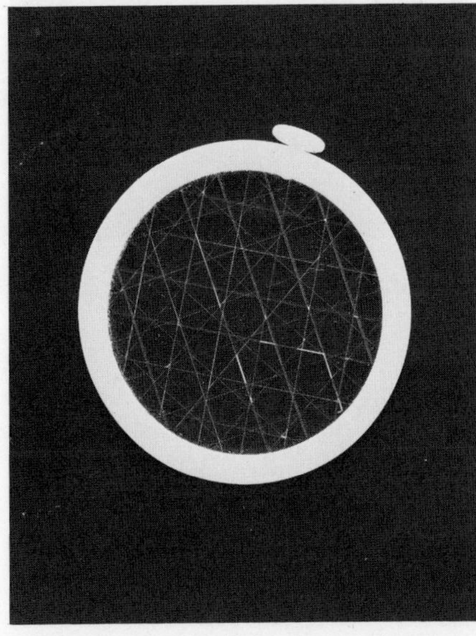

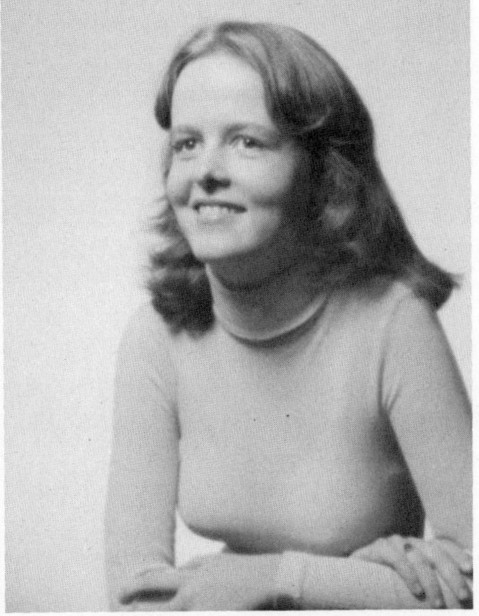

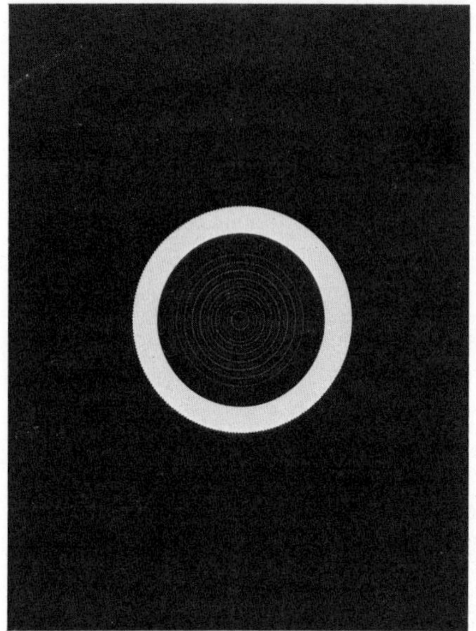

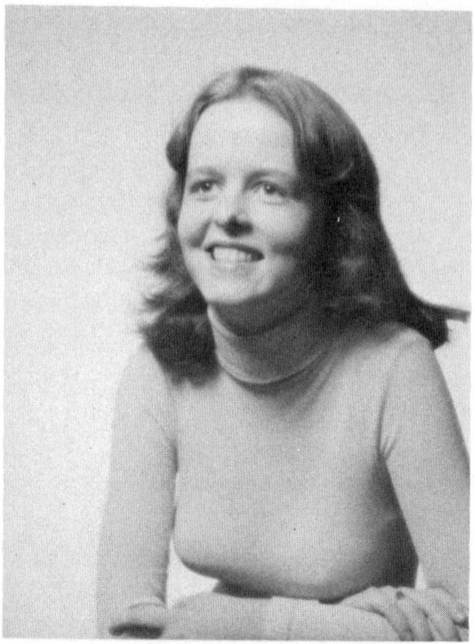

The Rollei-Soft disc and the moderately diffused image it produces at medium apertures.

desire the old-fashioned diffusion which you get with the soft-focus lenses made by Kodak, Verito, or the Pinkham-Smith, you are restricted to large-format equipment. These soft-focus lenses produce an image that is reasonably sharp at the prime point of focus, after which the sharpness of the image alters rapidly. In a head-and-shoulders portrait of a man, for instance, from the tip of the nose to the back of the cheek, (the frontal planes of the face) will be relatively sharp and crisp while the ears will be diffused and soft. Such lenses require a great deal of control in photography; the subject must be quite still, since the slightest movement would lose the zone of sharpness and ruin the effect. Another reason why these lenses were particularly difficult to use is that it is essential to focus at the same *f*-stop that you will use for the actual exposure.

Images that are unsharp or blurry due to focus or camera movement are not soft-focus images. In soft-focus images, there is an overall sharpness of the central subject, while the outer edges of the image are diffused or softened. Soft focus can achieve an extremely beautiful effect but is not a remedy or replacement for retouching, nor is it a remedy for poor retouching on a negative.

Diffusion Discs Optical discs are another method for achieving soft-focus images. These devices are similar to clear glass filters with a series of ridges concentrically set to diffuse the outer periphery of the image. The diffusion decreases toward the center of the image. In order to achieve the maximum effect with optical discs, the lens must be used at a wide-open or almost-wide-open aperture. As the lens diaphragm is stopped down to the smaller apertures, it eliminates the outer ridges of the disc and therefore reduces the amount of diffusion. Before using this device at a sitting, make a set of test negatives to determine whether the effect you get is what you want, and also to determine the best *f*-stop.

Among the diffusion discs marketed today is the Rollei-Soft. Occasionally you may find an old Kodak portrait diffusion disc, originally designed for use on enlargers, but which can achieve some pretty effects. Spiratone (136-06 Northern Blvd., Flushing, N.Y. 11354) offers a series of lenses which fit most cameras that accept interchangeable lenses. These utilize optics which have not been perfectly corrected and intentionally reduce image sharpness.

French Tulle One of the most successful ways to make diffused images in the camera is to use a black netlike material called French tulle. The black color prevents internal reflections. Not only does it make a very fine soft-focus or diffusion material for the camera, but you can also fit one or two layers of it permanently into a simple filter holder and use it in the darkroom over your enlarging lens.

Many so-called diffusion tricks are unsatisfactory for portraiture. Wrinkled cellophane, silk stocking, or shiny steel screening destroy the quality of the image both in black-and-white and color to the point where they are unacceptable. The French tulle will soften an image without producing a large amount of halation and is the most inexpensive and practical way for softening or diffusing an image.

French Tulle mounted in a metal adapter ring produces a pleasing diffusion without overly degrading image quality.

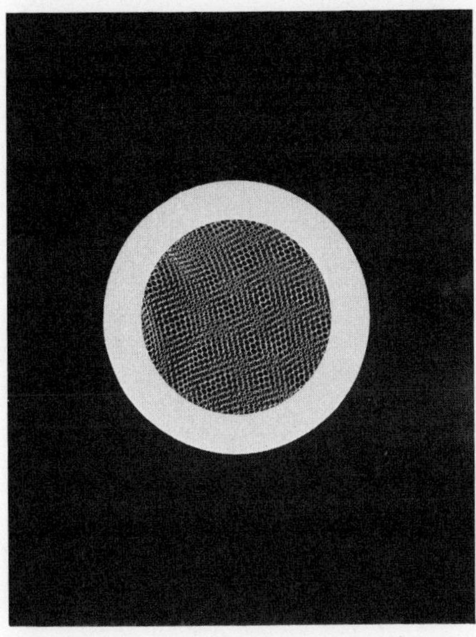

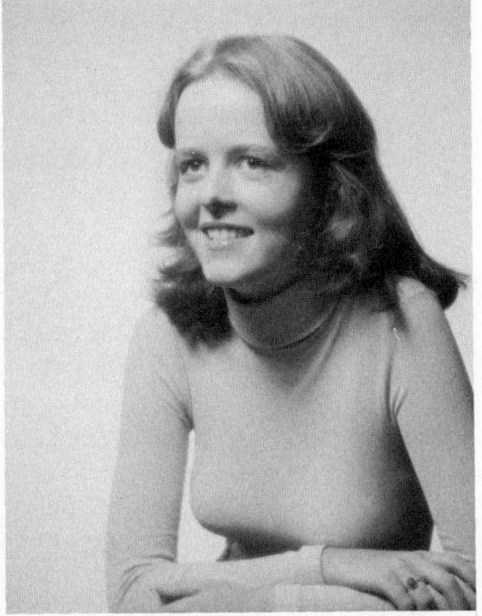

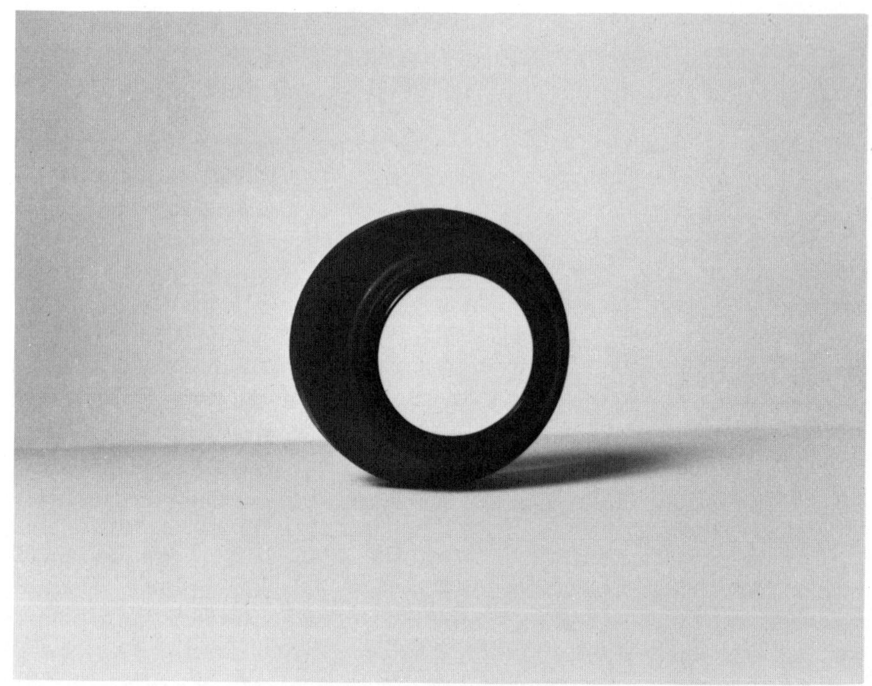

Regardless of construction material, it is essential to equip your camera with a sunshade to reduce the possibility of flare.

Chapter 7

Lighting Equipment

Light is the most important tool a photographer has at his disposal. You can make photographs by using a lighttight box with a pinhole and sensitized paper—without camera, lens, or film—but there is no way to make a photograph without light. "Photography" means painting with light, and light is a prime consideration to anyone involved with photography. The beginning photographer tends to concentrate on the quantity of light and getting sufficient exposure to correctly record the scene with the material he is using. Later he acquires the understanding that it is not the quantity but rather the quality of light that is the prime concern of the photographer.

If you want the best photographs outdoors, you have no choice but to return to a scene at the proper time of day to take them. In the enclosed environment of a studio, you can place the "sun" at any angle and at any time of the day or night. The controlled studio environment affords a freedom to the photographer which the outdoors does not. Although good photographs can be made indoors with virtually any type of light, including the glow of candles or a small incandescent light, you should strive to develop a lighting system that is reliable. If your lighting system permits you to know your precise exposure each and every time you use a specific film material, this eliminates the need for testing to determine exposure.

In addition, with a system that is properly balanced, you can achieve consistency in your work because you know in advance the amount of light that will fall upon the highlights, the shadows, and the background. The advantage here is one of simplifying your efforts so that you can concentrate on such important matters as pose, direction of the key light, and expression. If at each sitting you must struggle with lighting, exposures, and ratios for a given subject and film, the sitting can become an extremely difficult chore. Thus one key to

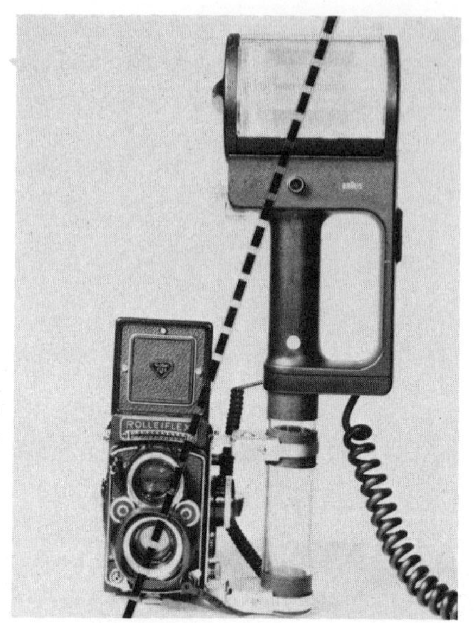

One of the better ways to improve lighting for assignments that do not permit a separate light on a stand is to mount the flash away from the lens. On a 2 1/4" x 2 1/4" format camera, turning the camera for horizontal or vertical photographs is not required.

The hot shoe elevates the flash, but when you turn the camera for a vertical photograph, the flash is positioned at the same level as the lens, producing poor shadows.

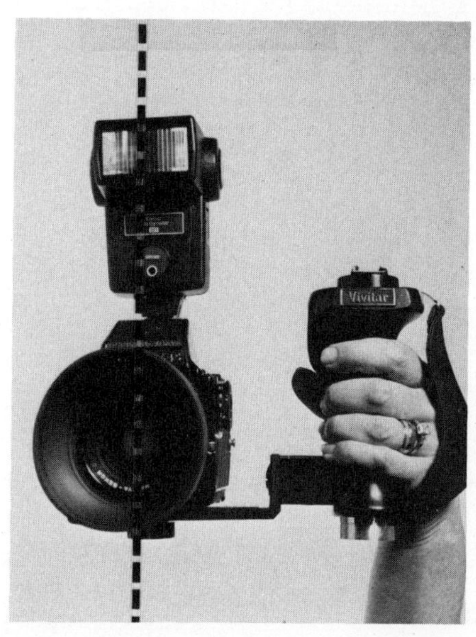

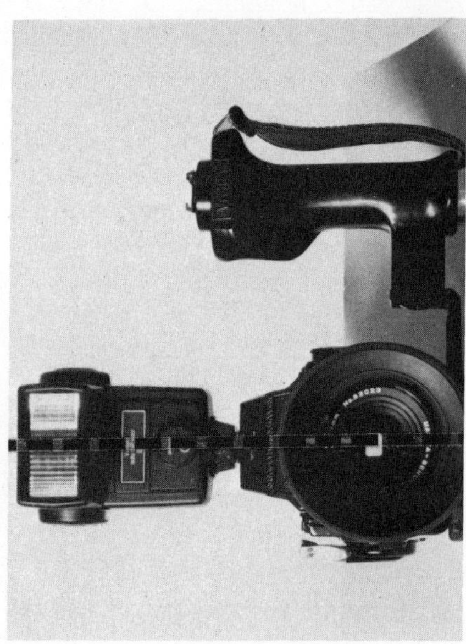

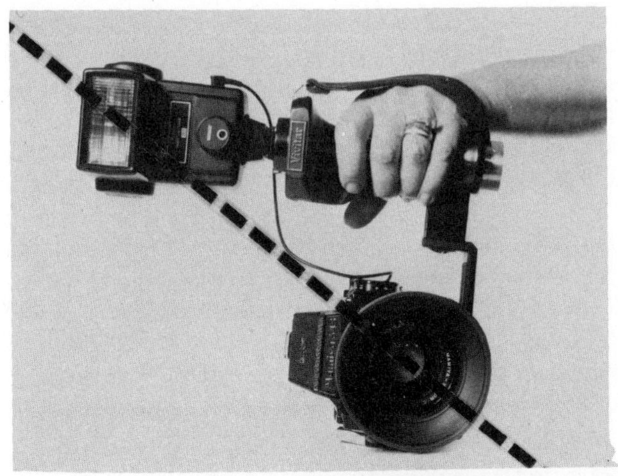

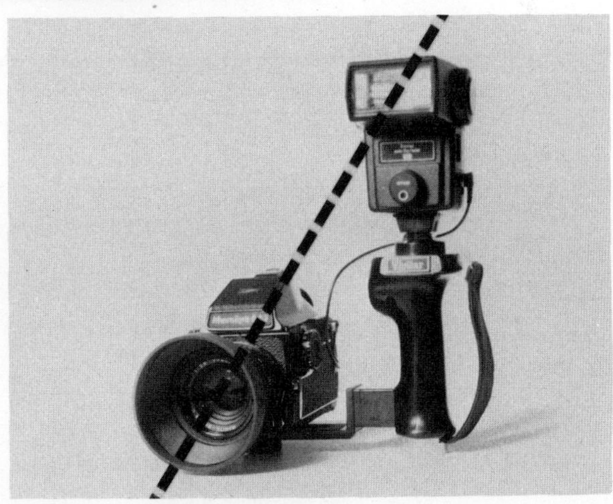

By mounting the flash on a suitable "L" bracket or grip, the flash is positioned above and slightly to the side of the lens, producing better lighting.

successful portraiture is to develop a method of working that offers consistency in exposure, control of light ratio, and frees you to concentrate on making the portrait.

This does not mean that lights should be so nailed down that they are never moved, or that the lighting is never altered for the individual subject. Developing a routine for lighting need not produce the sameness in your photography. What it does mean is that you can produce an unbelievable variety of lighting in a simple, direct method that is reliably repeatable, and you can set up all the equipment in your lighting system in such a manner as to make each sitting more predictable.

If you experimented with lighting and ran into problems, you may have decided that only bigger or more expensive lighting equipment would solve them. This, of course, is not true. You can achieve good lighting with basic equipment. More expensive electronic gear look impressive and offer you some conveniences, but the key to good lighting is understanding light itself and using the appropriate controls on your lights to produce the desired end product.

Since many beginning photographers cannot afford the investment in electronic equipment, one alternative is an inexpensive set of tungsten lights that are capable of reproducing controlled portrait lighting, have barn doors, an adjustable lamp socket, and adequate tilting controls that are easy to manage. Testrite manufactures such a unit (model #5W-100-3), as well as a variety of simple roller stands or standard stands that adjust adequately for portraiture. These lights use standard tungsten bulbs, and when used with blue-tinted commercial bulbs are more than adequate for producing high-quality color negatives as well as black-and-white photographs. They are suitable for individual pictures, pictures of couples, and groups of up to four people (see chapter 5). For a larger group, these lamps, which can accommodate 200-watt light bulbs, would have to be moved back too far, thereby requiring long exposures. For larger groups, Testrite produces lamps that can accommodate 500-watt bulbs. The only objection to these lights is that the barn doors on the inside are a highly polished aluminum, which makes controlling the light difficult due to the reflective surface. You can solve this problem by applying a coat of black matte spray lacquer to the shiny surface. A set of these lights will withstand the rigors of time for many years. Because of their flat pan construction, they throw an unusually even pattern of illumination and work quite well for making portraits. When using these lights, avoid photoflood lamps. If they are not available through your local photograph dealer, check the Appendix at the end of this book for the names and addresses of manufacturers.

ELECTRONIC FLASH

While there are many advantages to using electronic flash for portraiture, there are also some cautions. In producing professional-quality portraiture, your prime concern is the direction, quality, and control of light. This does not mean mounting a flash unit in the little bracket on the camera because direct frontal lighting creates all sorts of problems. It is the most aging and least flattering lighting you can use on a subject. For this reason, a flash should never be mounted directly on the camera for portraiture. Even on assignments that require flash, a special bracket that elevates the flash at least 14–16 inches from the lens will produce far superior photographs than one in which the flash is fixed directly on the camera.

In portraiture, the objective is to use light to shape the face; therefore, the light should be individually mounted on a stand and positioned approximately

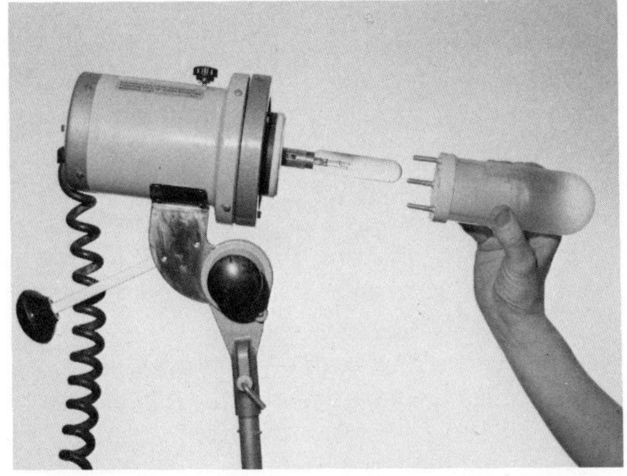

The modeling light (left) on this Photogenic flash is completely enclosed in a ground-glass cover containing the flashtube. This ensures that the modeling lamp and the flashtube throw the same light patter.

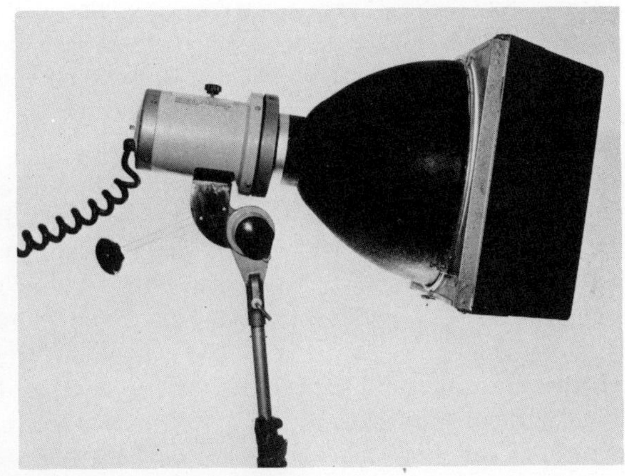

Rotating barn doors (right) permit you to control the pattern of light and at the same time prevent surplus light from striking the background and the lens.

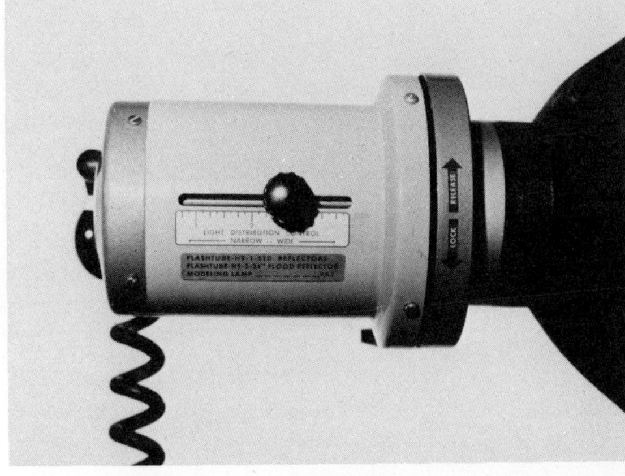

The tube can be easily positioned in the reflector with an adjustment knob atop the unit.

45 degrees from the camera. Most portable flash units do not have a modeling light—a tungsten light that shows the photographer the angle and direction of the light that will fall on the subject. However, some units have provisions for mounting a separate bulb near the electronic flashtube. Unfortunately, most of these fail to throw the same lighting pattern with the tungsten illumination as they do with the flash. In such cases, portraiture photographers are frequently frustrated because they see one image, as thrown by the tungsten illumination, and actually photograph something entirely different, as lit by the flashtube. A solution to this particular problem is to construct a Soff-Box (a trademark of Larson Enterprises, Inc.).

Before investing in an expensive electronic flash unit with built-in modeling lights, there is a way you can determine just how accurate the modeling light is. Regardless of the cost of the unit (and some cost thousands of dollars), if the pattern of light thrown by the tungsten light and the flashtube are not identical, you can never accurately visualize the end results.

Testing Electronic Flash To determine if a set of lights will record on film the same image that you see, make this simple test. Use a subject that will remain immobile during the test exposures, preferably a store-display head such as that used in the illustrations. If you have a camera that adapts to a Polaroid back, this will give you the test results more quickly. Otherwise, load your camera with the film you normally use and make one photograph of the subject or mannequin using the flash unit. Then disconnect the cord and, by using an exposure-meter reading and the same *f*-stop as before, adjust your shutter exposure because of the lower level of light produced by the modeling lamps. Make a second exposure using only the modeling lamps. Process the film and make two identical-size prints of the two exposures. Check the highlights and particularly the shadow under the nose and on the cheek line; this will tell you immediately whether the pattern of light is identical or whether there is a variation between the electronic flash and modeling light. If they are not the same, then what you think you see when you light the subject, will be different from the image recorded on the film. If this is the case, these lights will be more of a handicap and should be avoided.

Selecting Electronic Flash Equipment In some electronic flash units, instead of switching from one power output to another, you can use a variable device that permits intermittent changes at any point on a sliding range. This type of light is useful if you have to meter the amount of tungsten light falling on the subject each time you move the light. It can also be used provided you determine what the correct setting is for a given type of work, mark that setting, and then use it for that type of sitting. Fixed, push-button settings are more easily repeatable than a variable-output setting.

In purchasing electronic lights, buy those manufactured by a company that offers reliable, reasonably fast service should the unit malfunction. Some manufacturers supply schematics and have parts which you can purchase from them or a local electronics dealer. Find out what the dealer's policy is regarding repairs and the availability of schematics before you invest a lot of money in flash equipment. Unless you have had considerable training, don't try to repair the unit yourself. The capacitors (storage containers for the electricity) in these units can hold as many as 450 volts, and the novice can be injured seriously if he mishandles this type of equipment.

By using photo tubes or solid-state slave sensors connected to your flash unit, you can get automatic and perfectly syncronized light. This eliminates the need for long cables running in various directions across the room and makes your camera room safer for your subjects and yourself.

It is also important to have electronic flash units that recycle fairly rapidly—about two to five seconds. This way, you can proceed through a sitting or a series of sittings without having to think about recycling or wait for the lights to recharge. Sometimes waiting can cost you a good expression. Moreover, triggering the lights before the capacitors are fully charged will result in a less than full output of light. In exposing color film, this can result in unprintable, underexposed, or poorly exposed negatives.

Strobes offer the advantage of extremely short exposure times regardless of shutter speed. An electronic flash will produce exactly the same negative (in a room where there is little or no ambient light) at 1/25, 1/50, 1/100, 1/250, or 1/500 sec., because exposure is controlled by the duration of the flash. Most units will fire at about 1/650 sec. or faster, some going up into thousandths of a second. When using electronic flash, to photograph children or animals, you can be assured that you will not get subject movement because the flash will freeze any action. Most of the better units have accurate ready lights that tell you when the capacitor is fully charged and the unit is ready. In some of the poorly constructed units, the ready light is set up incorrectly and is deceptive. By putting a meter on the capacitor and adjusting the resistor, the manufacturer can set the neon bulb to glow when the capacitor is anywhere from 60–90 percent full. To get the full output of the flashtube so that you consistently get the same amount of light, a well-built unit is usually set to 85–90 percent of the capacity of the capacitor.

Here's how you can test your light to make sure that it is putting out a full charge when your readylight goes on. Make two exposures—the first, after the unit has been on for some time and is fully charged, the second, the instant the ready light goes on. The latter exposure will show whether the negatives have a matching density or whether the second is underexposed to any degree. This simple test can spare you grief later, because consistency will save a lot of time in production of good-quality, matching prints.

HIGH-INTENSITY LAMPS

Quartz lights, movie lights, and other high-intensity lamps are ideal for lighting large sets and are frequently required in in-plant industrial photography of large areas or machinery. Unfortunately, this type of lighting does not lend itself well to use in portraiture. This is not to say that you cannot make portraits with this type of lighting; but when you consider subject comfort, danger from extremely hot lights, and the fact that at close distances these lights rarely throw the flat, soft, even pattern desirable for portraiture, they are best avoided.

WINDOW LIGHT

One of the most elegant types of lighting is window light. True, you are limited to certain times of the day, but window light can produce that soft, wraparound lighting which shapes and forms three-dimensionally. To make portraits using window light, position the subject close enough to the window so that adequate light for an exposure will fall upon the subject, and make sure to exclude the window itself from the picture. If the pictures are made in a room where the shadow side of the subject is extremely dark, use a reflector to soften those areas for suitable lighting ratios. When using window light, be certain that the sun is not coming directly through the window, as this will cause undesirable contrasty, harsh lighting. If you cannot avoid using a window through which sunlight is streaming, transparent or translucent curtains can soften the light sufficiently.

THE SOFF-BOX

One of America's finest portraitists, Joseph Zeltsman, has done some interesting lighting experiments using a Soff-Box. These Soff-Boxes are lightweight frames covered with black cloth on four sides, highly reflective material on the inside, and a soft matte or white translucent cover on the front. They are equipped

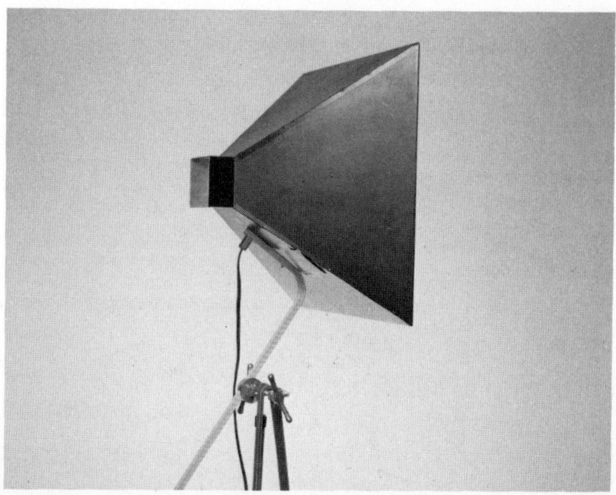

Basic construction shape of a Soff-Box without strobe mounted.

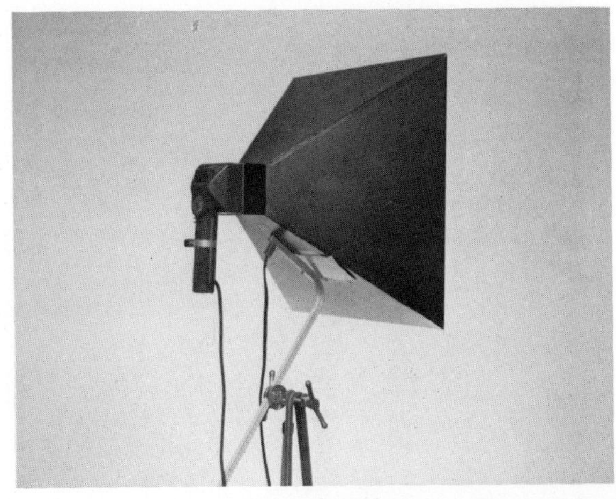

Soff-Box with Matador flash head fitted into the opening.

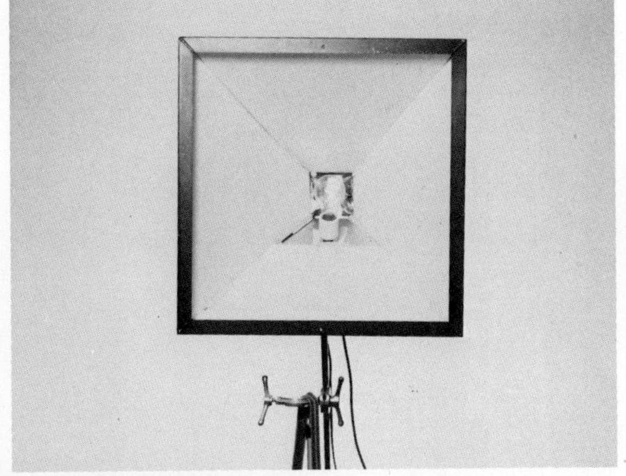

Soff-Box with barn doors and diffuser removed to show position of modeling light and socket. White matte board was used for reflector surface.

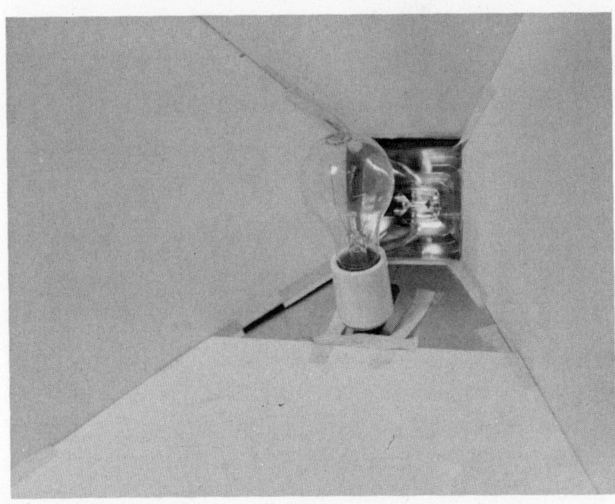

Closeup of modeling light and flashtube to show positioning.

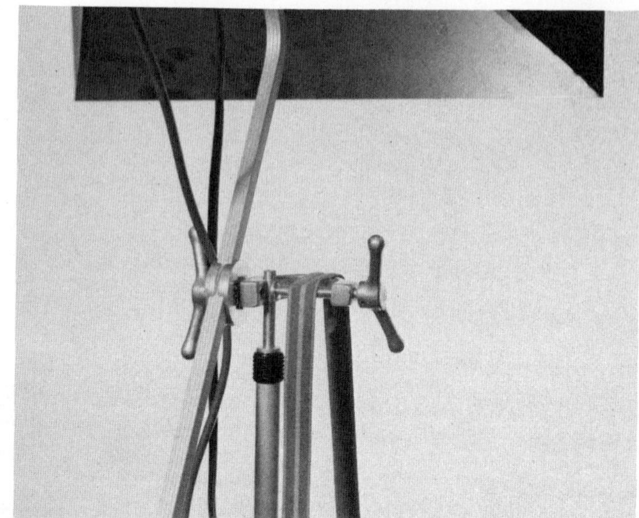

Mounting brackets for Soff-Box on conventional stand.

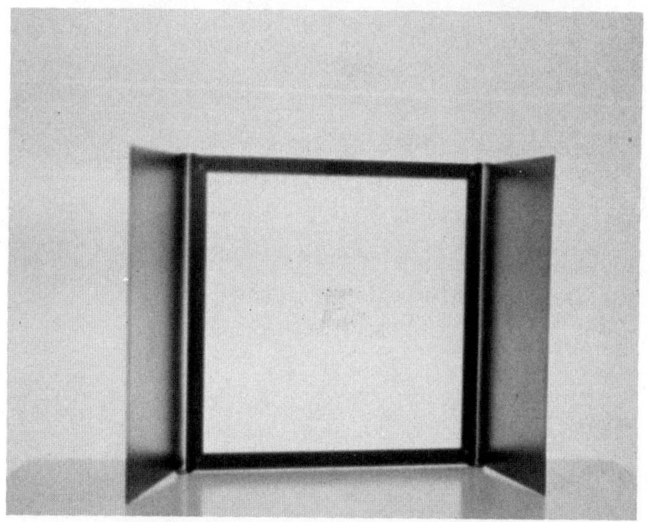

Barn door construction. Barn doors are completely covered with matte acetate diffusion material. The insides have been sprayed black.

with barn doors to produce controllable broad, soft illumination. Used as the main light, a Soff-Box produces a very satisfactory lighting pattern for portraiture. Soff-Boxes are relatively inexpensive compared to many of the large metal reflectors available and your only objection might be to its large size, particularly in a studio with limited space. However, you can construct a smaller, scaled-down unit to fit your main light using foamcore in quarter-inch thickness. Use tape to hold the unit together, some aluminum foil cemented down for your highly reflective inside surface, and a sheet of diffusion plastic matte acetate over the front of the box. Not only will your homemade Soff-Box produce admirable lighting for portraiture, but it is also ideal for the individual who doesn't want to spend money for electronic flash equipment or who wishes to use the electronic flash units he already owns. You can also construct similar boxes to fit medium-size portable electronic flash units. By adding a socket to hold a standard 75- or 100-watt bulb inside the Soff-Box structure, you can produce high-quality light for a very modest amount of money. At the end of this chapter is a set of plans for building your own electronic flash Soff-Box.

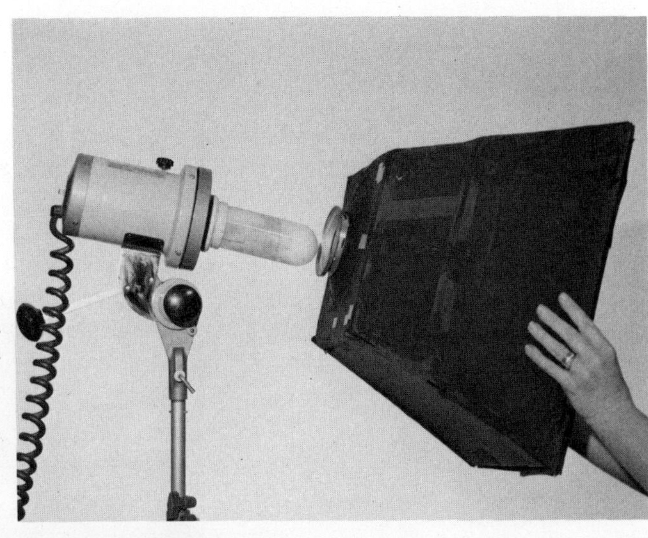

Homemade Soff-Box for the Photogenic studio flash unit slips over the flashtube and is held by a locking ring on the light.

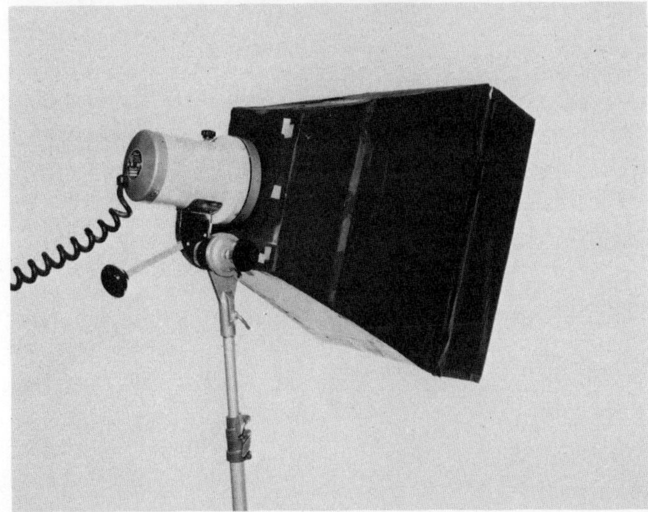

Assembled unit with barn doors.

BARN DOORS

Any light you use for portraiture *must have barn doors.* These are hinged devices that permit you to move the light around your subject, even to the point of almost directing it into the camera lens without causing extraneous flare which would destroy or degrade image quality.

To avoid background shadows, position subject away from the background; and if your main light equipped with barn doors is used correctly, it is impossible to get distracting shadows on the background. This is why controlling your light is extremely important and the use of barn doors on your main light absolutely essential.

REFLECTORS

Since the early days of photography over 100 years ago, photographers have used reflectors. Sometimes it was mounted on a stand and, by adjustment, resulted in a beautiful soft fill light that kept shadows from recording as inky black on the emulsion. Used properly, it did not destroy the modeling (shaping) of the main source of illumination. No modern commercial studio could complete many of its intricate, small-product photographs without the use of both large reflectors and small mirrors fixed in modeling clay to add touches of sparkle to illustrations.

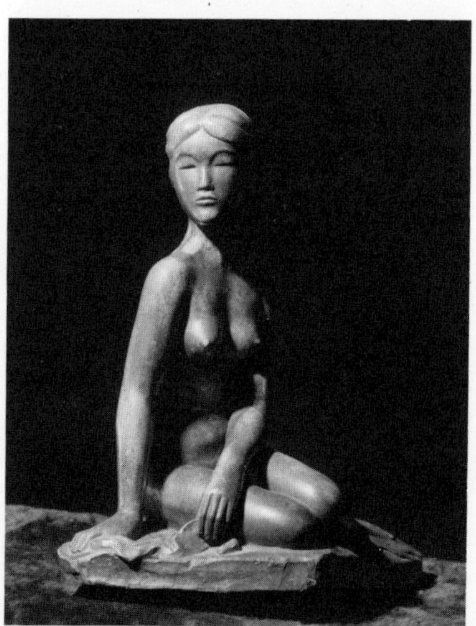

A 15-inch statue lit by a single light without a reflector.

For outdoor assignments, you can illuminate the scene with simple reflectors on large wooden flats. If you do a fair amount of location photography, you can adapt reflectors to your work. Take a lightweight material, such as foamcore, that will set up in a rigid form and yet be compact and portable. You can purchase this polyurethane material sandwiched between sturdy paper covers in 36″ × 40″ sheets. The lightest foamcore, which is three-sixth inch will enable you to build reflectors small enough to fit almost any camera case. Use glue to fasten aluminum foil on one side, and Scotch tape and a paper hinge for a folding leg that is adjustable to many angles. A 16″ × 16″ reflector (A) will fold to 8″ × 8″ × ¾″ (B) to drop into any camera case for ready access (C). A similar design could substitute ordinary white matte board for the foamcore.

A reflector lets you see and control shadow illumination visually. In the studio, reflectors work well with any illumination, including electronic flash with modeling lights. On location, you will find that a newspaper adds a lovely, soft glow to an outdoor head-and-shoulders portrait; that crinkled aluminum foil adds brilliance to portraits made in the shade or with backlighting; and that an outdoor still life peps when you add a reflector. Since outdoor light is never perfect, you can use a reflector to fill in hard shadows and reduce contrast, or to add brilliance.

This sculpture of the little mermaid illustrates how you can add fill light and maintain the feeling of three-dimensionality by the addition of a reflector. If you use window light in wedding and candid photographs, you will find that a reflector can add beauty to your subject. There is the additional advantage of using a single prime light and a reflector for taking portraits, which means that you only need to purchase one light rather than many.

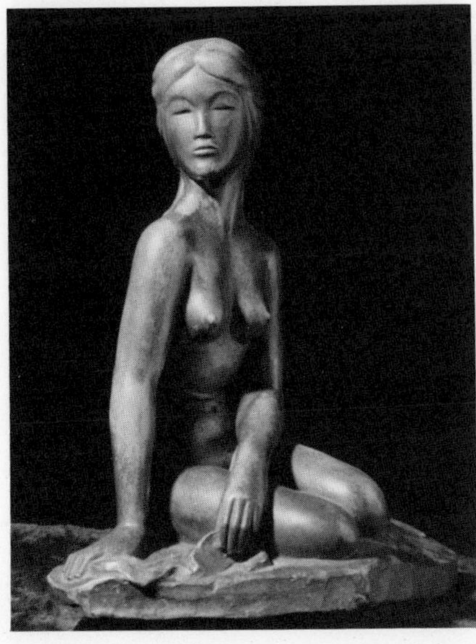

The same statue with the reflector added.

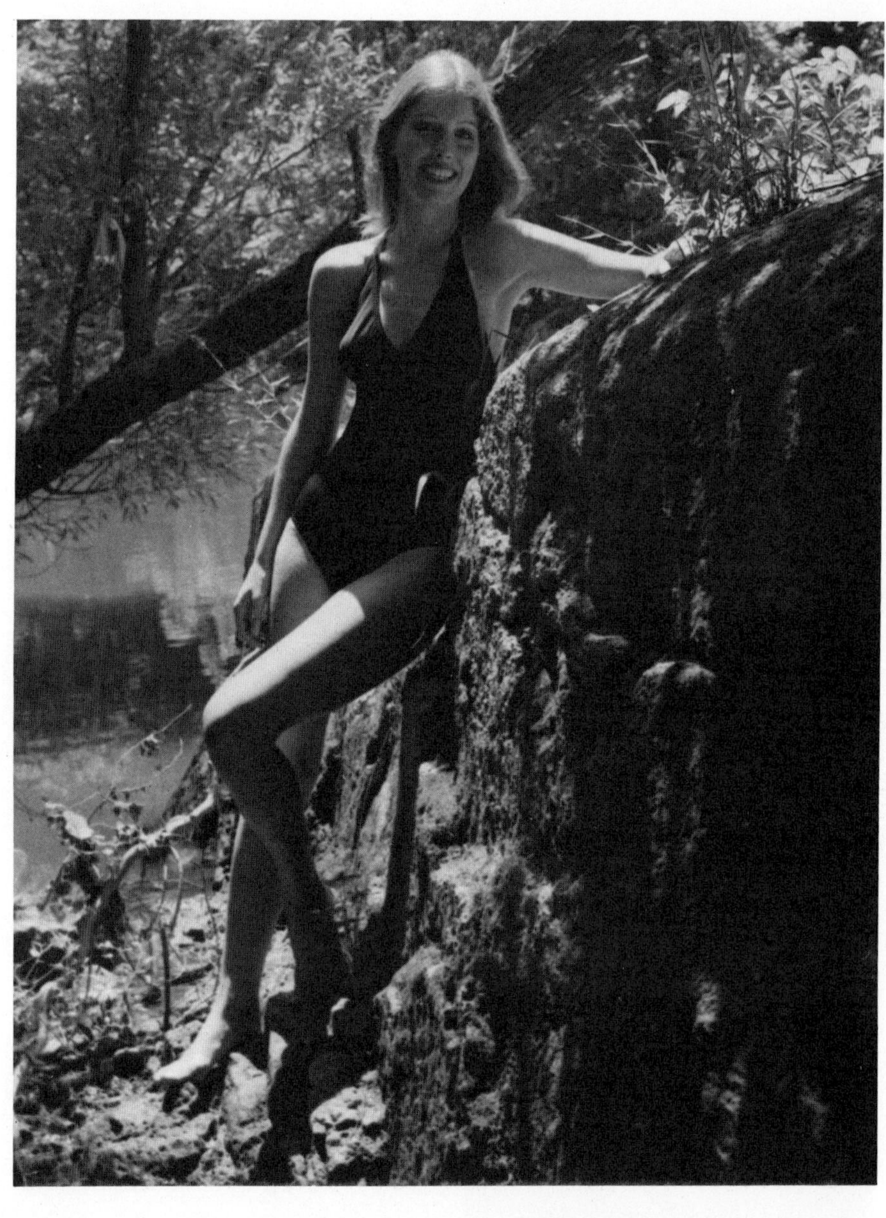

Harsh lighting outdoor often creates unwanted dark shadows. These shadows can be eliminated on the reflectors or flash.

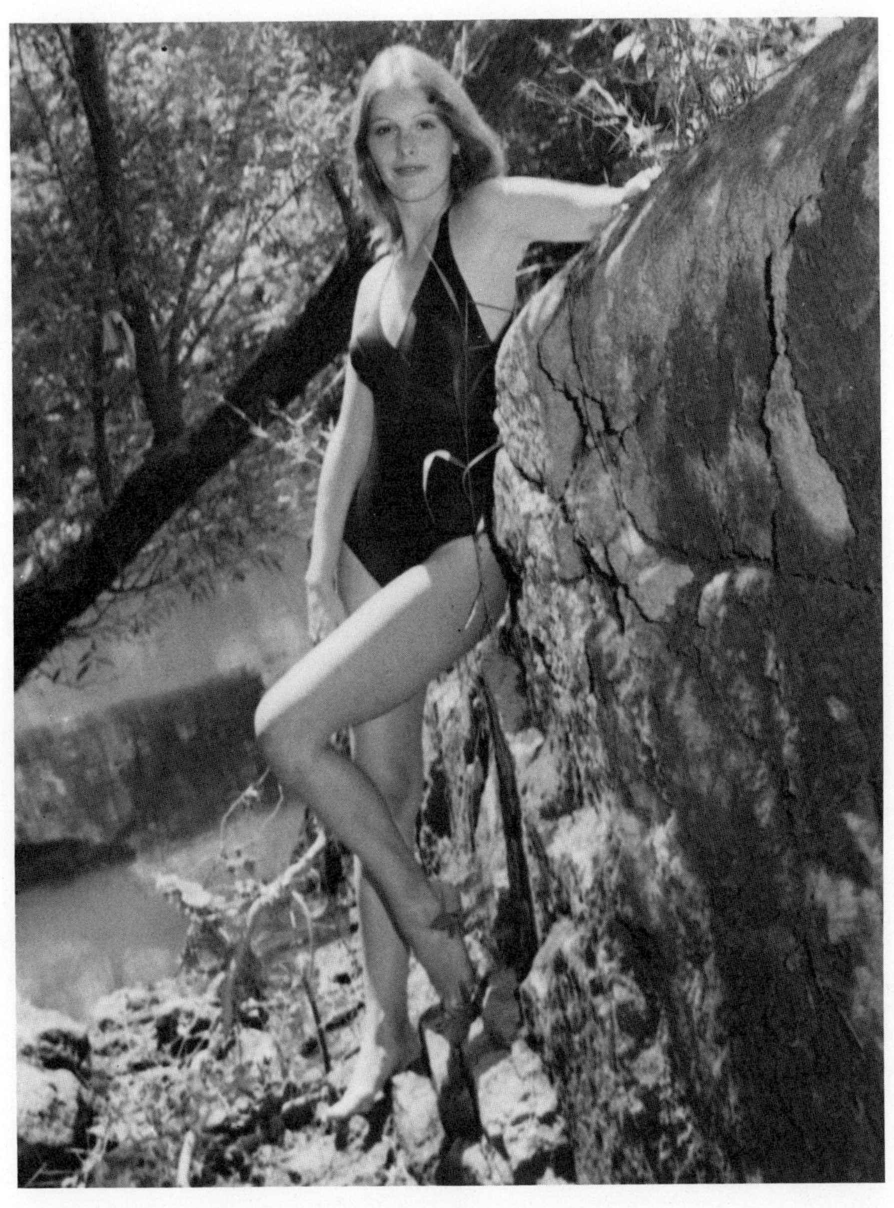

Outdoor assignments in harsh lighting conditions can improve considerably when a reflector bounces light to fill and soften the shadows. Or use a small portable flash instead. Take care that the flash does not overpower the natural light.

work with the light quite close to the subject and constantly change the positioning for each photograph, you might consider light stands with wheels. The ideal light stand is a sturdy unit that does not wobble, that has a good locking system for adjusting the height of the light, and legs that do not extend too far.

LIGHT STANDS

A multitude of light stands are available for use in portraiture. You should therefore take care in selecting a suitable one. Stands with devices that suddenly slam down can be disconcerting and annoying to both you and the sitter. For occasional use, a simple stand with tripod legs is adequate. Make sure those legs don't extend out unnecessarily; although the long legs make the unit more stable, they can get in your way while you work and cause lights to tip over.

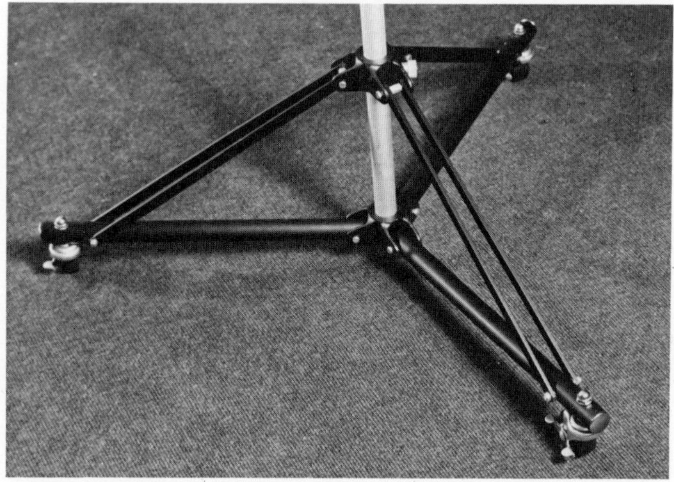

It is advantageous to have your lights on wheels to facilitate slight adjustments during a sitting.

Chapter 8

Lighting and Lighting Diagrams

It is essential that lighting diagrams be as specific and simple as possible. Think back to the number of times you saw an exciting image and decided to attempt a similar set up for one of your sittings. Invariably you had great difficulty in duplicating the mood of the original photograph. Sometimes the problem has to do with the facial structure of the subject, which is probably unlike that in the original picture. Each lighting must be adjusted for individual facial characteristics. Often the diagrams do not indicate that the photographer used barn doors, and when you attempt to duplicate the lighting, you get lens flare in your photographs.

Another problem with many lighting diagrams of the past is that they attempted to teach lighting in angles or degrees, all of them calibrated from the camera position. If, when you posed your subject the head was turned to a slightly different angle because it was required for that particular subject, and you used the angle in an arc from the camera, the lighting could not duplicate what you were trying to accomplish. Lighting discussions should illustrate the lighting in an arc designed for the frontal position of the face rather than the camera position.

In a standard portrait, the camera height is generally at the eye level of the subject, and the variations resulting from the facial characteristics of the subject, should be indicated for better comprehension. In each illustration where a camera is shown here, there is a plus (+) or minus (−), indicating not the height of the camera from the floor but rather the variation of the camera from eye level. The same plus or minus will be used for the prime source of illumination. Each drawing will also indicate whether the barn door was narrow, average, or very wide open.

A LOGICAL APPROACH TO LIGHTING

From birth we continually see all things in a very specific manner. Outdoors there is one prime source of illumination—the sun. If we accept the premise that in making photographs we should try as closely as possible to emulate real life, the logical conclusion has to be that a properly lit portrait is made with one prime source of illumination.

Some lighting methods of the past required you to place two matching lights on either side of the subject, with one farther away, and presto, you had portrait lighting! However, such lighting casts confusing shadows because even the more distant and weaker light will create shadows on the highlight side of the face. In addition, by placing lighting on either side of a perfectly normal individual, you cast shadows on the innermost parts of the eye sockets, near the nose, resulting in a cross-eyed subject.

While you could not conceive of a plumber who did not know the proper use of a wrench, or a carpenter who did not know how to swing a hammer, yet when it comes to photography, there are many who presume to call themselves teachers without having a thorough understanding of the prime tool of the trade, namely, light. To develop such an understanding, it is essential to recognize several inherent shortcomings in the materials used to produce photographs, after which it becomes easier to overcome them and produce better photographs.

Human Vision vs. Film Vision The first problem is that film does not record an image in the manner in which the human eye perceives it. Normal human vision can discern approximately 2,000 tones between pure black and pure white. On the other hand, a perfectly exposed and properly developed film (if there is such a thing) can produce only about 200 tones from pure black to pure white, and an extremely fine print can have as few as 40 tones. You view a film negative, color or black-and-white, by transmitted light. The minute you commit those tones to paper in the form of a print, the image must now be viewed by reflected light. You must therefore recognize that were you to photograph the thousands of tones you see every day and properly expose and develop the film, you could at best record only a small percentage of the tones of the original subject matter. Most prints today have a very small number of distinguishable tones because, with each error in exposure and processing, the tones of the original image are lost or compressed and prevent the photograph from best revealing the subject you photographed.

NATURAL LIGHTING

Another important consideration in lighting is the fact that almost everything you photograph, with the exception of charts or other pictures, is three-dimensional, each subject having height, depth, and width. Photographs can only record two of those dimensions and the dimension of depth is lost. A well-lit portrait can create the illusion of depth and this is a factor which helps a picture look lifelike. When you use direct frontal light, you lose the third dimension and the pictures acquire a pasted-on look. For recording an occasion such as a birthday party or other social event, snapshots with the light fixed directly on top of the camera make fine memories. But for the portrait photographer, this type of lighting is unacceptable because it sacrifices the feeling of depth. Each photographer must develop a natural lighting approach that requires a minimum of adjustment and consistently produces well-exposed negatives both in the shadows and highlights. The basic components of a natural lighting system are main or key light, fill light, and backlight.

Main or Key Light This prime source of illumination is used to contour and shape a face or figure. It is the substitute for the sun when you work indoors.

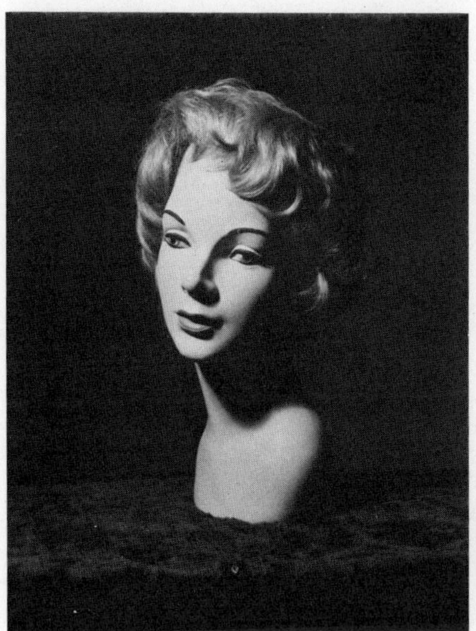

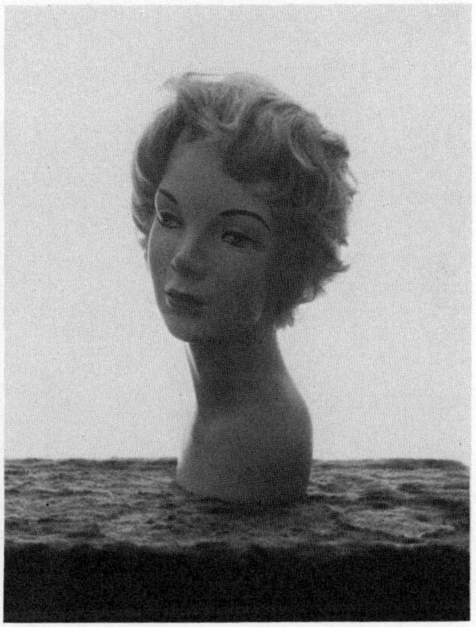

Key, or main, light (left) as the only source of illumination.
Fill light (right) illuminates the background.

Fill Light The fill light is designed to make up for the shortcomings of film materials. Were you to expose photographs only with the prime source of illumination, the lack of reflections or reflective materials in the studio would underexpose the shadows. It is well known that negative color films do not have the exposure latitude of black-and-white emulsions. This is true and usually negative color films will produce satisfactory prints with one-half *f*-stop under-

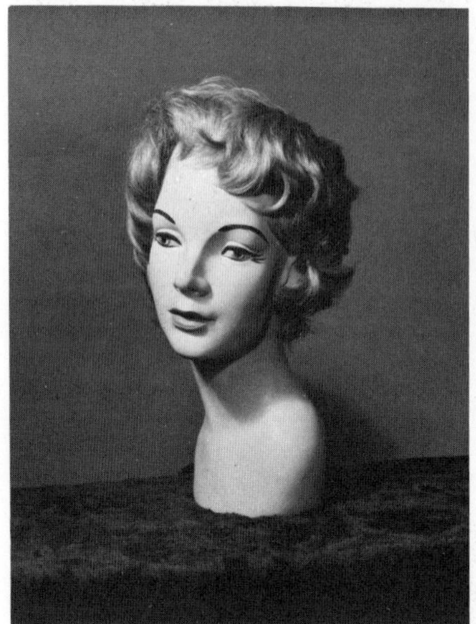
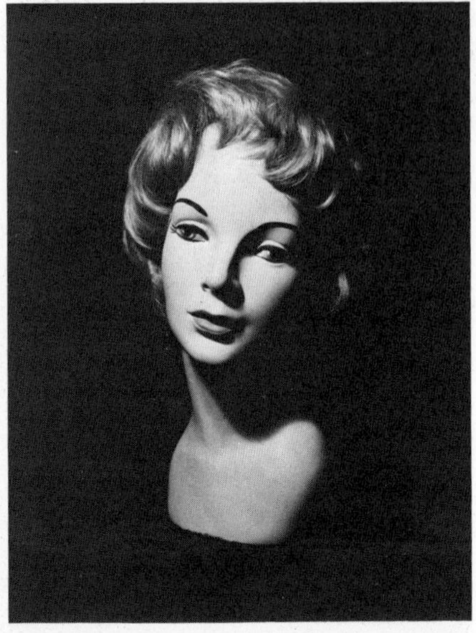

Combined key and fill light (left). Key light without a fill light (right).

exposure and up to two *f*-stops overexposure. The reason some photographers do not get optimum-quality prints from their color negatives is because they fail to get adequate shadow exposure. If the shadow areas do not have enough exposure, it is impossible to produce high-quality color prints from the negatives, since the development process cannot be varied.

You can base your fill lighting on a series of electronic lights—two, three, four, or more depending on the size of the room and the height of the ceiling. Paint the ceiling white so that it acts as a reflector and the entire ceiling area a light. Point the lights that are aimed directly at the ceiling straight up so that no light from these electronic flash reflectors strikes the subject. The result will be a soft, diffused illumination devoid of specular highlights. Fill-in illumination that causes specular highlights can result in a confusing image, as compared to the broad, soft light produced by the overall fill-in method described above.

In many cases, an umbrella light used as fill light produces a broad source of illumination while creating spectral highlights. When you use an umbrella as a prime source of illumination, it is difficult to gain adequate control over the direction of light, and lighting set ups that require light from the side or the rear cannot be achieved. It is possible to produce extremely beautiful photographs using umbrella lights. This is also true of bare bulbs and other large, diffused light sources. However, these approaches create a series of difficult problems, and the photographers who succeed in their use are the exception rather than the rule. Sometimes umbrellas or soft, overall lighting are used to standardize lighting to the point where no subject is individually lighted. This

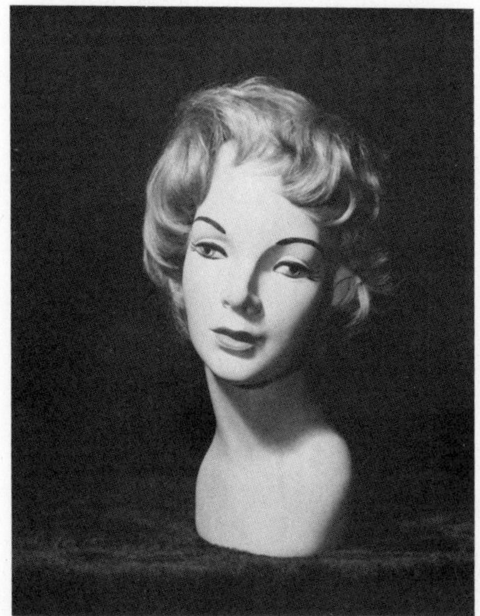

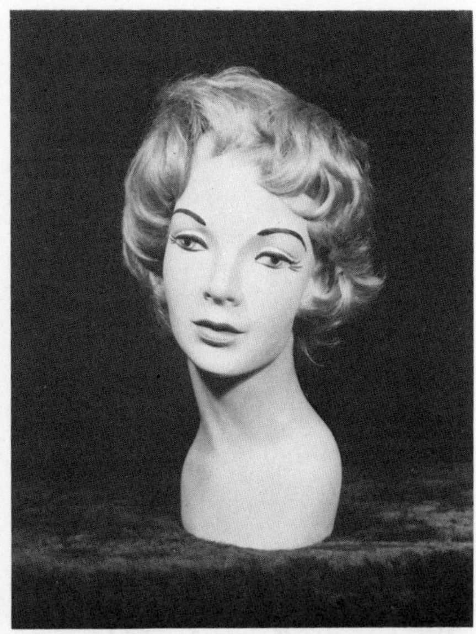

Balanced fill and key lights (left). Too much fill in relation to the key light (right).

approach is essential in mass-production photography; consequently, there is little variation, which eliminates problems in the rapid machine printing of these negatives. The usefulness of umbrellas for fine portraiture is questionable. They may be perfect for rainy days but not for making portraits.

Once you understand the function of the fill light, you must also learn to base the exposure of negative material on the fill light. If your studio portraits are made in a single location and much of your work is with negative color material, it is essential that your fill lights produce a flat, overall image with adequate shadow exposure.

Here is a simple test to determine the correct exposure once you have set up a fill-light system:

1. Position your fill light and camera as if you were photographing a subject.

2. In place of your subject, use a large piece of black velvet, wrinkled to create valleys and peaks. If black velvet is not available, any nonreflective black material will do.

3. With your lens wide open, make a series of exposures at one *f*-stop intervals.

4. Process the film normally and evaluate it.

The exposure frame with detail in the wrinkles of the cloth at the smallest aperture will be the correct base exposure. Unless you change your fill lighting,

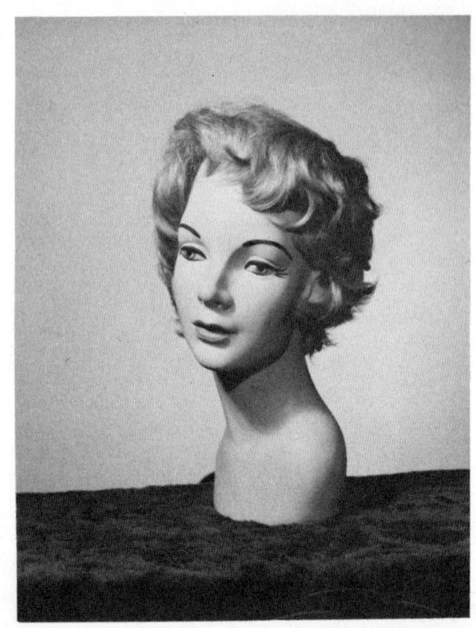

By adding a backlight, you obtain separation between subject and background, reinforcing the illusion of depth.

this will remain constant regardless of the position of your main light. This means that if you recorded detail in the black velvet at $f/8$, your exposure (with the same film) will remain at $f/8$ whether you are photographing a very small object or a large group of people. You will always know that there will be adequate shadow exposure in the darkest part of your subject. This is the key to consistently good prints in color and black-and-white negatives.

Of course, you cannot make photographs with fill lights alone. The results would be flat, lacking highlights that sparkle, and generally unattractive in appearance. Once you have established the correct shadow exposure, you can determine the distance at which to locate your main light by further tests. In subjects where you desire more brilliance or contrast, move your main light closer (by a few inches), and in subjects where you prefer less contrast, move the main light farther back (possibly 10–12 inches). One of the advantages of this system is that you never need to test for exposure. It will always be the same, and by merely moving your main light closer or farther away, you have total control over the contrast in the photograph.

Backlight The function of a backlight is to separate the outline of the subject from the background. Too many photographs fail because the background is over- or under-illuminated. The background light should produce just enough to separate the shape of the subject from the background. Large lights or spotlights that produce strong circular or oval demarcations can make the background more important than the subject. Conversely, a poorly lit background can cause a subject with dark clothing to merge into the background, resulting in a floating head and no separation between subject and background.

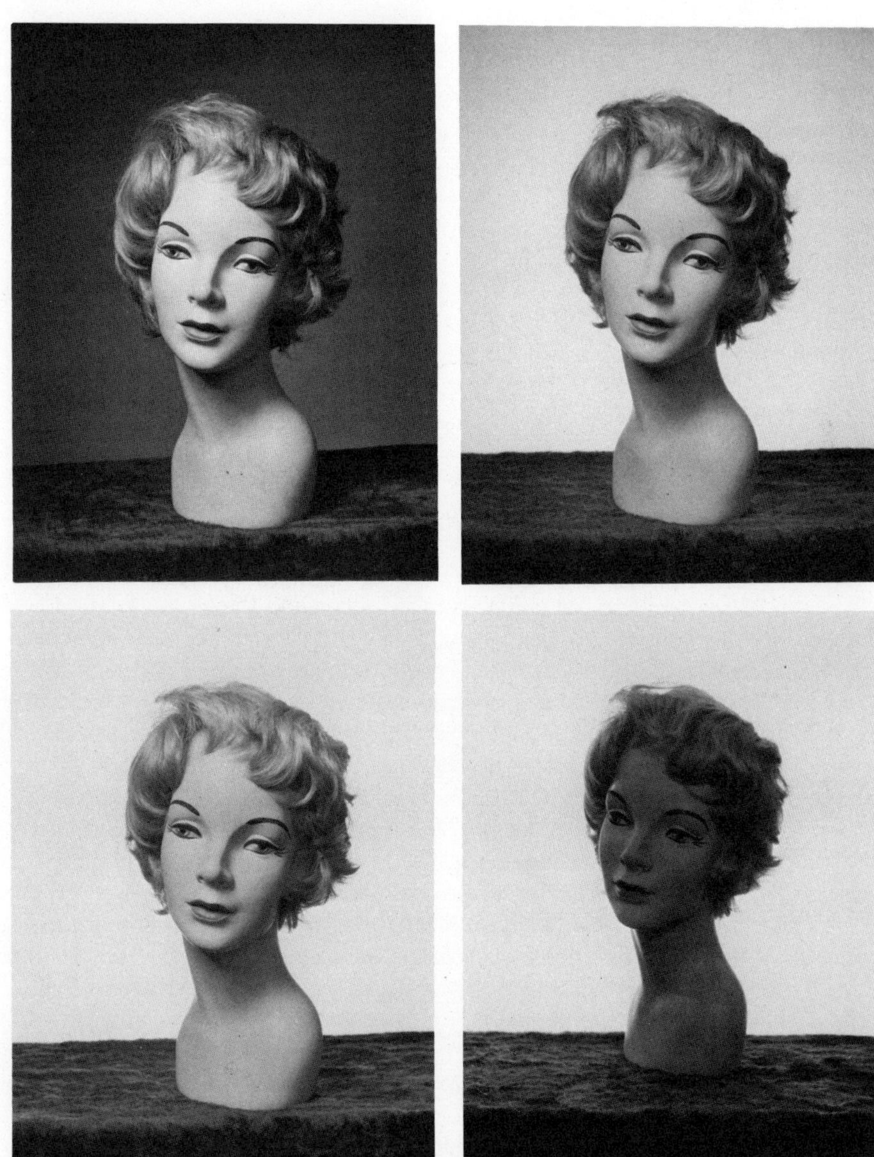

Background lighting can vary the mood of your portraits. Very little backlight (top left). Moderate background light (top right). Considerable background light (bottom left). Kicker light skims the hair and cheekbones adding a three-dimensional quality (bottom right).

An unusual phenomenon exists in lighting. Imagine the subject as the center point in a 360-degree circle; use a line between the camera and the subject as a starting point of 0 degrees. As the light is rotated around the subject at the same distance, its effect on the film intensifies radically. When you reach the 180-degree point, the light is directly behind the subject and therefore affects the exposure far more than the same light at the 0- or 45-degree mark. Since this is the usual placement of a background light (behind the subject), the intensity of the light striking the lens, because of its relationship to the optical axis of the lens, indicates that you need a only a small source and that it should not be mounted in the conventional type of reflector but rather in a shield to protect the lens from being struck by extraneous light. The illumination should be similar to a bare flashtube or a partially shielded bulb. This type of background light will cause a glow of light in the center, which gradually falls off and diminishes in intensity on the outer edges of the background. This keeps the viewer's eye in the center of the picture and eliminates the need for darkening the edges by printing-in each photograph.

Kicker Lights For most portraiture, the use of the main light, fill light, and the background light is sufficient. Occasionally you may use a "kicker" to accent a strong feature. This should not be confused with a hair light. If you use a bounce fill (ceiling lights) that gives adequate exposure in the darkest shadow areas, there should be no need for hair light. You also avoid the problem shadows created by a hair light as well as the trouble of having another light to adjust and watch. The kicker light is very small as compared to the main or fill lights, and it is pointed toward the camera lens to intensify its effect. Because of its angle, the intensity of the kicker will be greater even though it is a small lamp. It can add a lovely touch to some portraits and should be used on the same side of the subject and camera as the main light. This placement further enhances the concept of using one prime source of illumination. Directing it from the opposite side will produce unpleasant shadows, particularly in the subject's ear if it is visible. It also creates a second direction of illumination.

Cover the kicker with a snoot so that the beam of light is very small, approximately one to two inches in diameter at the opening. The rest of the light must be completely shielded so that it does not flare into the camera lens. A tiny light like this can be carefully aimed and directed at any point you wish to accent, such as the tip of the cheek, nose, or the edge of the hair, without throwing extraneous light on other areas of the subject.

Extremely beautiful portraiture can be easily accomplished using a single main light and bounce lights which illuminate shadow areas. For a permanent studio setup, the addition of a background light is ideal even though you might not use it in every sitting. It should be apparent from the discussion that you really do not require a great deal of elaborate equipment in order to produce quality portraiture. Once you understand the concept of using light to shape and form your subjects three-dimensionally, and that there is more to the purpose of light than merely supplying enough illumination to expose your film, you are on your way to making better photographs.

Chapter 9

Lighting Techniques

Start by studying the accompanying diagram. If you draw a line directly from the center or optical axis of the lens toward the subject, and another line from the subject's nose, you will see that they rarely coincide. In almost all portraits, the subject's head is turned, sometimes only slightly, sometimes more. The only exceptions are passport photos, where the subject is required to look full face into the camera; when a person is photographed after being arrested; and portraits of politicians for campaign photographs or posters. In the latter instance, looking straight into the camera lens helps create the illusion of honesty.

There are hundreds of lighting terms. Since the slightest turn of the head changes the angle and direction of the light, each time you turn the sitter a few degrees you are literally designing a new lighting. Variations in lighting from one sitter to the next depend primarily on the shape and size of the subject's features.

BROAD AND SHORT LIGHTING

When the face is turned even slightly from the camera position, you see less of one side than the other. The side that is less visible is the *short* side of the face, while the more visible side is the *broad* side. Thus if the main light is on the side of the camera and face where a larger segment of the face is seen, this is called broad lighting. Conversely, if the main light is placed on the side of the camera and face where you see less of the face, this is known as short lighting. Most subjects are flattered and are best photographed with short lighting, and many studio portraits are made with this lighting. Short lighting gives you the control

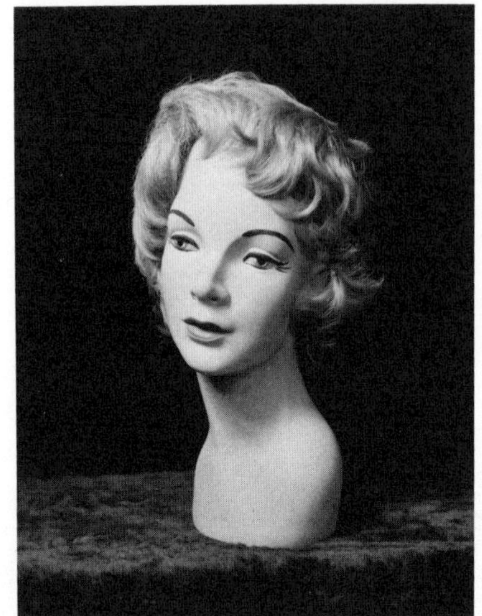

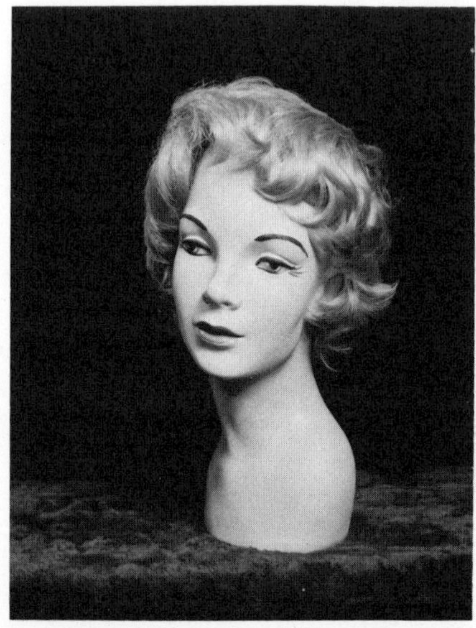

Short lighting (left) is probably the most flattering for most subjects because it shapes and narrows the nose and chin. Broad lighting (right) will widen a gaunt or thin face.

of narrowing the face, which is complimentary to most subjects. Broad lighting is appropriate with a very thin, gaunt subject because it widens the face and makes it appear heavier.

Often you hear talk about Rembrandt, rim, and edge lighting, all of which are minor variations of short lighting. If you determine the position of the light from the axis of the subject's nose rather than from the optical axis of the camera lens, and then set the light for short lighting while the subject is seated in a three-quarter or a profile pose, you will obtain these variations.

BUTTERFLY LIGHTING

Occasionally you will have need for glamor- or theatrical-type lighting. By elevating the light and bringing it in direct line with the nose, so that the shadow under the nose is equal on both sides, you achieve a third type of lighting which can be very attractive. This is commonly called butterfly lighting, as the shape of the shadow under the nose looks like a butterfly.

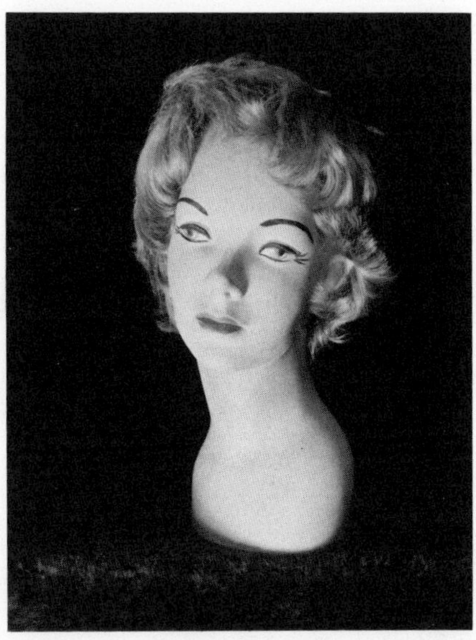

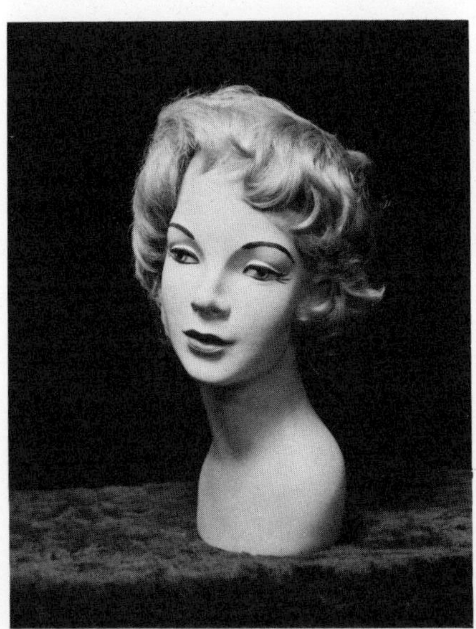

Butterfly lighting (left) is used mainly for glamour photographs.
Stage lighting (right) is not used in conventional portraits.

STAGE LIGHTING

There is a type of lighting that comes from below the subject's chin. If you were photographing a magician on stage or characterizing someone as a witch, this is the lighting you would use. Because the light comes from the same direction as stage footlights set in the floor, it is called stage lighting. Use it only in cases where the desired effect is one of mystery, drama, intrigue, or horror. Stage lighting should not be used in conventional portraiture.

SPLIT LIGHTING

Another experimental lighting that you can try is split lighting. To achieve it, position the light 90 degrees from the nose angle of your subject. Split light can be interesting and unusual when used on an appropriate subject; however, don't use it on someone with deep-set eyes, paunchy cheeks, or hair that projects in front of the face, as the shadows cast by these features will not make an attractive portrait. Don't be afraid to experiment, but always make the traditional

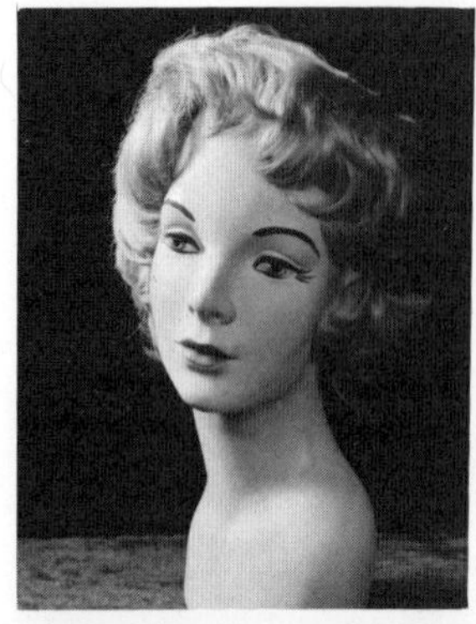

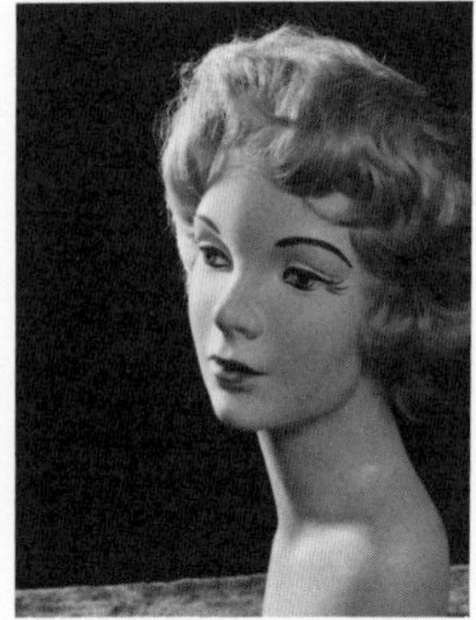

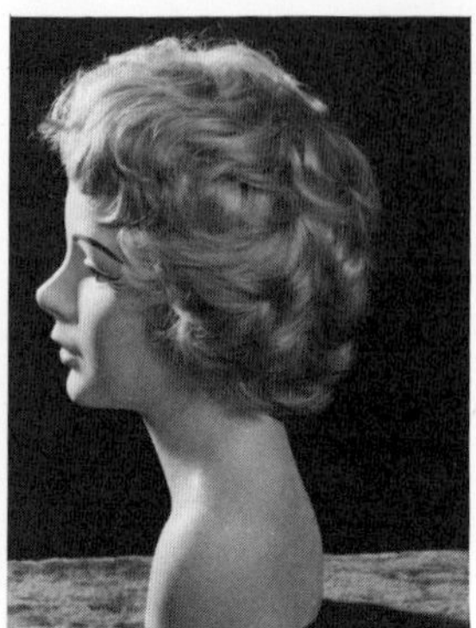

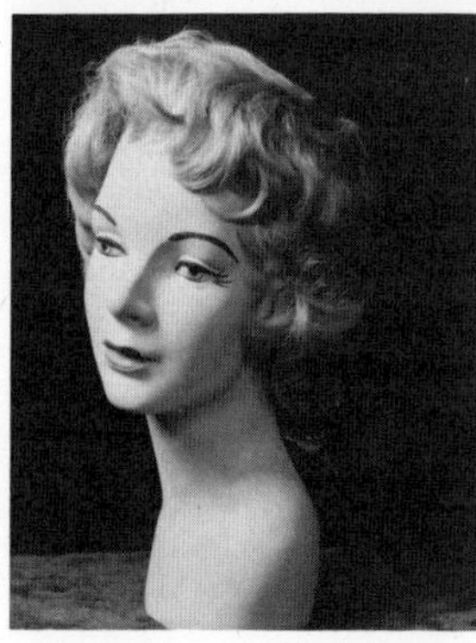

Two examples (top left and center) of split lighting. Rim, edge, or Rembrandt lighting (top right) are variations of short lighting and the camera position. To achieve this effect place your camera 90 degrees from its normal position, leaving the subject and key light in their original places. Watch the nose shadow (bottom); it follows the smile line and is halfway between the bottom of the nose and the top of the upper lip. This occurs in broad and short lighting.

photographs first so that you will have something on which to fall back should the experiment fail.

By simplifying the concept of lighting to basically broad and short lighting, it is easier to learn the correct placement of the main light for the most attractive lighting for a particular subject. By keeping your approach to lighting simple and repeating the basic techniques with each subject, you will quickly learn to make adjustments for variations in features. In so doing, portrait lighting becomes a simple approachable subject.

Chapter 10

Setting the Stage

The most important element of any sitting is the subject. If, when making portraits you have to concern yourself with little details and trivia, this affects your concentration on your subject. For that reason, it is advantageous to prepare in advance for a sitting. This way, the sitting will proceed effortlessly.

Your camera room should have a minimum of obstructions—wires, camera cases and lenses not required for a particular sitting, and other extraneous equipment. If you dislike wires running across floors and dangling in the camera room, arrange it so that they are suspended and retractable, overhead, or along walls. If wires cannot be avoided completely, arrange them in such a manner as to keep your safety and that of your subject in mind.

Never experiment with new lenses, films, electronic flash equipment, or cameras during a sitting. Pretest each piece of equipment, and once you have determined the correct setting and exposure and are completely satisfied with the results, only then should you use it on a paying job. This applies equally to location work, such as weddings and public relations (PR). Never use a piece of equipment without pretesting, because even new epuipment can be faulty. By pretesting in a given situation, you can determine the correct exposure and duplicate it consistently time after time.

Taking the manufacturer's word that a piece of equipment will produce so much light or a given exposure in a particular situation can lead to disappointment. They test the equipment under different circumstances, so it is up to you to pretest and determine for yourself the results you wish to accomplish. If this requires that you change the film's ASA or an *f*-stop, or that you use a light at a different distance, by all means follow your test results and forget about manufacturers' recommendations. Knowing your equipment will give you a confidence that is very important, and when you approach a sitting, you know that you can now concentrate on lighting, pose, expression, and, most important of all, the correct instant of making the exposure.

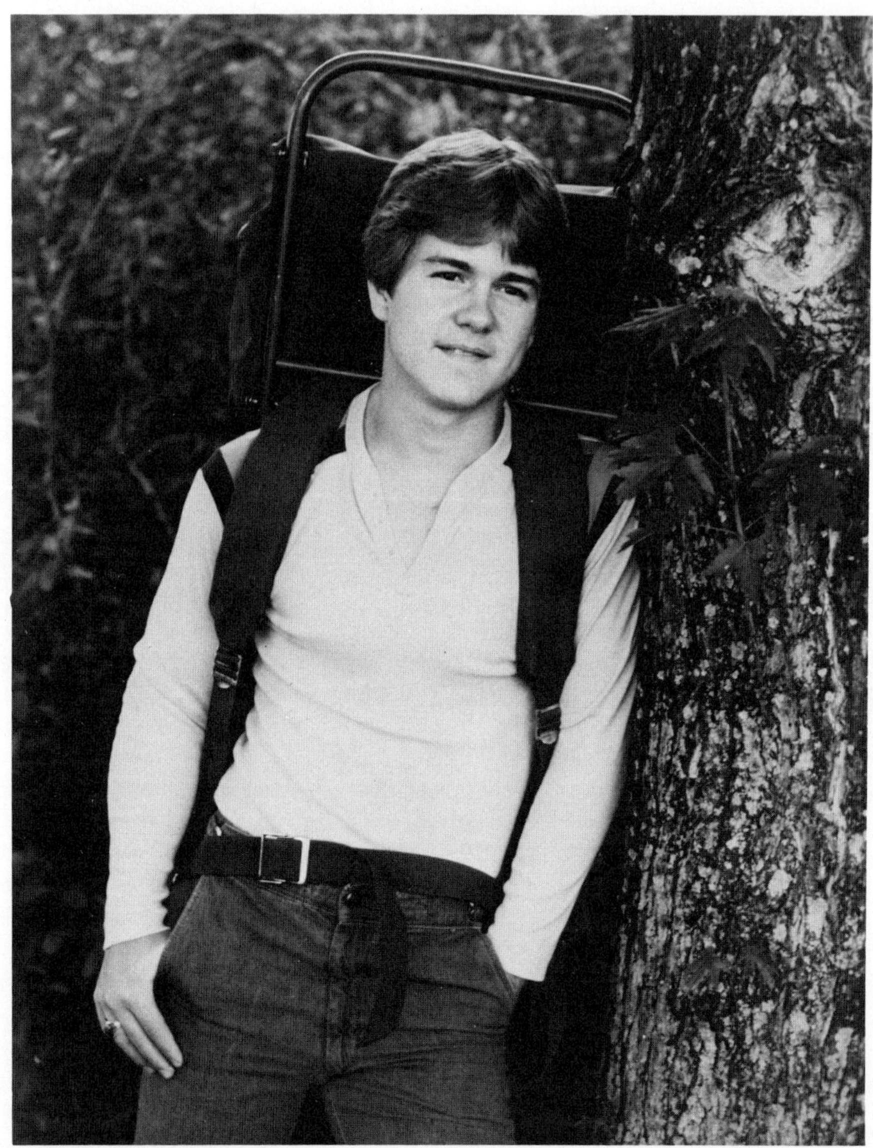

An informal portrait can often include a prop to heighten interest.
Photo by Monteith's Countryhouse Studios.

Chapter 11

Lighting and Lighting Ratios

Since the objective in portrait lighting is to achieve a realistic three-dimensional quality on a two-dimensional piece of paper, the illusion of a third dimension is created by lighting ratio. Ratio refers to the relationship between the amount of light on the highlight side of the picture as compared to the shadow side. This control of ratio is used for setting the mood of the photograph. In a picture of a lovely, young child with delicate tones, you may wish to reduce the lighting ratio to get a smoother transition of tones from highlight to shadow—often used in fashion or catalog photography, where the clothing is the subject. On the other hand, if you want to show a strong, dramatic picture, such as might be used for theatrical work or in a character portraiture to bring out powerful lines in a man's face, you could use a ratio of stronger highlights and darker shadows. Ratio is a useful tool in slimming a subject, as a high-ratio photograph, one with dark shadows and bright highlights, makes the subject look less heavy. Conversely, a low-ratio photograph will make a thin subject more substantial.

In a lighting system where the shadow fill lights are always the same and determine the *f*-stop, you control the ratio by moving the main light slightly in or out. These movements are never extreme and are not the same for each subject. By positioning the light 6–12 inches farther from the subject, you reduce the contrast between highlight and shadow and obtain less contrast in the finished photograph. By moving the main light 6–12 inches closer, you increase the contrast of the photograph and the ratio between highlight and shadow for a slenderizing or dramatic effect. Note that all these changes are controlled with a single light, indicating that you can achieve various lighting ratios using one light.

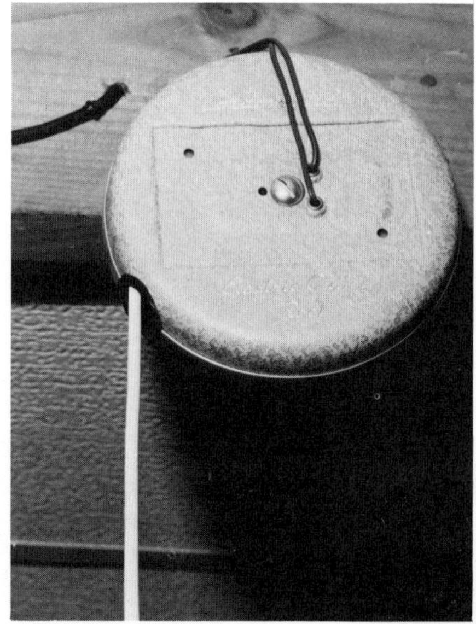

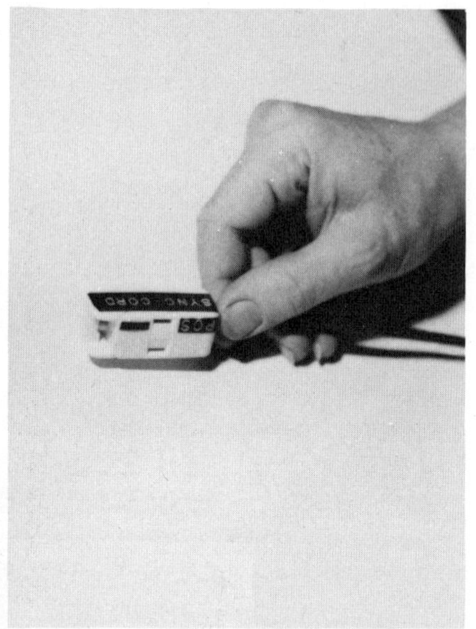

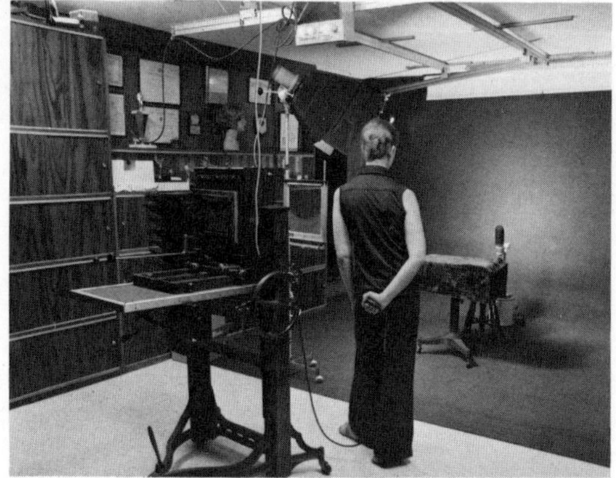

A cord-retracting device (upper left), commonly used in service stations, was rewired for use as a permanently mounted synch cord. Cube tap (upper right), marked with + polarity for camera synch cord. The camera room as it is set up for a sitting. The subject is not included here to enable you to see the placement of the background light.

CONTROL DEVICES

Using barn doors on the main light gives you considerable control as to where light falls on the subject. Occasionally you will require additional controls, for instance, when you wish to darken the upper part of the head of an individual with a receding hairline. In this case, you can use a cardboard shield or a head screen to block the light. The latter is a stable, adjustable short stand with a

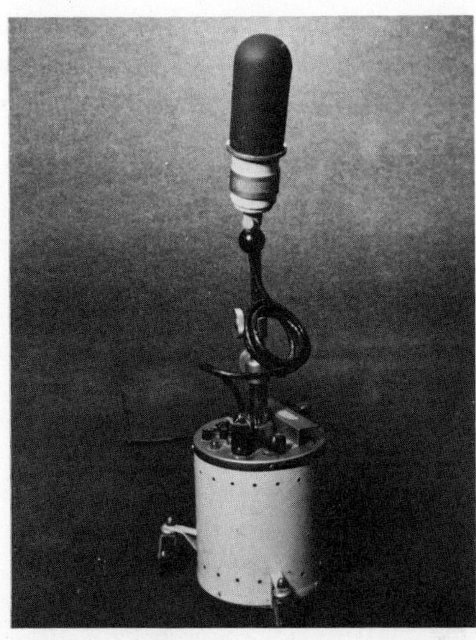

Background light on casters with flat, open reflector that can be placed directly behind the subject or moved about.

gooseneck segment in the upper part. Attached to the gooseneck is a large piece of opaque plastic. One side is straight while the other has notches to soften the light falloff. This is placed in the appropriate position in front of the main light to cast the shadow where you require it. Although referred to as a head screen, this equipment has many uses in controlling extraneous light in any photograph.

LIGHTING FEATURES

The type of lighting system used in a portrait studio materially affects the results. A good system need not be expensive, nor does expensive equipment guarantee the best results. If you plan to buy lighting equipment, here are several features you should consider:

1. A sufficient amount of light to make exposures at the desired *f*-stop. Portraits should be made at one or two *f*-stops below the widest aperture of the lens (for example, an *f*/3.5 lens at *f*/5.6 or *f*/8). This will produce the sharpest images with a softening of the background. Buying extremely large and powerful lights for portrait studios is wasteful because of the added cost, bulk, and maintenance.

2. A reflector large enough to evenly illuminate without being drawn back too far from the subject. The flashtube moves back and forth in some lights and may be adjusted to the most desirable pattern of illumination.

3. A consistent light output so that you can standardize exposures. If the neon ready light is not accurate, you will get reduced intensity flash.

If you suspect this problem with your equipment, an excellent way to check it is to take a flash meter, *fully* charge the light, wait 30 seconds after the ready light goes on, then fire the strobe. Repeat the procedure, but fire the unit as soon as the ready light goes on. Both readings should be identical; if not, your ready light is inaccurate and you must allow additional time for your unit to come to peak. Varying light output can be disastrous for a sitting or sequence of color exposures.

4. Barn doors, or a similar device, so that you can control the light in any direction and eliminate the possibility of background shadows and lens flare. It is sometimes desirable to angle the light so that it points in the direction of the camera. This creates a three-dimensional effect and brings out skin texture. If you don't shield the light to prevent it from striking the lens, this causes internal reflections in the lens which materially degrade image and color quality.

5. If you use electronic flash, a modeling light system that produces the identical highlight and shadow pattern as the flashtube is imperative.

6. A sturdy stand on casters and with large knobs for quick adjustment of lamp height and angle. Ceiling-suspended rail systems are expensive but excellent, provided you have a permanent place to work and at least a ten-foot ceiling so that they may be installed with adequate clearance. You must be able to elevate the light sufficiently so that the rails do not show in large group portraits.

7. A background light with a flat pan reflector and a solid base to prevent tipping. Poor background lighting is responsible for many poor prints. Since the eye is naturally drawn to the lightest part of a photograph, too strong a background will detract from the subject. If it is tilted up about 15 degrees, the light will fall off the outer edges of the photograph.

Caution: If your lights are from more than one manufacturer, or of the same make but different models, it is a good idea to test them to ensure that they produce similar color balance of light output. To do this, simply photograph a color patch and a black-and-white gray scale on color transparency film with each light, and check the processed transparencies for major differences in color rendition. If one light is off-color, you can place filters over it so that it balances with the rest of your system.

REPAIRS

Unless you are skilled in handling high-voltage electronic equipment, *do not try to make your own repairs.* The capacitors in electronic lights can give a 400- to 500-volt shock, and you can further damage the circuits by poking around in the unit with a screwdriver. If you don't have back-up equipment, make sure you have schematics from the manufacturer on each piece of equipment you purchase. With these as a guide, an expert repairman can fix the unit quickly. For each of your lights, try to keep spare flashtubes, high-voltage tubes, fuses, modeling lamps, and other replaceable parts handy. This often means that you can unplug and replace a defective part in a matter of minutes.

Chapter 12

Selecting Film

If you have been doing photography for any period of time, then you surely have run into some of the strange characters that photography attracts. Imagine being on location, your equipment all set up, only to have a stranger tear down the road in his car, jump out, run to his trunk and remove his camera, come right up to where you are standing and ask what exposure you're using. You tell him and then watch as he sets his camera, exposes a single frame of film, puts the camera away, jumps back into his car and drives off without ever asking what film you were using, whether black-and-white or color, or anything else. And there are those who will use a particular film because it is the fastest available, because some super pro uses it, because it's the only kind available in a particular camera store, and for many other silly reasons. No manufacturer can anticipate the brilliance of your lenses, the type of lights and reflectors you use, or the subject matter you will photograph. They can only give general ideas and suggest that you make tests to determine the best materials for your needs. The selection of film materials also must be based on your needs. Select films because their speeds permit you to work at *f*-stops you consider desirable; because they are consistent in quality; and because you feel you get the best result from them under your working conditions.

BLACK-AND-WHITE FILM

Photographers still do a fair amount of black-and-white portraiture, and you may find a medium-speed panchromatic film ideal for your purposes. By selecting film made by a large manufacturer, you are assured of an adequate supply of the same material over a long period. This standardizes and eliminates the need for constant testing and experimentation and makes producing quality negatives a relatively simple procedure.

COLOR FILM

This discussion of portrait photography covers only negative color film which, with its long, soft tonal range and great exposure latitude, is ideal for portraiture. Color transparency materials lack these characteristics, and a slight error in exposure results in wasted film. To date, the processes for printing transparencies are ideal for industrial or commercial photography but lack the softness and lower contrast ranges available with negative color films.

If you rely upon custom labs, you know that many don't process or print the amateur-type films. Yet Kodacolor II negative material is preferable for portraiture to the professional Vericolor II. True, Vericolor is a fine film and produces excellent work, however, Kodacolor II is not quite as finicky when stored, is slightly more brilliant, has a greater exposure latitude, and offers a finer grain structure.

Film manufacturers know that the amateur will run under a tree and make a picture in deep shade, then run out into the brilliant sunlight and make another picture, often forgetting to adjust the camera. For that reason, they engineer more latitude into amateur films. If you process and print your own film, it is certainly worth a trial roll of Kodacolor II to determine whether you find this film pleasing for your color work.

DO-IT-YOURSELF PROCESSING

A question that often arises is whether or not you should process and print your own film or use a custom lab. There are many factors to consider in making this decision. You may want to keep your operation as self-contained as possible by doing your work yourself. The finest color labs cannot be responsible for delays and losses in transport or the mail. Good labs are hard to find, and those which produce consistently high quality work are very busy. As such businesses expand, however, there is often a noticeable change in the quality of their work. Rather than subject yourself to those possibilities, you may prefer to do it yourself.

Processing Color Color processing is relatively simple. It is easier to learn to make a good color print than to make a good black-and-white. Yet many people in the photographic industry are deathly afraid of color processing. Actually, if you can read a clock, chart, thermometer, count to 7, and load film into a lighttight tank in the darkroom, you have all the skills required for processing color.

You should try processing your own film not because of the economic factor, but because the chemistry you use over a certain period before discarding it, will produce consistently higher quality results than chemistry that is replenished. In the replenishment process, a good engineer can accurately predict how much of each chemical needs to be replaced at the end of each 80 square inches of film. Unfortunately, nobody has yet devised a method for removing the by-products of development from the chemistry. Since all color materials begin as black-and-white emulsions that record the image in three different layers, the first stage of processing is the developing of the black-and-white image. As the exposed silver is turned into metallic silver by the developers, bromide is released. These bromides act as restrainers and slow down the development process. Replenishment chemistry being stronger than the initial developer, overcomes this bromide drag. In some systems where the chemistry is used for 3, 6, or 12 months, a tremendous amount of chemicals are added to the developing agents in order to overcome the ever-increasing bromides that are released into the developer. This system must be monitored with absolute precision, otherwise the developer will reduce the film quality by increasing grain size and will require you to develop the film to a higher contrast than is desired for optimum results. For highest-quality results, use a developer for a fixed number of films and then discard it. This means that you will have to increase developing time for each roll processed after the first. By using this simple system and with today's self-loading tanks, film development becomes a routine procedure.

If you feel that it is more practical to use lab processing, check out those in your area. Expose three, four, or five identical rolls of film and send them out to the various labs for processing. Compare the prints you receive and determine which lab did the most satisfying job. This does not guarantee that this particular lab will always do a good job, but such a test can tune you in very quickly to those which do mediocre work.

Some professional photographers send film out for processing and then do their own printing. This is similar to putting the cart before the horse, because if the negative is damaged, there is no way to improve the quality in the printing. If you have neither the time nor facilities to set up your own color lab, the wisest procedure is to process the film yourself and then send it to a lab for printing. This way, if a print does not meet your standards, you can always make another. But at least you have a good negative with which to start.

Color Language If you spend thousands of dollars on lab color printing each year, a working knowledge of the process will enable you to better communicate with a lab technician. When a print is poor, a technician will frequently use such words as "cross over," "contamination," "improper exposure," or "subject failure," in an attempt to convince you that the fault was with you or your equipment rather than with the processing. If you are thoroughly familiar with the process and speak the "language of color," technicians will respect you more and work harder to produce a better product.

PRETESTING

Companies such as Eastman Kodak, Ilford, and the many others around the world deserve high praise for producing consistently uniform, high-quality photographic products, particularly when you consider that the layers of emulsion of a color film or paper are approximately 1/1500-inch thick, and that their uniformity is extremely difficult to produce with regularity. The quality control of these materials is also superb. However, you must be aware that from the moment of manufacture, color material is constantly changing.

Photographers take many things for granted. Some believe that a given *f*-stop, say, *f*/5.6, on every lens will transmit exactly the same amount of light. Many also believe that if the shutter speed is set at 1/200 sec. that this is precisely the amount of exposure they will get. Neither of these assumptions is true. If you were to test a half dozen of any brand of the better cameras, you would find variations which could cost you points in producing a high-quality image. In addition, temperatures can radically alter shutter speed. Photographers also look upon exposure meters as super computers. Yet a meter can see only a certain amount of light; it cannot determine the quality, direction, or nature of that light nor select the prime area where exposure should be determined.

For all these reasons and more, it is essential that you pretest all equipment. Test your camera, lens, and electronic flash with a given film. Determine what is the correct type of negative for your printing equipment. An ideal negative for a condenser system in not ideal for a diffusion, cold-light, or grid system. Once you determine how to adjust for the variables, you can standardize the technical aspects of photography and concentrate on the artistic endeavors. Use a manufacturer's recommendation only as the starting point for your own experiments, not as hard-and-fast rules that will work every time. Try the exposure test with wrinkled black velvet cloth, described earlier. If you can determine the exposure that will give adequate detail in black velvet, there is no subject that will cause underexposed shadow areas under the same lighting and exposure conditions. Once you have determined the correct exposure and the film that best suits your needs, stay with that combination for as long as possible.

To assure consistency, purchase film in bulk. When negative color material is stored at 50 F or below, changes in the film are almost nonexistent. By purchasing film in bulk, refrigerating it, and using it (after the appropriate warm-up time) as needed, you will discover that the filtration required in making color prints stays within very close range over a long period. Some manufacturers recommend freezing the film, but refrigeration is adequate. This reduces the warm-up time and the film can be used 10–15 minutes after removal from the refrigerator.

Nothing will help you produce better photographs than experience. When you use a material for a while, you learn its advantages, shortcomings, and limitations. This means that each time you load your camera and expose that material, you are gaining additional knowledge about that particular film. The constant search for finer grain and faster, super emulsions can only lead to confusion and put obstacles in the way of making good negatives and photographs.

Chapter 13

The Camera Room

Camera room requirements vary. Usually they will grow in relation to the number of sittings that are done in the area and on the kind of photography you do. Some people operate portrait businesses in trailers, basements, living rooms, and other cramped places. On the other hand, there are commercial-industrial photographers who have enough camera room to accommodate several automobiles or a small airplane.

If you plan to photograph large groups, for example, obviously the room will have to be a suitable size. Most of your photography may consist of individual portraits and pictures of groups with as many as 12 people. An adequate camera room is one that is approximately 16′ × 20′, with a doorway through which you can back the camera when necessary. The ceiling should be at least 8 feet, although a 10- or 12-foot ceiling is preferable. Neutral or white ceilings and walls prevent color casts, which create problems in color portraiture. Install adequate electrical outlets if the room does not have them, or place them in such a way that wires are not strung across the floor from one side to the other.

If there are windows in the area, cover them with opaque shades so that the ambient outdoor light will not affect your pictures. One advantage to having windows is the occasional use of window light for making photographs. This lighting can add interesting effects to your sitting as well as variety.

BACKGROUNDS

In recent years, many mass-production operators of the 88¢ photos have fallen in love with the multicolored, glopped-up, painted backgrounds. These work best when photographed moderately out of focus. Unless it is the main subject, backgrounds should not intrude in, or detract from, a portrait. Backgrounds should also be simple.

A background recommended by Tony Witchers, of Topeka, Kansas, consists of a wide piece of congoleum nailed to the wall along the top, with the pattern facing the wall. The backing material is painted with a medium gray rubber-base paint. Cut the bottom flush with the floor and secure it with a narrow strip of moulding. You can get many years of service out of this simple and inexpensive background, which is preferable to paper backgrounds, the rolls of which develop lines and fail to stay flat, casting horrible shadows on the background or showing unsightly ripples and distracting highlights.

Permanent Structures If you decide to install a permanent seamless background for full-length posing, try some quality indoor-outdoor carpeting that is dark enough to suit your needs and without strong or obvious texture. Make curved supports from ¾-inch plywood. Install these metal "L" brackets at 16-inch intervals, and curve the background area against the wall. Notch the curved supports to permit installation of an electrical outlet (117 volts AC) so that you can plug your backlight directly into the background under a small flap. Take a piece of ⅜-inch masonite, slightly grooved on one side so that it will flex, and nail it firmly at each support. Mark an opening for the electrical outlet before firmly attaching the carpeting along the top of the wall. Cut the flap on both sides and the bottom only, so that when the light is removed the opening virtually disappears.

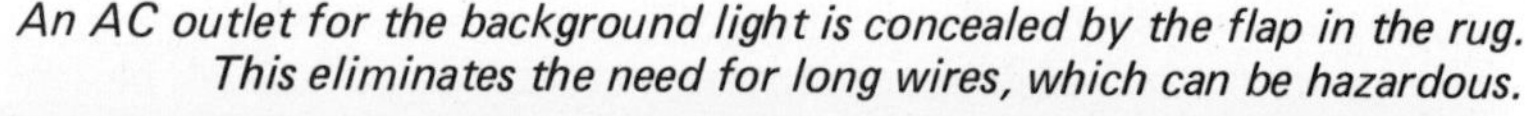

An AC outlet for the background light is concealed by the flap in the rug. This eliminates the need for long wires, which can be hazardous.

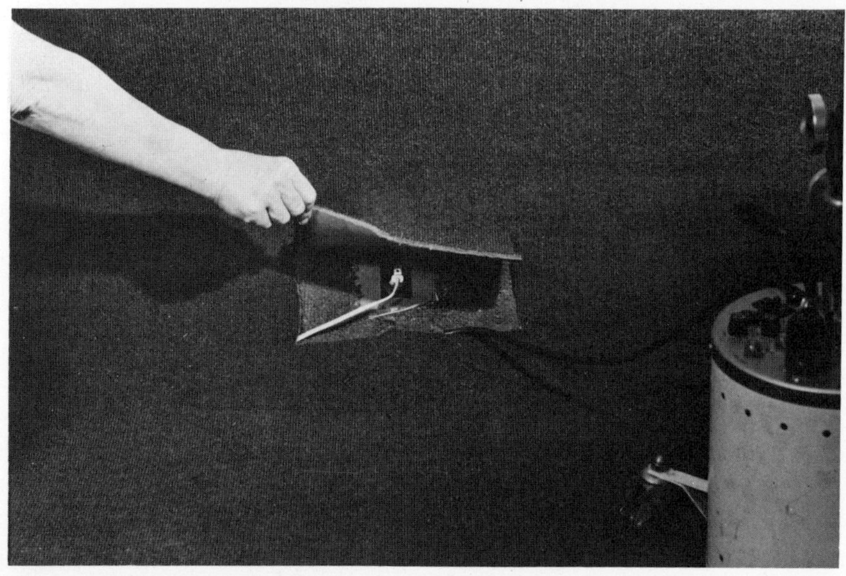

Temporary Backgrounds If you can't turn your living room wall into a permanent background, almost any neutral-colored wall (gray, beige, tan, white) will suffice and can be made as dark or as light as you wish, by adding or eliminating a background light. By placing your subject away from a solid background, and if no illumination from the main light falls on it, it will photograph very dark because the fill light falling upon it will underexpose it. As long as there are no breaks, such as doorways, windows, pipes, or radiators, these backgrounds can produce extremely nice results in portraiture.

Another suggestion is that you purchase a heavy-duty window shade large enough to act as a background for one or two people—a shade seven to nine feet wide is ideal. Paint it with a medium or dark neutral rubber-base paint and set it up on a stand or some hooks as needed. Several companies make painted canvas backgrounds which can be rolled up and stored when not in use. However, such backgrounds should be photographed well out of focus rather than razor sharp. Since large custom window shades are expensive, it might be worth it for you to visit a local manufacturer and purchase one at a bargain. Occasionally they will have large shades stored away that the customer refused because they were too short. Larger shades can be cut down to size, but smaller ones cannot be stretched. Sometimes you can purchase these "goofs" for a very modest sum of money since they have little value to the establishment and just take up space. But be certain that the shade is mounted on a heavy duty roller.

POSING BENCHES AND TABLES

Some of the companies that sell equipment specifically for the camera room are listed in the Appendix. If you wish to improvise, you can use a seat or bench

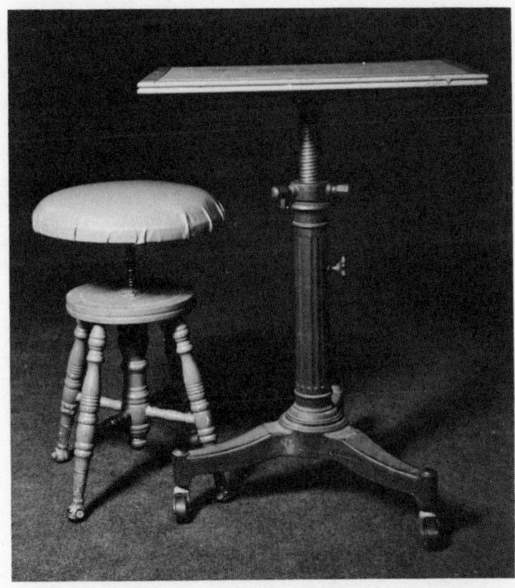

A sturdy piano stool and adjustable table are ideal for posing. Such a stool is often available at garage sales or used furniture shops.

whose height is adjustable. Since the seating height of each sitter will vary, an old piano stool or a backless bar stool that moves up and down will do nicely. If you do sittings only occasionally, large books placed on a conventional bench to elevate the subject to the correct sitting height will work just fine.

A posing bench must be adjustable. Use the posing bench to stabilize the subject; if the subject moves or turns her head, use of the bench permits the same plane of focus when the pose is resumed. With adults and children over three, you can seat the subject, stabilize the arms and proceed with the sitting without being overly concerned about refocusing for each photograph.

The table height must also be adjustable so that the subject is seated in a proper plane and is comfortable. A wobbly table can make the sitter insecure. In a head-and-shoulders portrait, these tables are indispensable. If you don't want to buy a table that is adjustable or one that has an arm that raises and lowers, you can produce the same effect using a low table and some books with a cover over them. Never use a chair or permit the subject to sit back and lean away from the camera. Leaning back gives the feeling of fatigue or old age and results in sloppy posing.

Props and Toys Be constantly on the lookout for unusual props and toys. One of the most terrific devices for getting and holding a youngster's attention is a "squeaker." They are inexpensive and can be purchased in quantity from Peirce (see Appendix). When concealed in your hand, you can squeak your nose, Mommy's nose, and the child's nose and make a game of making the picture. Squeakers are also great for capturing the attention of a pet. With little ones who

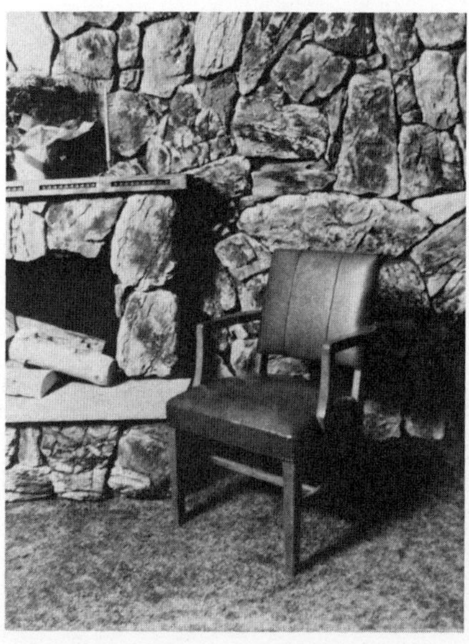

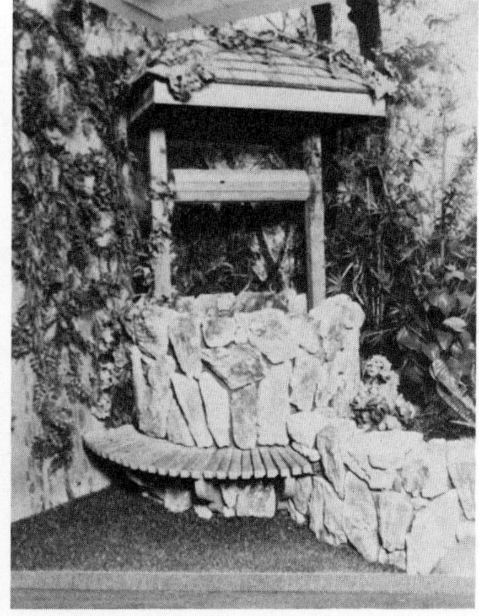

do not respond well to this toy, try blowing soap bubbles; the device is an inexpensive little bottle of sudsy material that comes with a plastic loop. Blowing bubbles can delight a child who has never seen them before and turn an otherwise difficult sitting into a success. Or ask Mommy to bring along the child's favorite stuffed animal or toy for use in the sitting. When you photograph a child with his or her own toy, the child feels more at home; at the same time, you add a personal touch to the picture.

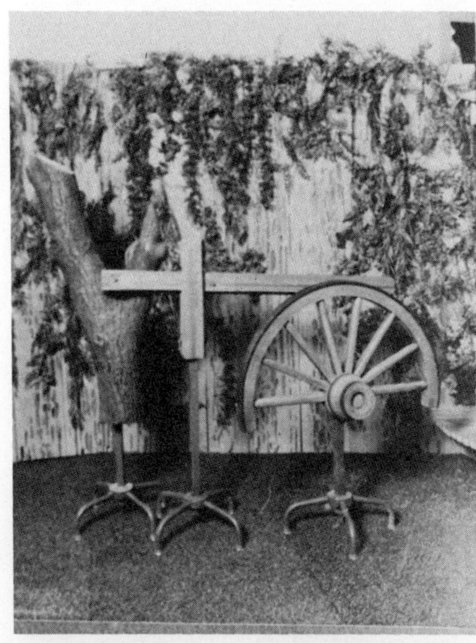

Photographs of five different studio props (two opposite) providing a wide variety of scenes for interesting portraits. Courtesy of Don Peterson.

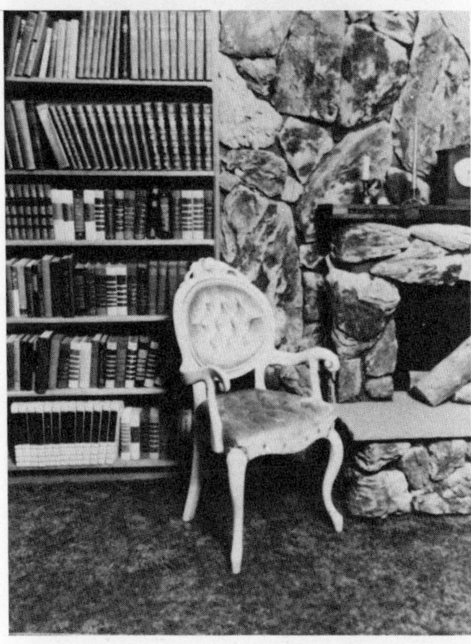

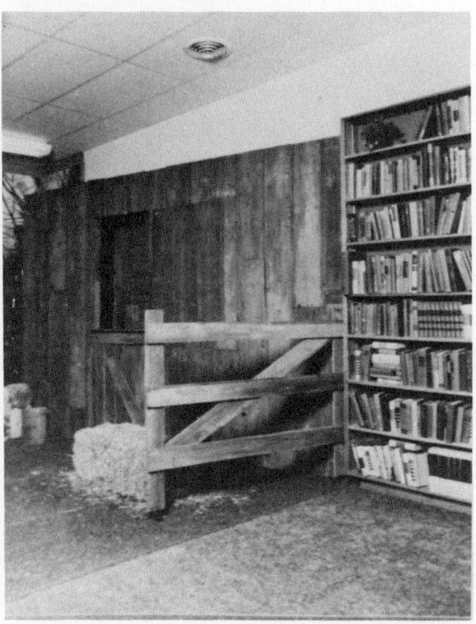

POSING PLATFORMS

You can use a configuration of four boxes, designed so that they may be used singly or in combination. They permit you to create a situation where a subject can be seated on what appears to be a floor and yet not produce camera angle that is extreme. The boxes can be used in all types of portraits. They make an ideal flat surface for photographing pets and other animals and, in combination, can be used for photographing groups or couples for love portraits.

The boxes are constructed of ½-inch plywood. Once they are formed and nailed together, they can be left unfinished, or painted a color to match your background, or covered with carpeting. The boxes themselves are never visible in the actual photograph. When not being used, stack and store the boxes in a corner and keep the carpeting nearby.

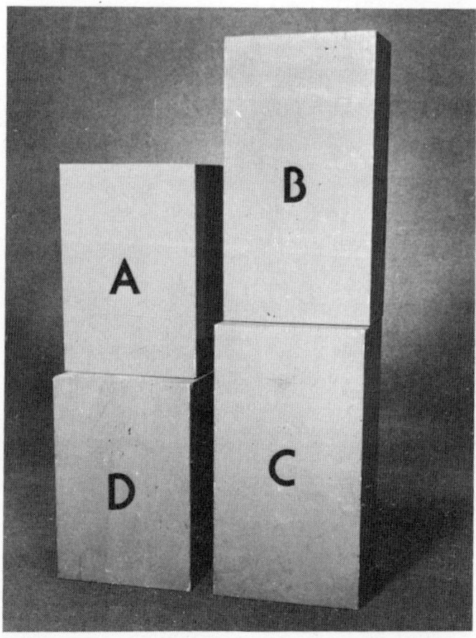

Four boxes of varying sizes can be used as posing platforms. Suggested dimensions are:

Dimensions of Four Posing Boxes

Box A	=	*28″*	x	*12″*	x	*20″*
Box B	=	*36″*	x	*12″*	x	*20″*
Box C	=	*16″*	x	*36″*	x	*20″*
Box D	=	*16″*	x	*28″*	x	*20″*

Chapter 14

The Time, Place, and What to Wear

THE RIGHT TIME

In setting up the time for a portrait special attention should be given to appointments made for small children. They should be photographed at the time of day that is best for them as individuals. The best time to photograph infants is immediately following a meal or after a nap. The child is rested, satisfied, and will respond best to the "play" of doing a sitting. But if the infant does not respond, it may be that stomach cramps or the cutting of a tooth are distracting the child to the point where getting good photographs is extremely difficult, if not impossible. In such instances, it is better to reschedule the sitting.

Young ladies sitting for engagement portraits respond best in the early evening; the pressures of the day are over, they have had their dinner, had time to relax a little, and these conditions all contribute to producing a successful sitting, particularly if the sitter is nervous or tense. Compare this to a young lady who rushes in to have her portrait made during her lunch break. Deadlines make it more difficult to achieve the proper relaxed mood for best results.

Many men try to avoid having their photographs made because they find the experience unpleasant. Because of this, try to reassure the male subjects prior to each sitting, that the work will proceed as rapidly as possible and with a minimum of fuss and delay. Once the subject realizes that you will be considerate of his feelings, he will cooperate.

THE RIGHT PLACE

Portraits can be made at home, in a specific outdoor setting, on location, at a place of business, or in the studio. Working in the studio offers the photographer the greatest advantage, however. Sittings can be scheduled at any time, and all the camera and lighting equipment are ready for use and do not require transportation. Transporting lights, backgrounds, and camera equipment can be done but incur additional effort in setting up and breaking down the equipment for each sitting. The practice of the mass-production photographer working in the customer's home, particularly for portraits of children, has decreased considerably over the last 25 years. In today's market, it is far more efficient for them to place their equipment in a mall, shopping center, or large department store where there is heavy customer traffic. This means they can set up their equipment once and operate for a certain number of days as compared to moving from place to place.

A portable lighting unit available for location photography. Courtesy of Spiratone. Keep in mind that outdoor assignments cannot be photographed very far from the nearest electrical outlet.

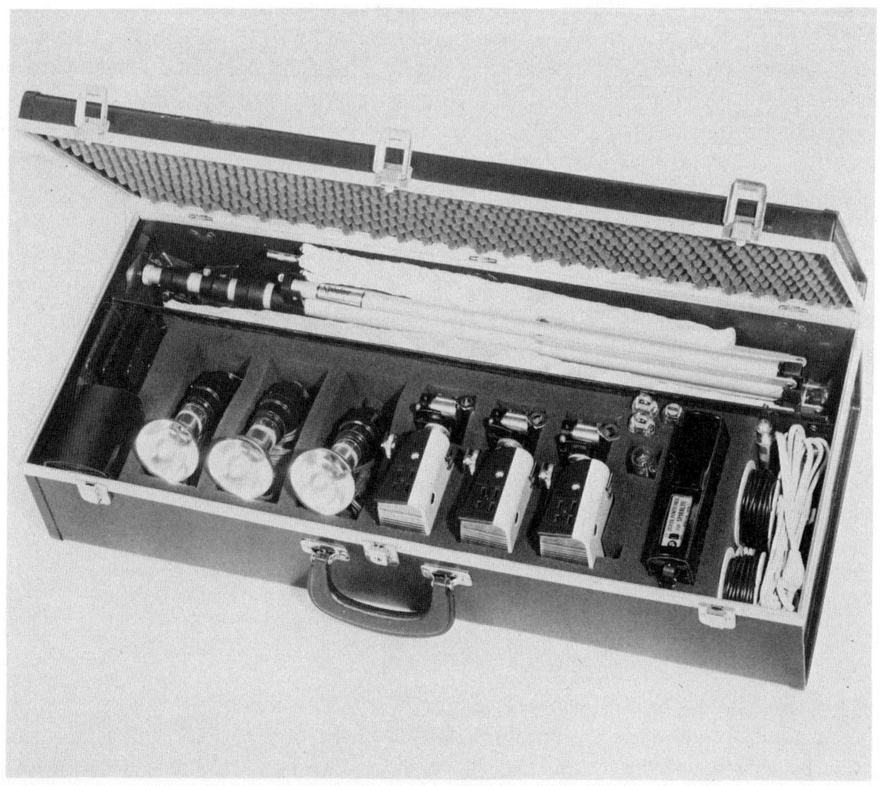

With the miniaturization of the camera, flash, and other pertinent equipment, working on location or in and around the clients home is more feasible today. Whether this approach will function well for you will depend on the area where you do business as well as the weather in your part of the country. In warm climate, you can work outdoors all year round, but in many places, such as the northeast, outdoor photography is limited to four or five months a year. Inclement weather can result in cancellations of outdoor sittings, and waiting for the sun to shine can be a problem. The photographer also has to contend with the sky appearing through trees, possibly causing strong distractions in the background. If these cannot be avoided, you must correct the print later to eliminate them.

When and where you do your portraiture is really something you must decide on the basis of the clientele you wish to attract and where you feel most comfortable working. Working in the customer's home or outdoors reduces overhead if you do it exclusively. On the other hand, having a place where people can come, and where you won't have to move equipment, can be advantageous. Some photographers do both, using the outdoor settings when weather permits, and working in the studio at other times. Remember that there is a radical difference between making outdoor snapshots and outdoor portraits. High-quality outdoor portraiture calls for considerable control, and it is rare that nature will give you the perfect lighting situation that will make great portraits. Consider the pluses and minuses of working outdoors and make your own decision.

If you plan to venture into the great outdoors for location photography, it will serve you well to plan ahead. If you can find a series of locations and note when the sun is in the best position there, it will simplify your outdoor portraiture. Some photographers go to extreme lengths to have beautiful, elaborate locations right in their backyards or on their property. If you can afford this, it is of course simpler than traveling to a nearby park or wooded area to make photographs. Once you use a location successfully and it suits your needs, then return trips to the same location are very practical. Having a half-dozen or more location spots that are convenient to you and your clients is ideal and can save you disappointment and hiking through woods to find a proper spot. Interesting tree stumps, fences, or rock formations that photograph well can be used again and again from slightly different angles and positions so that the photographs do not look exactly the same, yet require a minimum of moving around to accomplish good results.

THE RIGHT CLOTHING

When a customer makes an inquiry or appointment, discuss clothing for the sitting. Distracting clothing can interfere with the quality of a portrait, particularly in group photographs. Uncoordinated mixed colors and various types and styles of clothing permit the clothing to dominate the picture. In a portrait, the subject's face is the most important part of the picture, unlike a fashion photograph where the clothing is more important, or a theatrical photograph where the character and mood must dominate. Likeness is the vital factor in a portrait. The only true area of likeness is in the five front planes of the face, and therefore any part of the picture that is more powerful than the subject diminishes the importance of the sitter.

So suggest conservative clothing. Once the client has stated a preference for informal, semiformal, or formal portraiture, make whatever recommendations you can about clothing. Clothing with extremely high contrast, such as stripes, plaids, checks, or very bold designs, should be discouraged. However, there will be occasions where a mother wants her little girl photographed in a dress that Grandma made. In that case, you have little choice but to do what the customer wants.

Even with the loveliest model the arm closest to the camera can be a distraction. Covering the arms with long-sleeved clothing (opposite) can reduce the intensity and bring more attention to the subject's face.

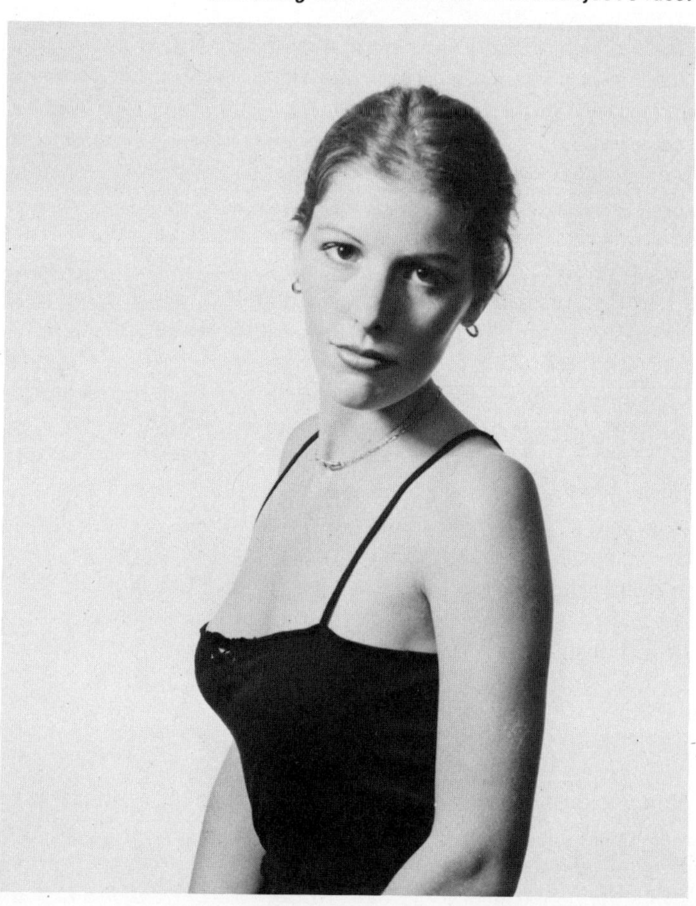

Cool colors photograph well—blues, greens, grays, aqua, turquoise, soft beiges, dark browns, and black. These colors make the skin tone the strongest color in the picture. Soft blues and faded denims and jeans are also very attractive. Because you do not want to compete with skin tone, try to avoid such colors as yellow, pink, red, or orange.

With ladies, the bare upperarms are most unflattering. The camera sometimes makes arms appear very large and heavy even with the most slender subject. Therefore, suggest full-length or three-quarter sleeves for female subjects. V- and high necklines are most flattering while square and boat necklines make the individual look heavier.

Don't feel that a customer will object if you make clothing suggestions. If made correctly and in the spirit of helpfulness, people appreciate the assistance. During the consultation, advise them that you have a dressing room available

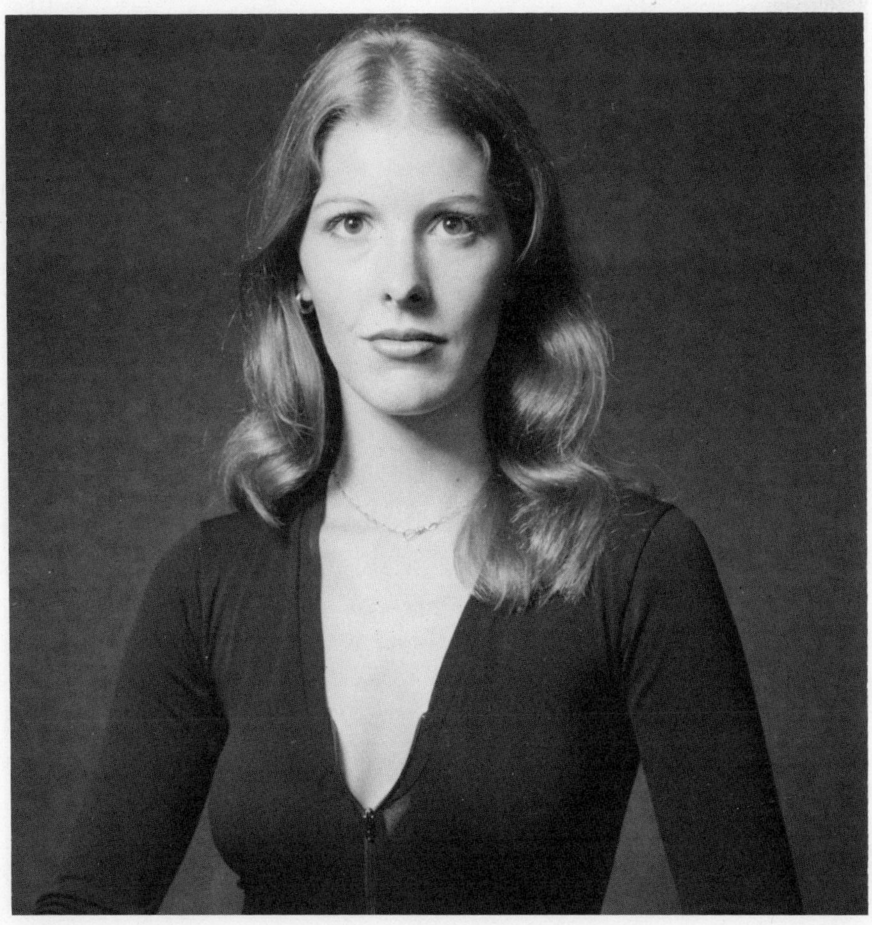

and would be delighted to have them bring in a number of outfits from which you can help them select the most appropriate. If the young lady has a favorite dress, offer to make photographs in several outfits. Changing the poses and clothing gives you the opportunity for sales of prints from more than a single negative.

MAKEUP

Some states prohibit anyone who doesn't have a degree from an accredited school of cosmetics from applying makeup professionally. If you reside in one

This series of photographs (pages 94-100) demonstrate in gradual change in the model's face as the different cosmetics are added. We begin (below) by showing the model without makeup.

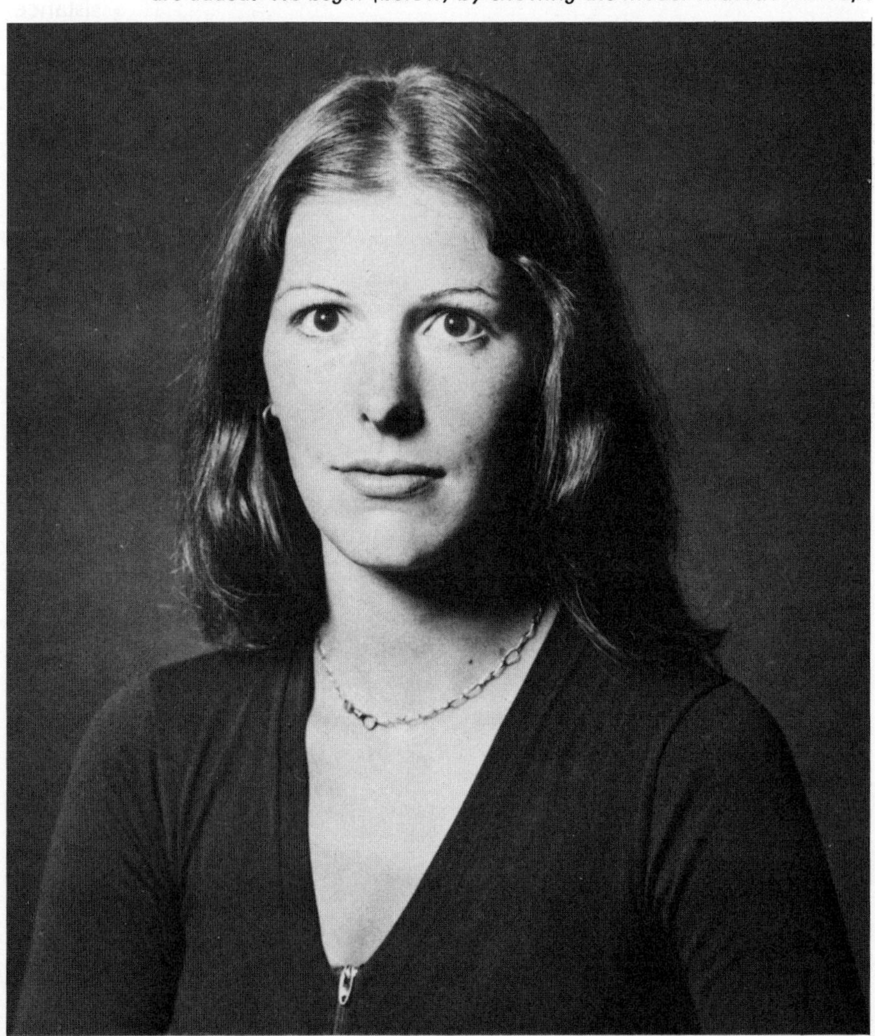

of these, it is best to have the subject apply her own makeup under your direction. Also remember is that some people have allergies to cosmetics. Before applying makeup, ask each subject whether she is allergic to normal cosmetics. If she is, she may be able to use special hypo-allergenic products.

Makeup offers several advantages to the photographer. In engagement and bridal pictures and those of women in general, checking the makeup prior to the sitting and helping the customer adjust it or adjusting it yourself can be beneficial. If you use makeup to cover blemishes or minor skin defects, it simplifies having to retouch the negative or print. Applying the makeup also gives you a few minutes to get the subject relaxed and time to observe her facial

The base makeup has been applied.

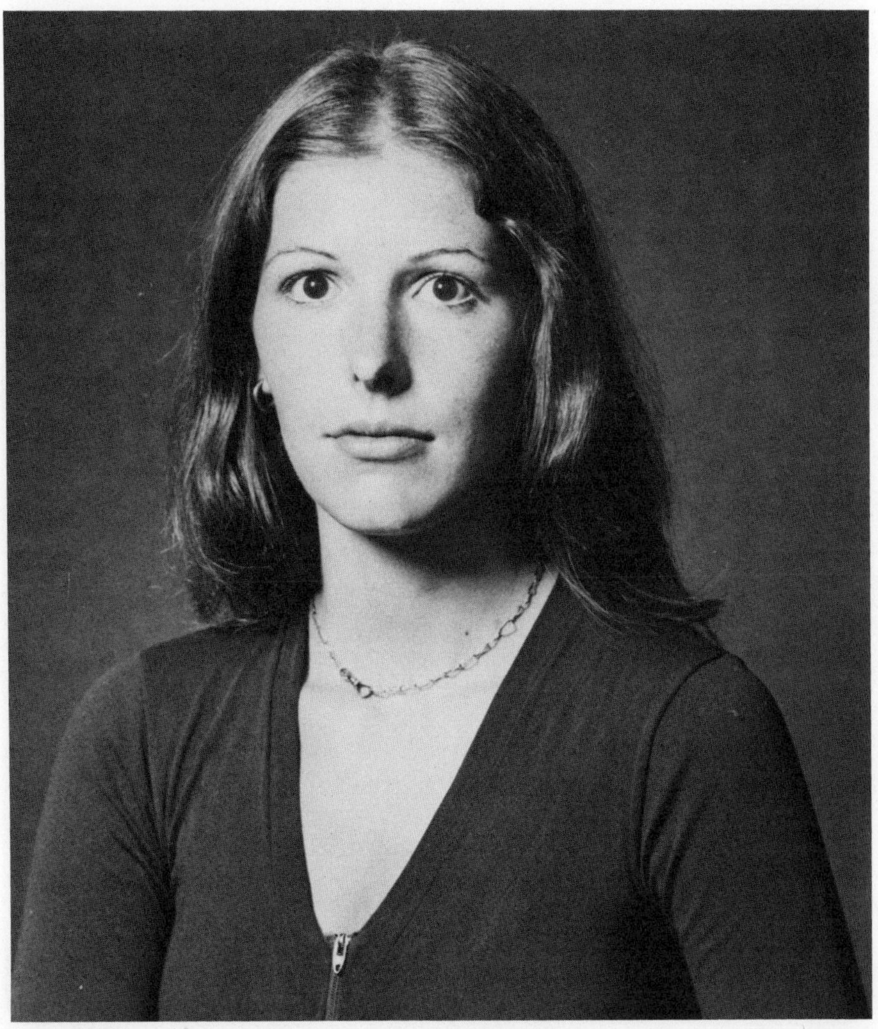

characteristics, helping you to decide which angle the face should be turned to minimize the little defects of which the subject may be self-conscious. If you are aware of these factors, you can avoid errors in posing and lighting. It is not uncommon for a young lady to remark that she has been photographed many times but that nobody has taken the time and trouble to help her with her makeup. Knowing how to apply makeup is an advantage, and even though it does take time and some study, it can be a plus to your business.

Eye shadow and mascara have been applied here.

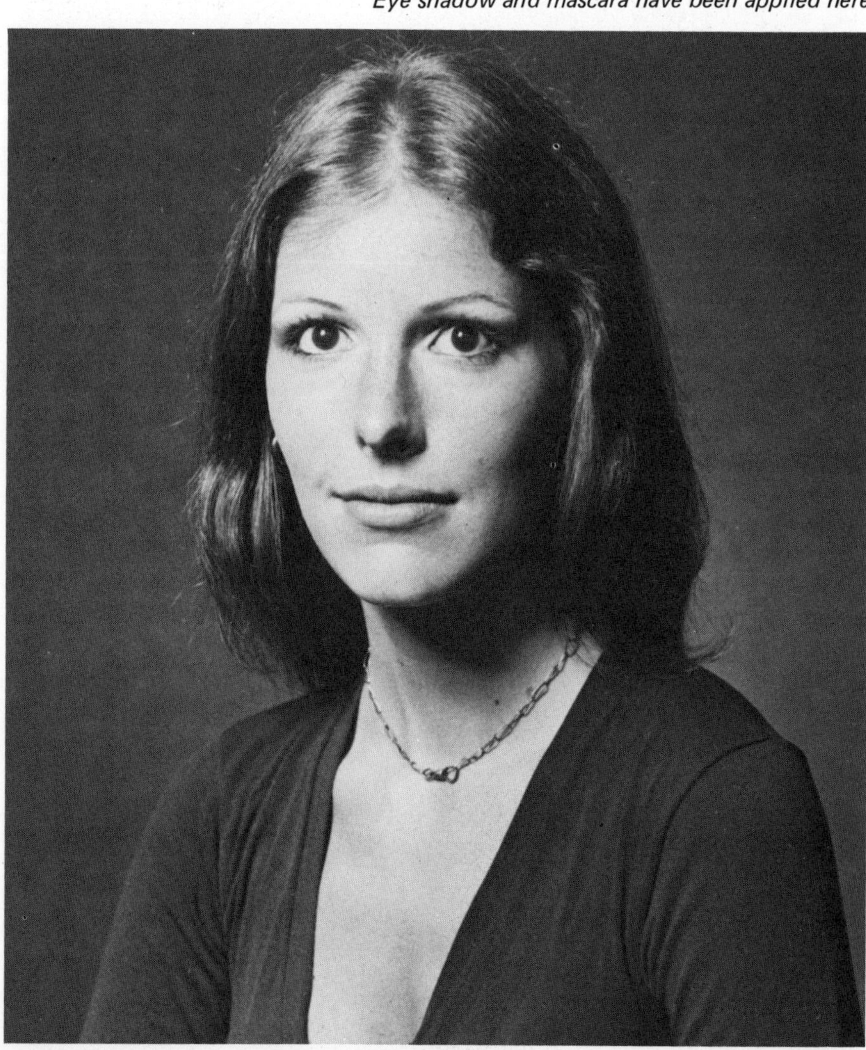

For portraits of a small child or strong character portraits of a man, the forehead, cheekbones, bridge of the nose, and tip of the chin should be highlighted softly with a touch of cleansing cream. With a child, ask the mother to apply the cream, or make a game of applying by gently dabbing and spreading it on the child's face. With a male subject, ask him to apply it on his face and on the knuckles of his hands if these are to appear in the picture. This gives strong spectral highlights. Use Albolene or other unscented cold cream, available in drugstores.

After the eyeshadow and mascara were applied, the eyebrows were then shaped.

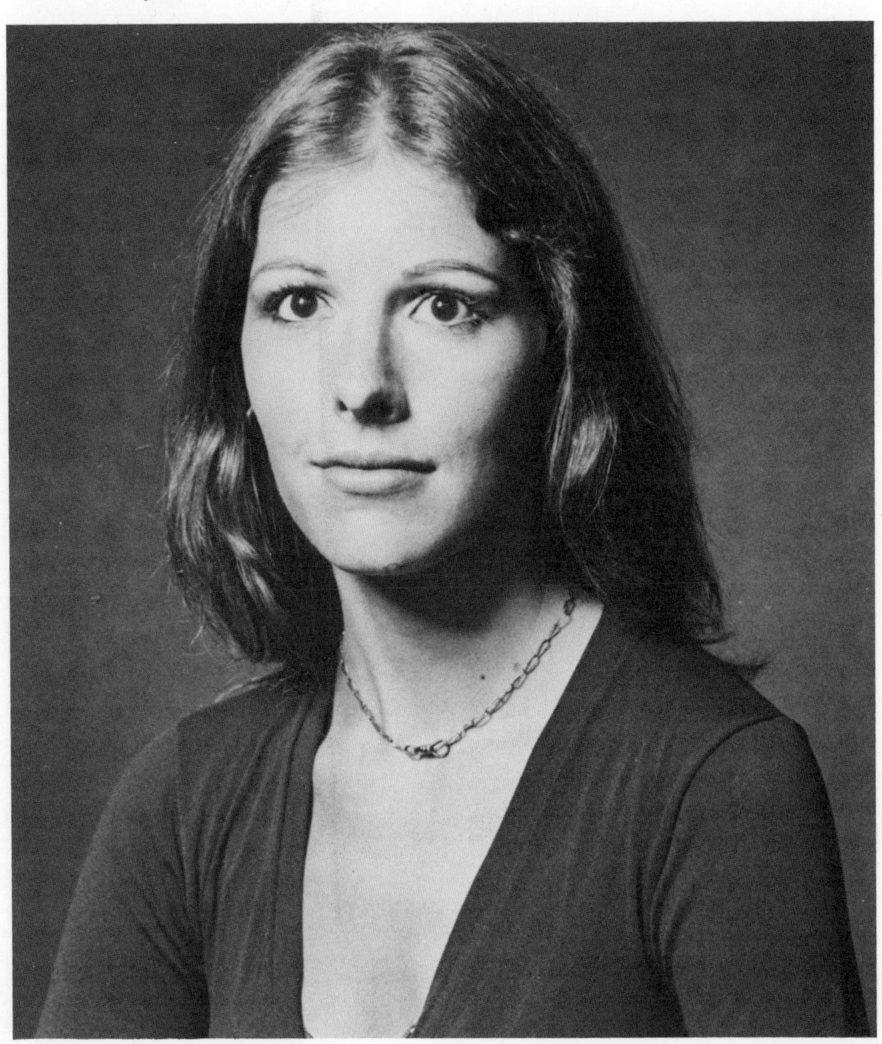

If a young lady has very attractive eyes, use makeup to accent them by intensifying the eyebrow arch, the upper and lower lashes, and adding a very soft nonreflective eye shadow above the eye on the upper lid. A clear pink or red lipstick is best. Avoid lipsticks that have a bluish or cyan cast because the coloration sometimes fluoresces and can photograph badly. The makeup base should closely match the skin tone. Occasionally a girl will have such clear skin

Blemish remover (Erase) has been applied to cheeks and forehead.

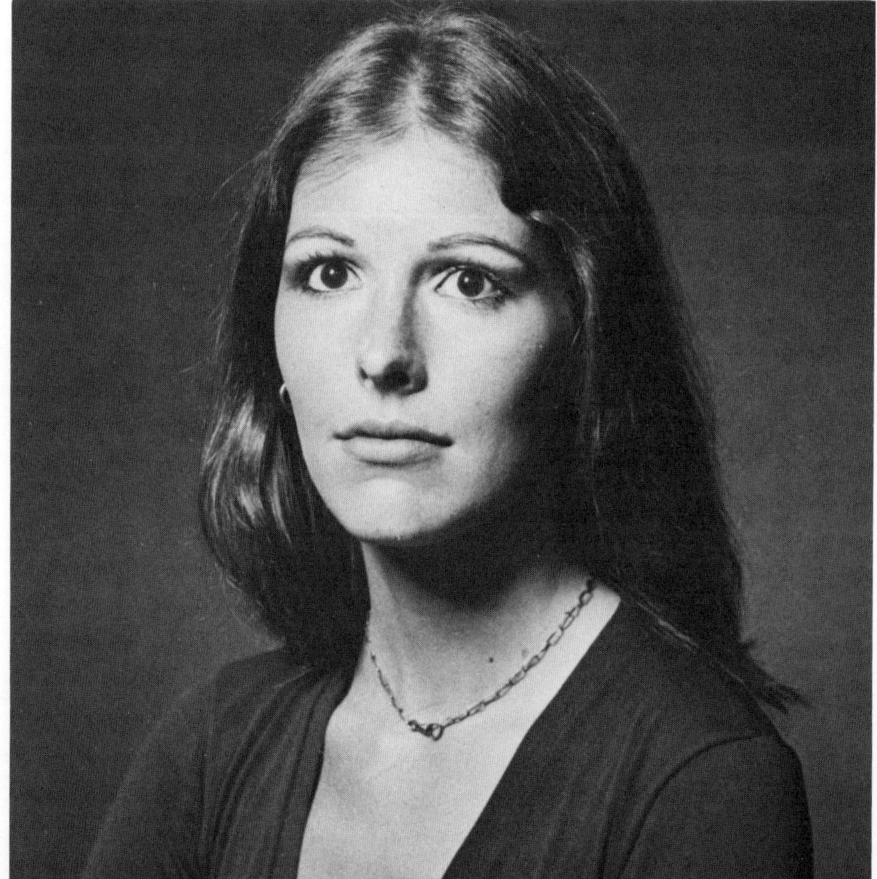

that no makeup base is required. With most, however, a light layer of base will cover some of the discolorations and blemishes that could be difficult to retouch. Products such as Erase, which are formulated to cover blemishes in skin tones, can be advantageous. Even if you feel that makeup will not materially add to the appearance of a young lady, the psychological effect is important. When a woman feels that she looks her best, she assumes an air of grace and self-confidence.

Lipstick has been applied and stray hairs on the forehead held in place with hairspray.

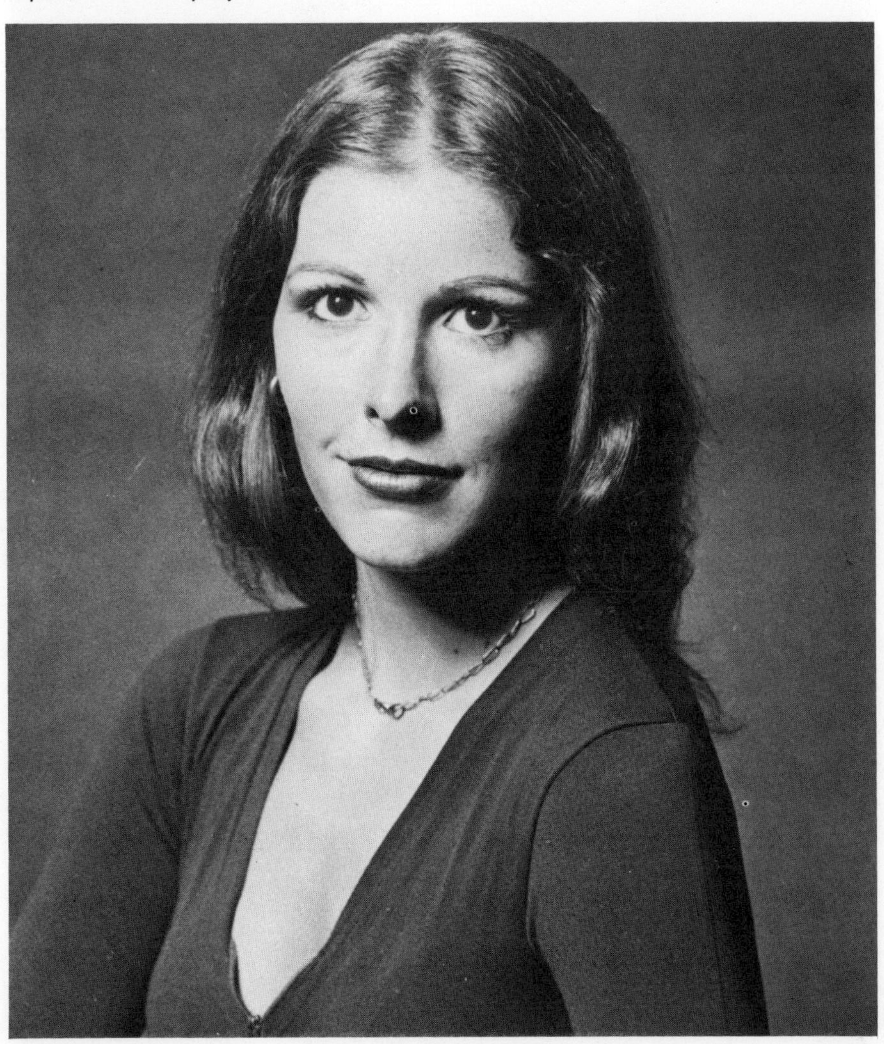

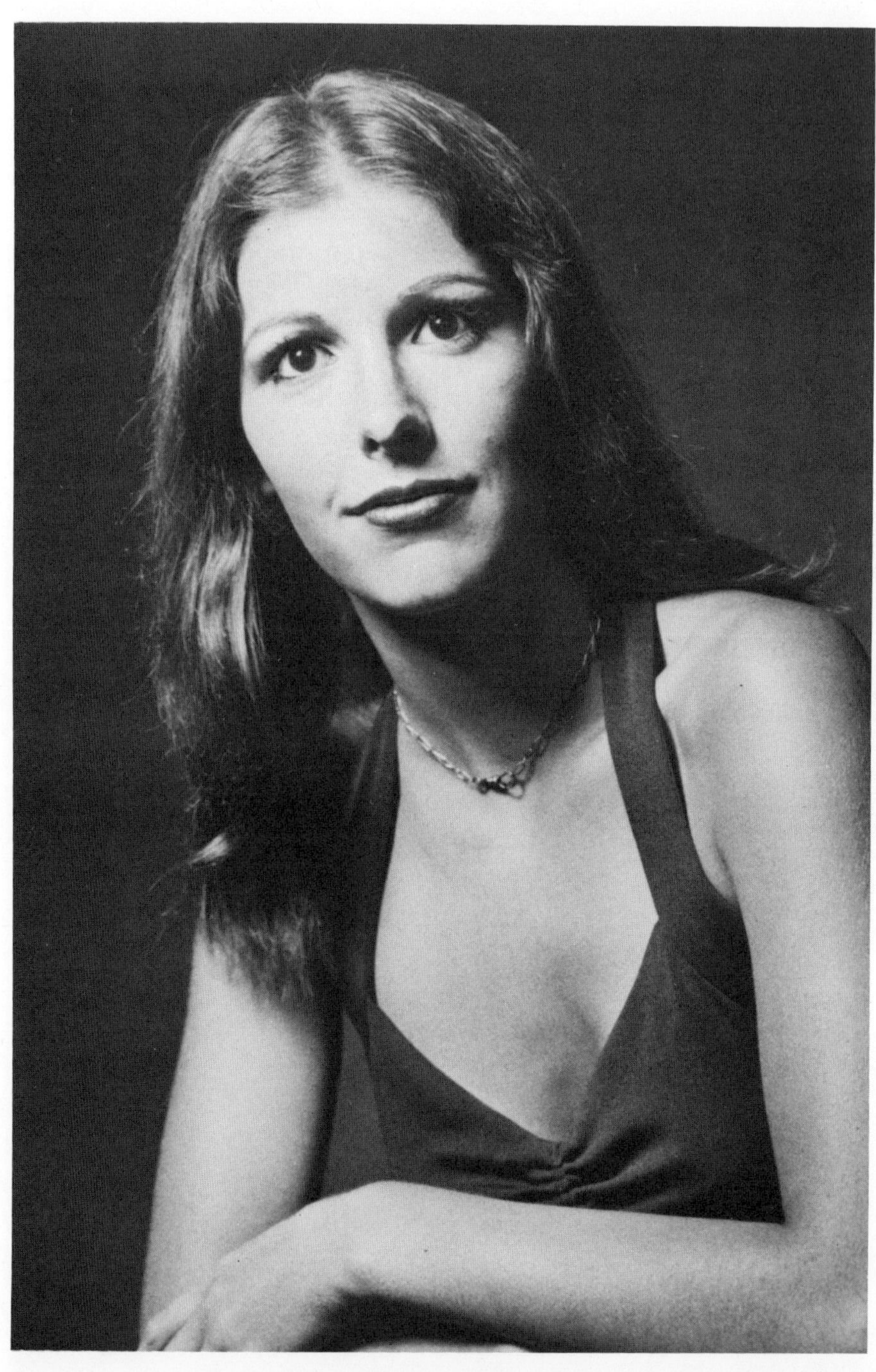

The model has changed into the dress she will wear. The makeup and clothing are now complete and she is ready for the final portrait.

HAIR STYLES

When discussing clothing and makeup for the portrait, pay attention to the subject's hair style. Mostly your concern will be that the hair is smooth and that no stray hairs are poking out along the outer edges, although these can be smoothed down by moderate use of a nonaerosol hairspray. Don't spray directly on the subject's head but rather spray some of the product on your hand and gently touch the area that needs repair. Use as little as possible to avoid the plastic, overcoated look produced by too much spray.

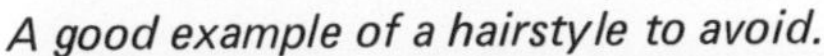

A good example of a hairstyle to avoid.

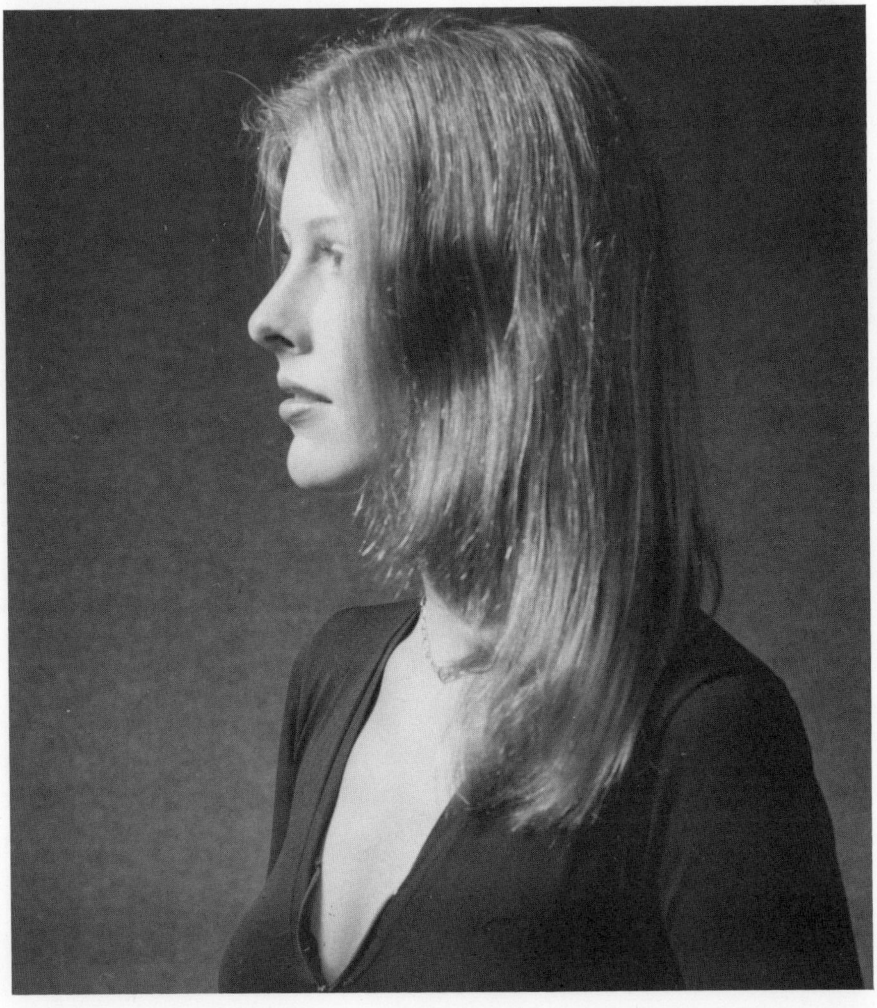

Occasionally a female (most often a teenager) will come into the studio with a hairstyle that is extremely unflattering for her facial characteristics and bone structure, for example, a short, round-faced young lady with bangs that come down to her eyebrows or below, resulting in a Porky Pig look-alike. To get your message across, explain to the customer that if she were learning to draw a face in art class, she would first draw an egg-shaped configuration, then subdivide it into thirds—the top third at eyebrow line, the middle third at the

An otherwise excellent picture is marred by the long hair hanging down on the forehead.

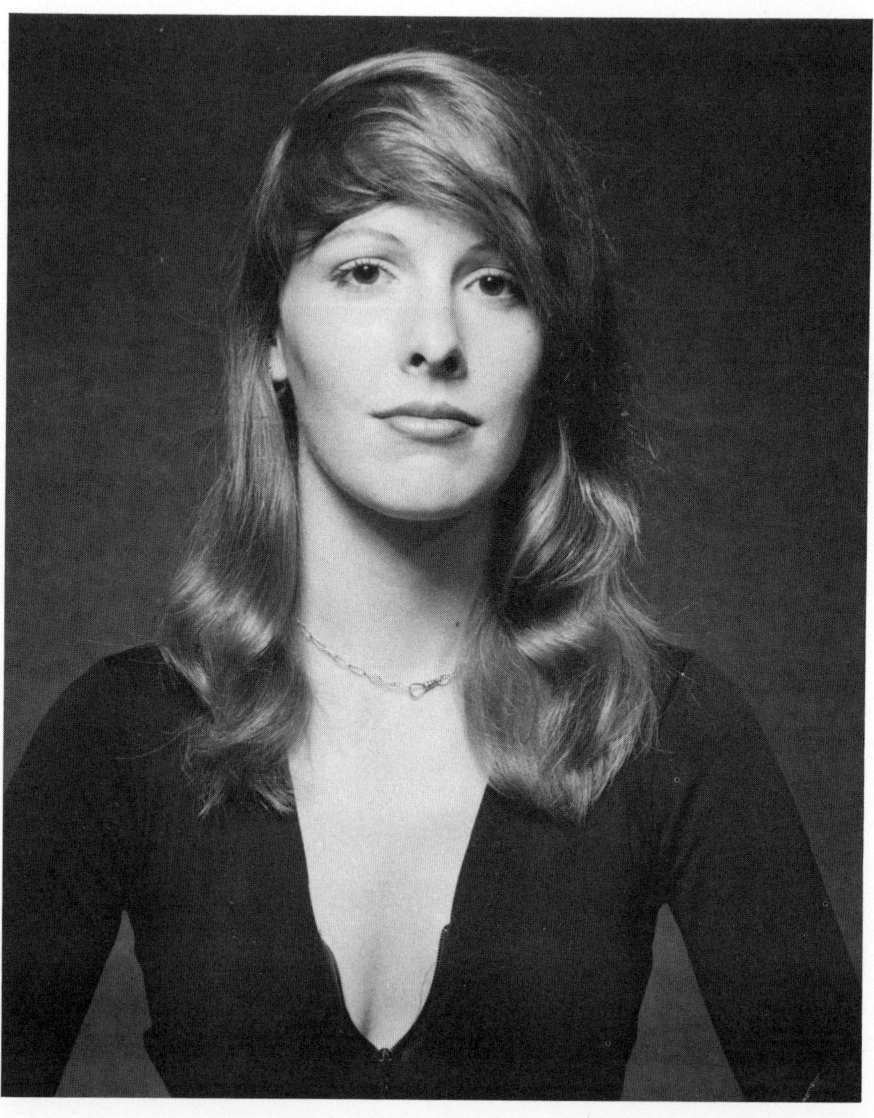

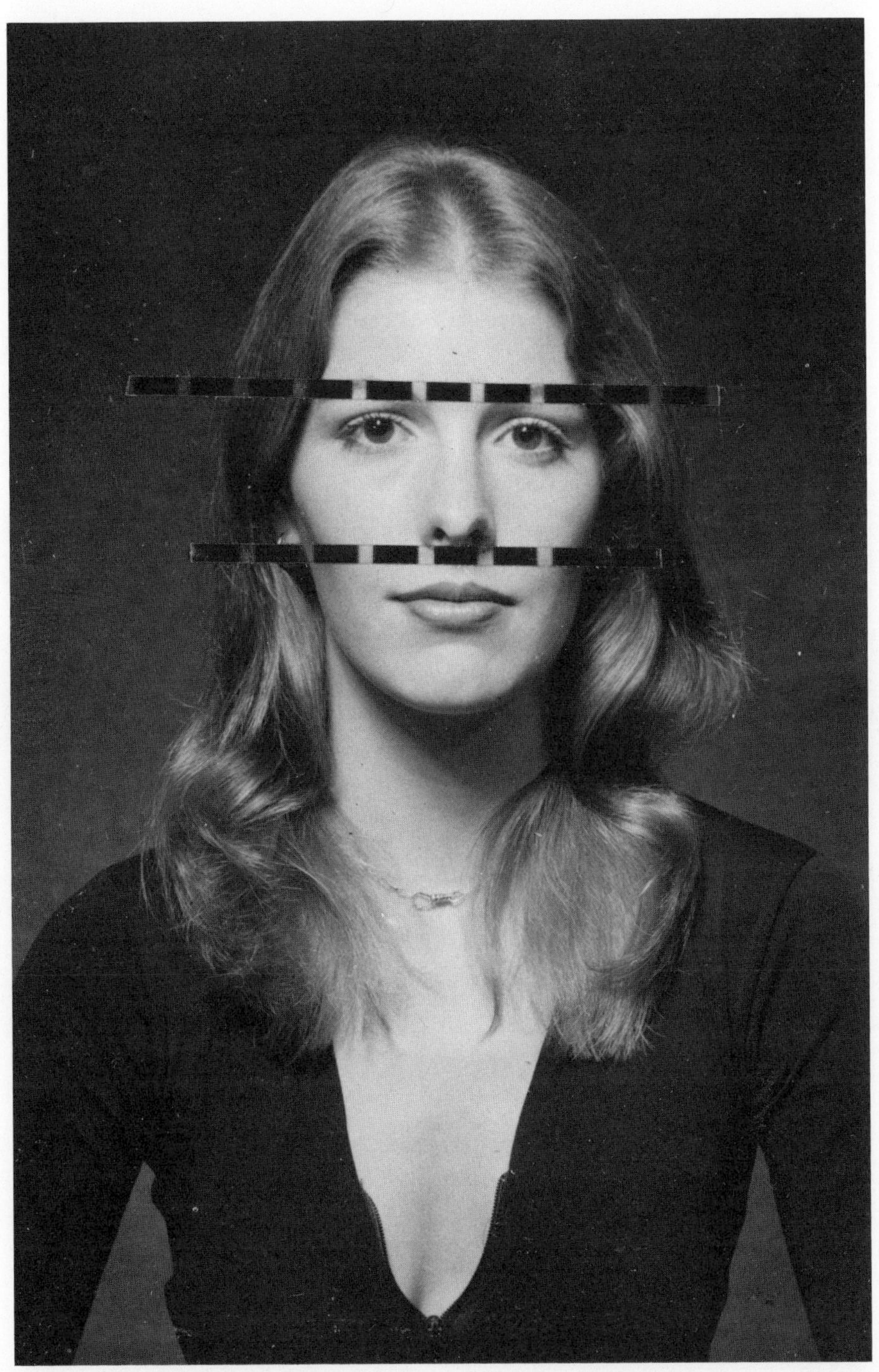

The "rule of thirds," indicating the symmetry of the face.

nose line , and the final third at mouth. Tell her that if the top third is removed (by covering it with hair), this makes the face appear shorter and wider. Many will see the point and change hairstyles. Try to part the hair to reveal the forehead. If the only reason for bangs is to conceal blemishes on the forehead, explain that the combination of makeup and retouching will remove these completely. If a young lady insists, "But that's *me,*" back off and suggest making some photographs in the style she prefers as well as additional poses with another hairstyle. This suggestion is seldom refused. Once the subject sees the proofs and compares, she usually will select the portrait with the hairstyle you recommended.

Older women, like to make appointments for a sitting immediately following their weekly visit to the beauty parlor. Often she leaves looking as though she has been plasticized or vulcanized, wearing the "hairstyle of the week" whether or not it fits her features. If you find out that the lady is going to visit the beauty parlor just before a sitting, schedule the sitting for at least 24 hours after the hairstyling. In the case of children's haircuts, three or four days eliminates that fresh-trimmed look. With some teenagers today, there isn't much you can do about hairstyling except keep it out of the eyes and try to make sure that the hair is combed back sufficiently so that it does not cast shadows across the forehead or cheeks when the lights are positioned.

If gaps or open spaces in the hair show up in the proofs, this means you were not very observant during the sitting. An ideal way to find these intruding gaps as well as objectionable stray hairs is to turn on the background light and stand at the camera position while the subject is in normal placement for the photograph. Turn the main light away so that no illumination from the front falls on the subject. By watching the outline, it is very easy to see the hair flaws and correct them rather than having to retouch or having the customer hate the portraits because the hair looked terrible. Another way to do this is to place a lamp behind the subject in the makeup area. By momentarily turning off the overhead lighting, you can readily see any flaws and correct them.

Chapter 15

Building Rapport

When someone calls or stops in to make an appointment for a sitting, first find out the purpose of the photographs. Pictures of a young lady for her family and pictures for a boyfriend or financé require different types of sittings. Very often the conversation enables you to get to know more about your subject and the pictures required.

People must like you personally before they will go out of their way to do business with you. When your clients enjoy a visit to your studio, you can rest assured that they will bring their friends as well. If you run a successful studio operation and deliver a reasonable or high-quality product, you can be more successful by improving the pleasure or fun factor.

You will find that the silly things you do to entertain children completely absorb parents as well. Among the toys selected to entertain a child during a sitting are: a tickle machine or peacock feather, a bubble machine, stuffed spring animals, hand puppets, and squeakers. To keep the youngster occupied when the parent is selecting proofs, equip your reception room with challenging action toys. The Dyna-Diver, from Diversion Dynamic Inc., is a simple scientific toy that appeals to young and old. The most rambunctious little darling can be kept busy for an amazing length of time with such a toy. A bean-bag chair is also fascinating to children. Moreover, it will hold an infant securely and firmly while the parent transacts business. A bowl of inexpensive plastic "rewards" for the kids is also a good idea. Novelty companies sell these trinkets and you can give them to the older children. Not only do children remember a happy experience, but parents are grateful for your interest and perhaps a few minutes of peace and quiet.

CAMERA-ROOM MAGIC

One of the problems a photographer faces in making a portrait is overcoming the shyness of a subject. People are fascinated by magic, and a simple trick or two can work wonders in relaxing a shy or nervous subject. The tricks that work best are brief, small, easy to store in a desk drawer or pocket, and inexpensive. Things that can be handled in the studio are coins, cards, rubber bands, paper clips, rope, and pocket tricks, which do not require any real manipulative skills. Don't use tricks that require razor blades, matches, knives, explosives, or other dangerous objects. Children love to experiment and may try to duplicate your tricks at home. Youngsters love wild tales, so devise stories of witches, pirates, ghosts, and robbers to go along with your magic.

For infants who cannot understand tricks, a simple stunt with a coin that sticks to your forehead will hold their interest. The peacock feather, or tickle machine, also works well with young children. Another attention-getter is the dime-store bubble machine. You can capture a variety of expressions with the help of this simple toy. Stand in the area where you wish the child's eyes to look and blow bubbles from there. You will see how well you hold the child's interest. A long air release is a must in this case so that you can move away from the camera.

Before rushing out ot the nearest magic shop, remember that the best tricks are those with audience participation. The object is not to prove that you are The Great Houdini or Thurston, but to relax folks and to hold their interest. Try to understand what people like, and you will be on the road to a successful business operation.

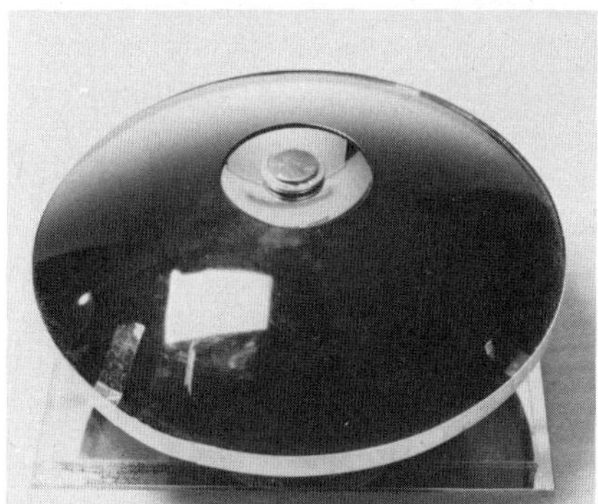

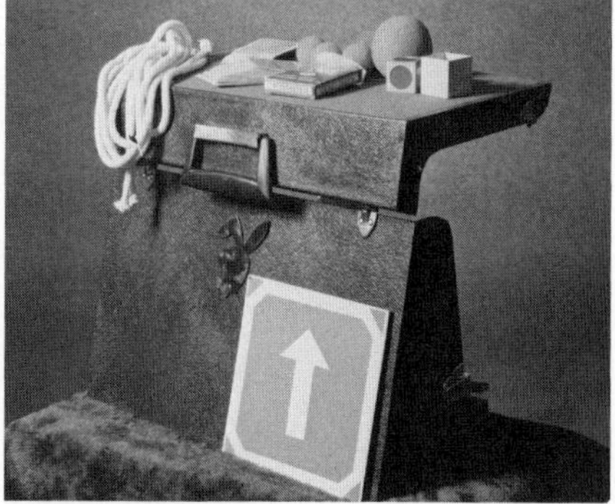

This optical illusion (left), obtained from Edmund Scientific, is a real conversation piece. The saucer-shaped disc appears to have several coins balanced on top. When the viewer reaches for a coin, his fingers pass directly through it.

This magician's worktable (right) is always ready with cards, rope, sponge balls, and other small tricks to relax a nervous subject.

Chapter 16

Subject Characteristics

HUMAN IDIOSYNCRASIES

Many people go through life seeing but never observing. Seeing is the visual action that we do automatically. But to observe is to select and remember certain characteristics and be aware of them on a conscious level. A photographer who makes pictures of people for a living has to consciously separate what he does from the many visual images to which he is constantly exposed on TV, theater screens, and the stage. Most people are interested in pictures that make them look good and present them in the most flattering manner. In order to accomplish this, the photographer must have the ability to observe the subject and determine what kind of photographs will please that particular subject. Remember that no one is ever satisfied with what he or she has. While women with straight hair want it curled, those with the curly hair want it straightened. A short person wants to be tall, while a tall person wishes otherwise. The overweight person wants to be thin, and the thin person wants to gain weight. Young girls strive to look older and older women want to look younger. And so on. Understanding these human idiosyncrasies can help you in your approach to making successful portraits people will like.

Skin Color People who are very pale and alabaster in complexion prefer to have their skin tones darker in a photograph. On the other hand, dark-complexioned people prefer lighter skin tones. Hardly anybody prefers "natural" color. Your objective should be to produce pleasing color. Observing masculine and feminine traits and noting them will give you information about your subjects and how they should be posed, lighted, and what expression will best flatter them.

Shape of Face Observing the subject's features is what it is all about. The shape of the face will determine the angle at which your main light should be positioned. A narrow face calls for a somewhat more frontal or broad lighting to widen the face. A round, pudgy face calls for a three-quarter position and short lighting with relatively strong shadows on the side of the face closer to the camera in order to slim it.

Hairline If the subject's hairline is normal, then no adjustments in lighting or pose is required. If someone has a receding hairline, use a lower camera angle and shade the top of the head slightly with the barn doors or a head screen to improve the picture.

Forehead Foreheads refer to the plane of the forehead: some are flat and go straight up before they recede at the hairline; others lean back from the eyebrows to the hairline; and still others protrude at the hairline and recede in the direction of the eyebrows. The normal, flat forehead requires the standard camera and head position. For a receding forehead, raise the camera angle slightly and tip the subject's head forward so that it appears to recede less. For a protruding forehead, raise the chin and lower the camera to bring the forehead to a more normal configuration.

Eyes Consider how deep the eyes are placed in relation to the forehead and cheeks. With many subjects, normal lighting does a good job and little change is required. For subjects with deep-set eyes, lower the main light to illuminate the inner aspects of the eyes and eyelids. For the subject with protruding eyes, elevate the main light. The expression of the eyes is very important in a portrait. Referred to as the windows of the soul, it is with the eyes that a subject really smiles, not the mouth.

You must also be aware of whether the eyes focus correctly. To photograph a cross-eyed subject, where at times the muscles in the eyes do not coordinate and move together, suggest that the subject look at a distant point. Make the exposures only when the eyes are straight. Don't show any proofs in which the eyes appear crossed. Crossed-eyes are more prevalent in young children and often they outgrow this. Photograph a cross-eyed youngster in profile. Work from farther back and take the photographs only when the eyes are perfectly straight.

Occasionally among older people you will encounter a wall-eyed subject—someone with the tendency to look at opposite walls and who has difficulty positioning the eyes straight ahead and in one direction. The solution to photographing wall-eyed subjects is to give them something close at which to look. This forces the eyes to look together so that they are parallel. Make your exposures when the eyes are straight.

One important thing the photographer must observe about eyes is that few people have both eyes exactly the same size. Sometimes this difference is relatively small and therefore insignificant. In those cases where the difference is obvious, you must be aware of it. In posing the subject, position the smaller eye closer to the camera, as it is enlarged due to the angle of the lens. You thereby minimize the fault. Posing the subject with the larger eye closer to the camera will exaggerate the fault, resulting in a photograph which the subject may consider unacceptable.

Eyeglasses Occasionally someone will come into the studio to have a photograph made and will grope around and squint strongly when looking at the photograph displays. This is a clue that this individual wears glasses but has removed them because he or she does not want to wear them in the picture. Rather than embarrass the subject in such an instance, try poking fun at yourself. If you wear glasses, point to them and explain that you really don't need them—except to see! This generally relaxes people. You can then explain that if they wear glasses most of the time, people get used to seeing them that way and a portrait without glasses would make them look like someone else. Depending on the cooperation from the individual, suggest that the sitting be done with glasses if possible. If the subject insists on not wearing them suggest that the poses be done with and without the glasses. If this fails with a male subject, ask him to hold the glasses in his hand and include them in the picture, and explain that they are a prop and will add to the likeness in the picture.

Glasses present several other problems. Glasses of average or moderate optical correction may cause no reflection problems. But if the lenses are like magnifying glasses and will distort the shape of the eye due to their correction and curvature, there are a number of ways to handle the problem.

1. You can remove the glasses and have the person hold them, or remove them from the picture completely. This is not the most satisfactory way of solving the problem but there will be times when you have no other choice.

2. If you are aware of the problem in advance, you can have the client bring in an old pair of glasses and use the frames with the lenses removed.

3. Sometimes a very concerned customer will discuss this problem with you in advance, in which case suggest that they stop at their eye doctor and borrow a similar style of empty frames for use in the photographs. This is frequently done on television, where actors wear blank frames to retain their likeness and eliminate the problem of reflections from thick lenses. If the lenses are fairly large, sometimes raising the earpieces about a half inch above their normal position will tilt the lenses down and eliminate reflections. From the camera position, the glasses will not appear tilted.

4. People who wear contact lenses are most sensitive about having someone else's hands around their eyes. The moment you notice this, reassure them that you will be extremely careful not to disturb their lenses.

5. An ever-increasing problem in eyeglass styling is the use of extremely dark or tinted lenses, some of which darken when in bright light and lighten in low levels of light. This type of lens radically alters the color of the eyes in color film and often obscures much eye detail. People with this type of glassses usually have a conventional pair as well, so request the subject to wear the regular glasses for the sitting. Explain that the tinted lenses will alter eye color and that little can be done to the finished photograph to change this. If this is what they want, then fine. Otherwise, request regular glasses, empty frames, or no glasses.

Noses Comedian Jimmy Durante, who was endowed with a huge nose, used to make fun of it by saying, "There are a million good-looking guys, but I'm a novelty." The average person with a large nose does not feel this way nor is a big nose a joking matter. This is evident by the millions of dollars spent annually on rhinoplasty surgery to alter and adjust the shape of noses. It is important, therefore, to try to minimize the size of the nose. When you photograph a subject with a long nose, you can shorten it by tipping the head up and lowering the lights to reduce the amount of shadow area under the nose. A slightly lower-than-normal camera angle is also advantageous.

A nose that appears broken can be straightened by turning the head and finding the most flattering camera angle. A nose that shows a sharp break in it from one side of the face will be relatively straight and normal looking from the opposite side. Noses that are relatively broad in the septum are best photographed with the head in a three-quarter pose and with short lighting. This shapes the nose so that it looks much narrower. This pose and lighting tend to narrow the other features of the face as well.

For people with tiny "button" noses (most frequently seen in children), tilt the head down, raise the light slightly to increase the amount of shadow under the nose, and take the photograph from a higher camera position.

The Mouth The mass producer of photographs has decided that all pictures should be of people smiling. Yet you would be hard-pressed to find more than a handful of paintings (of the millions that have been done in the last 500 years) of anyone with a huge, grinning smile. The painter always maintained that the mouth should be at rest in a very relaxed position, with perhaps the slightest suggestion of a smile at the corners, and that the expression in a good portrait is in and around the eyes. Although a smiling picture is pleasing the first few times a person views it, after a while one begins to wonder what the idiot is grinning at. Unless there is a specific situation that requires a smile, try to capture an expression of a sparkle in the eyes that suggests a happy, relaxed mood without resorting to a large grin and display of teeth. Typical of this is Da Vinci's "Mona Lisa," where the artist managed to capture a spiritual, mystical smile in the eyes of his subject.

Strive to photograph the subject with sparkling eye expression and a relaxed mouth expression. The only time you should break this rule is when your subject has a down-curved mouth. About one-third of all people have upcurved mouths and therefore a very natural, pleasant expression; one-third have straight mouths, and the slightest pull of the muscles upward gives them a pleasant expression; and one-third have mouths that curve down. In this latter case, use a soft, partial smile because it eliminates the unhappy look in the subject.

Regarding the subject's teeth, there is little the photographer can do in posing or lighting to correct problem teeth. These must be made either in negative retouching or positive retouching directly on the print. However, the portrait of a subject with irregular or discolored teeth should not be retouched in such a manner that they become unrecognizable. Excessive retouching creates a phony look and should be avoided. Moderate retouching or partial correction of faults is usually satisfactory.

Often the parents of a youngster wearing braces will instruct the child not to smile for the portrait. Consequently the child presses his lips together creating an unpleasant expression. To relax and deal with such a child, tell him up front that if the braces show in any of the pictures, they will be retouched, and that braces are only temporary, not something which will be part of his appearance. Most of the time this relaxes the child, who then responds in a more natural way. For this type of subject, take a number of photographs with the lips gently closed as well as several exposures where part of the teeth show. If the parents decide that this is the pose they like best, retouch the braces and minimize or eliminate their visibility.

This same approach applies to subjects with irregularly spaced or missing teeth. If you let them know that you can repair the defect about which they are sensitive, you eliminate their fears and they relax for a successful session.

Ears Ears don't play an important role in portraiture in most cases. However, some subjects have ears that resemble flaps or barn doors. For this type of subject, confine yourself to a three-quarter pose of the head, which conceals one ear, and although the other ear is pointed toward the camera, this angle flattens and diminishes its size. Ears have very little to do with the likeness of a person. For that reason, when part of an ear is objectionable in a picture, there is no reason why it cannot be toned down or completely removed with retouching.

Chins Chins which vary radically from the normal either recede or protrude. Protruding chins can be corrected by lowering the head and raising the camera slightly above its normal position. For receding chins, raise the head and lower the camera. You can improve multiple chins by altering the angle in which you pose the subject. By leaning the subject forward almost to a 45-degree angle and raising the head, most of the extraneous chin area will be reduced in size. Higher lighting, which casts a strong shadow underneath the chin, and elevating the camera position a little above the normal position, can also be useful.

Neckline A V-shaped neckline can elongate a face and produce a more flattering overall result. In older women, where heavy lines and creases create serious retouching problems, high necklines or a scarf can be extremely flattering while concealing the problems. In most cases, such subjects are aware of the problem areas and are most cooperative.

Hands In many portraits, particularly of couples and groups, use hands to put the subjects together in a harmonious composition. Photograph a couple not as two separate people, but as two people joined as one. In a family group, try to form a composition that gives a feeling of unity and togetherness. Hands belong in a picture *only* if the subject actually uses them to express himself or herself. You must be constantly aware of what the subject does naturally and not attempt to force a person into a pose simply because it looks good. Just prior to the sitting, and in the dressing room, if makeup or hair adjustment is required, observe the natural actions of the subject. If, during a conversation the subject uses her hands in an expressive manner, stands with a hand rested against her chin or forehead, or touches her glasses at the temple, she should be photographed in a pose that is close to what she does naturally. When a subject stands with his hands jammed into trouser pockets and never elevates them or uses them to express himself, this person should not be forced into an artificial hand pose.

Head Positions A photographer should also be aware of whether the subject in a natural situation tends to turn the head consistently to the right or to the left. Many people are either right-headed or left-headed; it has to do with the comfort of the subject. Try a little experiment on yourself. Turn your head sharply over your right shoulder and hold it for 10–15 seconds, then bring it back into a straight frontal position for a few seconds. Repeat the same thing in the direction of your left shoulder. You may find that one direction is comfortable while the other causes low-level discomfort in the neck muscles when you turn your head. Now imagine trying to photograph a person whose head is turned in such an uncomfortable direction. It can cause discomfort which leads to fidgeting and unnatural expressions. By posing a subject so that the head follows in the most comfortable direction, you have a greater chance of capturing a relaxed expression with the subject truly at ease.

From the preceding, it should be obvious that each subject you photograph is truly an individual. In order to make a fine photograph of a subject, all these factors and many more must be taken into consideration. Each subject should be posed, illuminated, and photographed from a vantage point that will best represent that subject. Every portrait subject is an interesting and exciting challenge, some more challenging than others, but challenging nonetheless.

Chapter 17

You Are the Director

If you could spend a half hour watching a group of aspiring student photographers in a studio situation with a model, you would quickly learn what not to do in making a portrait. Some will mumble or half whisper directions to the model; others will give confusing instructions; and a few will boldly march up to and start pushing her into the position they want. Frequently they are so embarrassed that they will rapidly make exposures as the model moves about, hoping that one of them results in an acceptable picture.

Some with motorized cameras will make rapid-sequence exposures as they move about the subject, working on the assumption that if they take a picture from every angle, they will find one that will make an attractive portrait. But good portrait photography is done with precision and intent; it is never by accident. If a photographer understands the good and bad features of a subject and places that subject in the correct pose and uses the correct lighting, then by creating the proper mood and expression the portrait will be a pleasing one.

Many photographers suddenly awaken to the fact that beyond the technical capabilities and an understanding of the requirements of the basics of good portraiture, they must also function as the director, developing a theme or idea, and be capable of communicating specifically what they wish to record on film. A good director must be explicit and his directions *loud, clear,* and *understandable.*

Adolf "Papa" Fassbender always insisted on this simple rule: "Don't touch the subject." Keep this in mind, because if you have done your homework and learned the basics of direction, there is no need to touch the subject to accomplish the desired pose. If a jacket needs straightening, a tie needs adjusting, or a sleeve needs to be pulled to eliminate a crease or wrinkle, first tell the subject precisely what you are going to do before doing it. Approaching someone and adjusting their clothing for them can distract or even annoy people. It is best to give directions from a reasonable distance and make them explicit so that your subject knows precisely what to do.

A handy way of accomplishing this is as follows: When the subject enters the camera room, first ask her to stand at the camera position while you assume the basic pose, showing her what you want. Then changing places, ask her to do likewise. Once the basic pose has been achieved, make adjustments verbally. By initiating the action yourself, for example, lowering your chin when you want the subject to lower hers, or raising yours when you wish the subject to do the same, you gain complete control.

Even with smaller children, you will find that by making a game of placing a hand under a chin, folding an arm, or placing a hand on a hip, you can get them to duplicate whatever pose you desire by doing it yourself and asking them to follow suit. If you want a child to stand in a fixed position, here's a little trick guaranteed to work: Drop a penny or small coin on the posing area and ask the child to place his right foot on it. Do the same for the left foot. If you tell the child that he can have the coins if he does not move his feet until you are finished with that pose, rest assured that those feet will not move.

Once you have established the correct basic pose and are satisfied with your lighting, your next task is to guide the subject, through conversation, to the correct quiet or high-peaked expression. Catching the moment when the subject is at her best is crucial in portrait photography. If you wish to establish a quiet or relaxed mood, the conversation and subject matter should be muted. Talk about pleasant, relaxing things which the subject enjoys doing or seeing. At the instant she assumes that longed-for expression, make your exposure. For a happy or joyous mood, when photographing a child, for example, raise your voice, make your conversation light and airy, and try to build the happy, relaxed feeling that makes it possible for such an expression to follow naturally.

CONSIDER YOUR SUBJECTS' FEELINGS

Each subject, regardless of his or her motive for coming to your studio, has feelings of apprehension. Some photographers will march a subject into a camera room, direct the person to sit in a position that is not always comfortable, and then expect the subject to turn on whatever expression they demand. With professional models or trained theatrical people, you could expect that kind of response because they are performers, but for the customer who walks into your studio, the approach must be different. It is up to you to produce the kind of pictures they want and to minimize defects. If the subject is a child who is wearing braces, or going through the indignity of having lost one, two, or three front teeth, you may be faced with a youngster with tightly pressed lips and a grim expression. In such a case, take several photographs with the compressed lips, but explain that you can make retouching corrections on both the negative

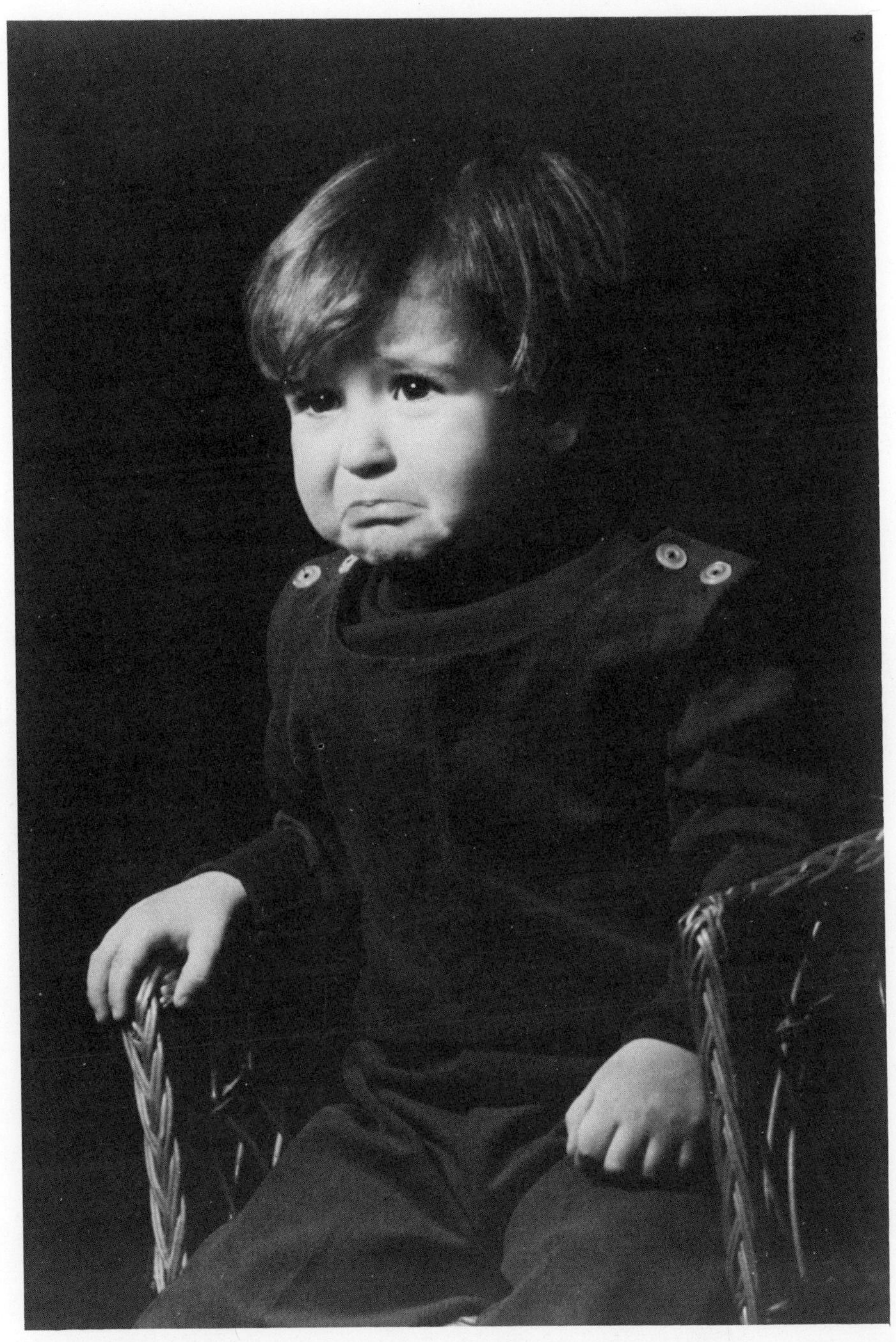

A good portrait photographer can turn what the layperson might consider a setting "disaster" into a marvelous portrait.

and the print. Rather than take a grim series of pictures with which the parents certainly will not be pleased, endeavor to make a number of exposures with the child relaxed. In most cases, the braces or missing teeth which every one thought would look horrendous really do not look bad at all and with a modest amount of retouching result in very lovely photographs. If a parent is still unhappy upon viewing the proofs, explain to her that what she doesn't like can be corrected.

At each sitting, it is your responsibility to be considerate of a subject's desires and to work within that framework whenever possible. When you disagree with your client, it is best to try the portrait both ways, thereby leaving it up to her, as the final editor, to select whatever she prefers. Being overly forceful can turn the subject off and make her uncooperative. For a successful portrait sitting, the full cooperation of the subject is a must.

Chapter 18

Approach to Posing

You are now in the camera room. All the discussions and preparations have been completed and you are about to start making photographs. This is a critical time. In the first two or three minutes, the impressions you make upon your subject will have much to do with how well the sitting will go and how the photographs you make will be. This is no time for hesitation or a halting approach. You must immediately take command and tell your subject precisely what you want done. At this point, you are not just a photographer, you are the director and must set the stage for the picture. The only way to do this properly is to be well prepared.

CAMERA-ROOM PREPAREDNESS

By this time, you, the photographer-director, should already have made some important decisions: the direction in which you will pose the subject, whether it will be a standing or sitting pose; and whether any chairs, boxes, or props will be used (if so, they should already be in place). Once the subject is in the camera room, do not hesitate in starting the sitting. Most important is the decision of whether this will be a head-and-shoulders, bust, three-quarter, or full-length pose. The preparations vary slightly for each, and you should move the subject into position, demonstrate precisely what you want, and immediately proceed to set the lighting for that particular pose and facial expression. Although you can tentatively place your lights at first, realize that you cannot place your lighting and then move the subject. This will alter the lighting. The best sequence is first to pose the subject, then set the camera position, get your lights precisely where you want them to be, then start making exposures.

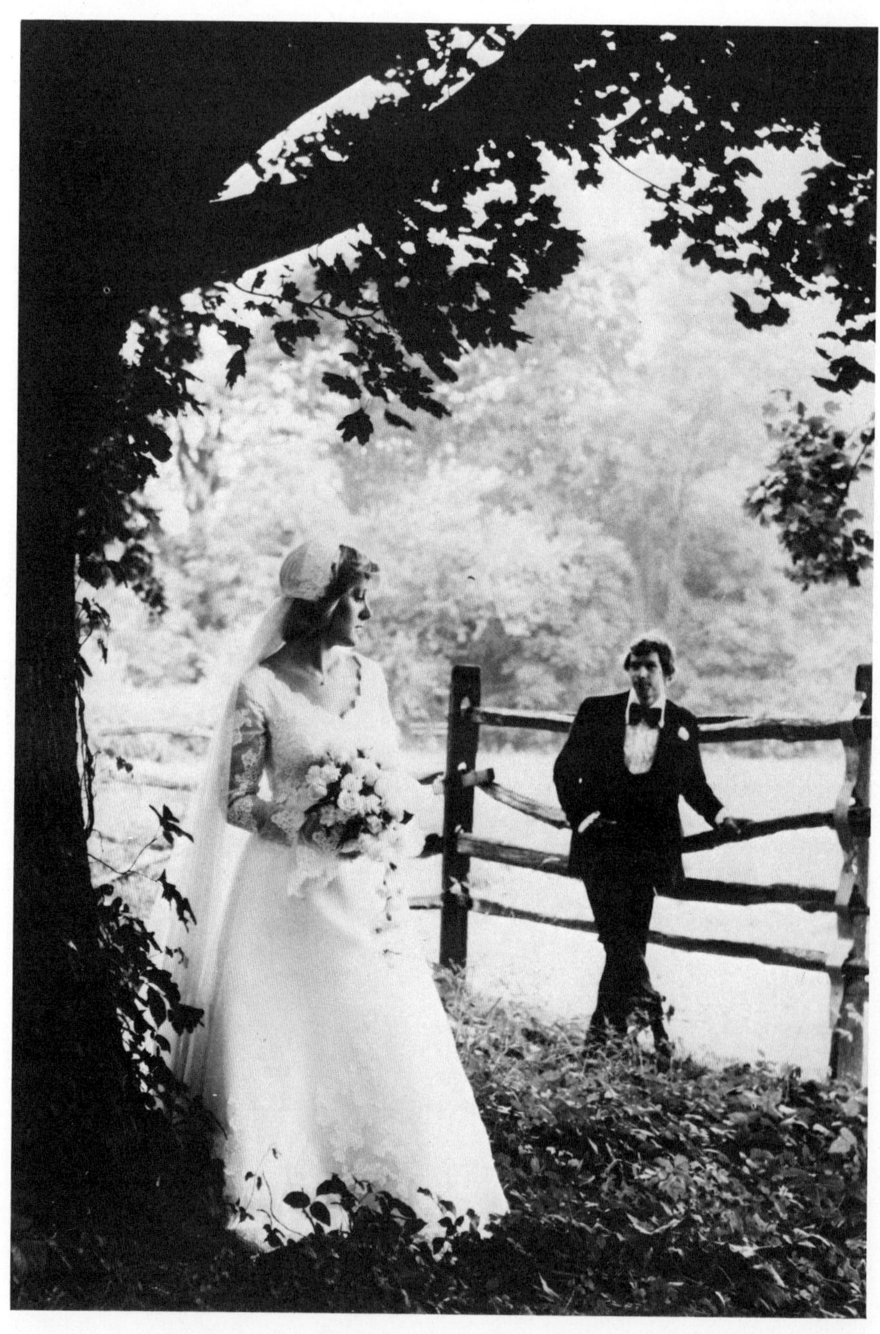

Make full use of the natural surroundings in any outdoor assignments. The rustic mood here heightens the contrast with the formal wedding attire.
Photo by Gerard Photography, Inc.

POSES

Sometimes, based on the subject's needs and wishes, you know in advance what the poses will be. If a photograph is intended for a one-column cut in a newspaper, you start with a simple head-and-shoulders pose. A three-quarter or full-length pose will not suit these requirements. When photographing a bride, a three-quarter pose can be very elegant and shows much of the detail in the dress. But make some full-length poses when the wedding gown lends itself to being draped and arranged to show detail, lace, and other fine work. A full-length pose is also extremely attractive when photographing children.

Whenever a customer remarks favorably about one of your sample photographs, note this and make several similar poses. Even when this type of pose is not totally suitable for this sitter, having a few to show that you are trying to please them demonstrates an effort on your part. Offer the sitter a variety of poses rather than limiting yourself to a single fixed concept. Start a sitting with a pose that you feel is appropriate for the subject. During the session, alter that pose so that the customer has a variety from which to choose when the proofs are presented. This may lead to additional sales. In every sitting, make the standard portrait poses; then after satisfying yourself that you have done your best, do some poses that vary considerably, not only in posing but in lighting, expression, and mood. Often the customer who came to the studio for a traditional picture gets excited about photographs that are different and will buy them.

If you plan to make a head-and-shoulders photograph for publication, you don't need to concern yourself with hand position or whether cuffs show. The photographer arranging the pose in the viewfinder or ground glass should know the approximate composition of the finished photograph. Even though you allow additional space for final composition, the decision of where the picture begins and ends is extremely important.

If you plan to take a head-and-shoulders photograph with the subject in a standing position, the placement of the subject's feet and the distribution of body weight are extremely important. Even though the lower segment of the body does not show, the placement sets the position of the spine and the angulation of the shoulders. Begin any standing pose by arranging the feet. Start sitting poses by the proper seating of the subject. These poses will suffer greatly if the spine is not straight and head and shoulders erect. Make every effort to avoid poses that are uncomfortable or ungainly to the sitter.

It is important to recognize that the basic body position for a male subject differs from that of a female subject because of the shoulder slope. You can determine shoulder slope by drawing an imaginary line across the body that reaches from the top of one shoulder to the top of the other. In a man's portrait, one side of the line should be higher when the face is turned in the direction of the lower shoulder. This leaning attitude psychologically depicts strength, aggressiveness, and forcefulness. In a woman's portrait, both shoulders should slope down away from the head.

BODY POSES

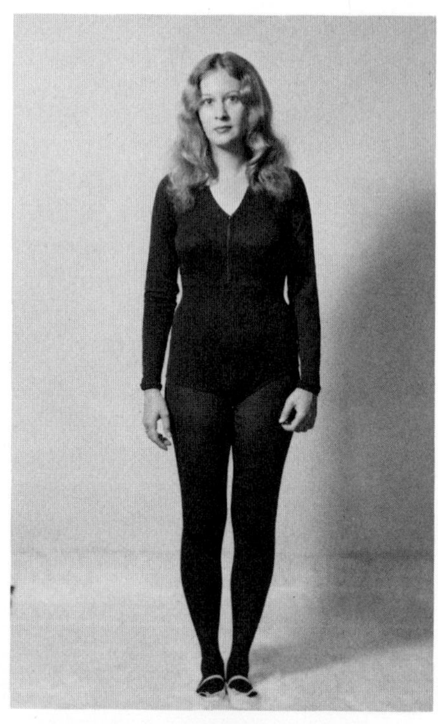

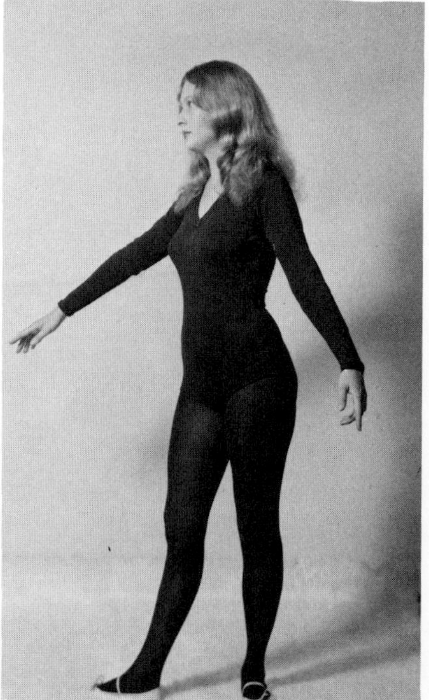

A flat-footed pose (above) squares the body. Separating the feet (left) in a ballet position improves weight distribution and shoulder position.

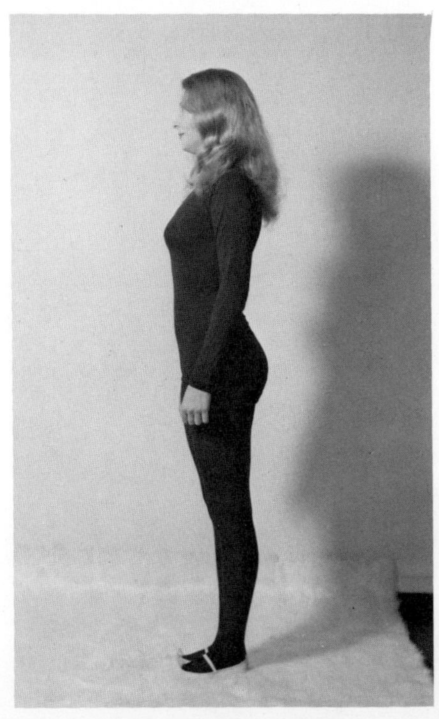

Flat-foot pose (left and below) from the side illustrates how the angles of the body are altered.

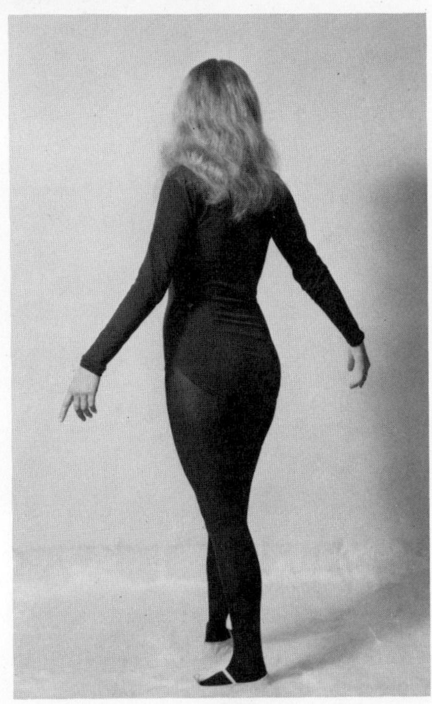

POSTURE

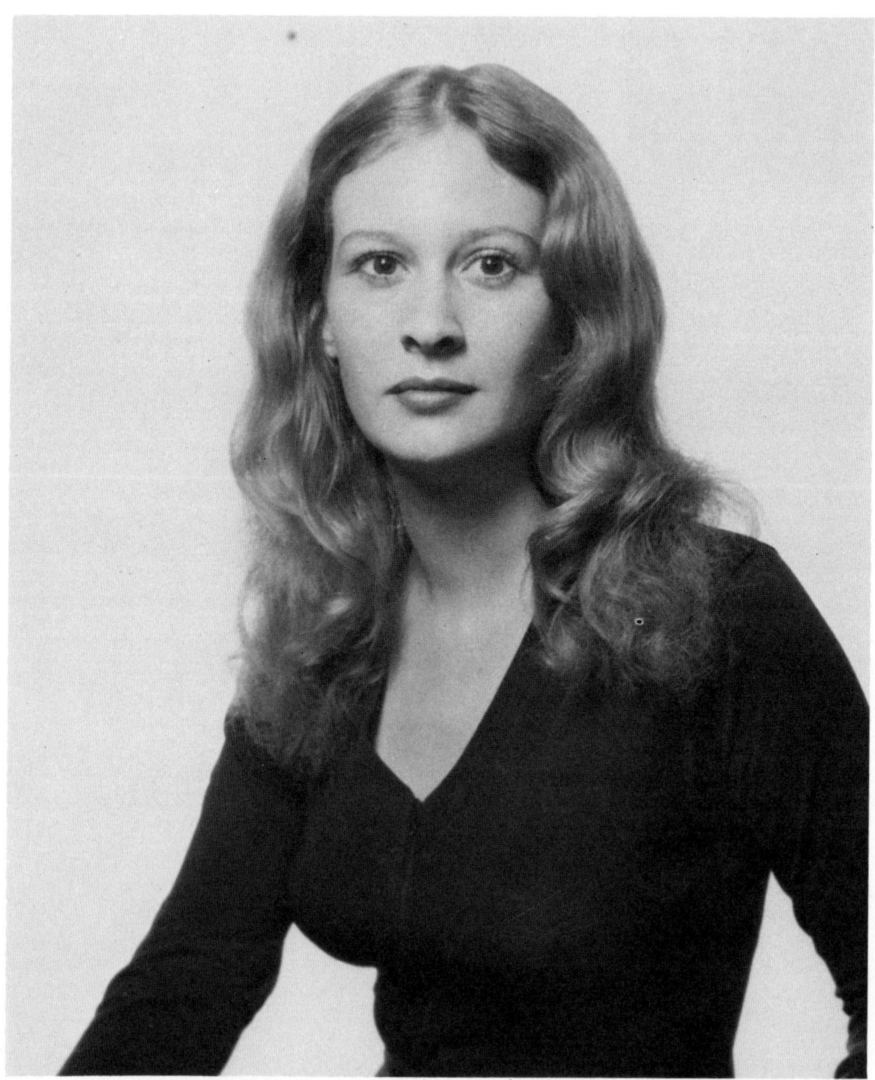

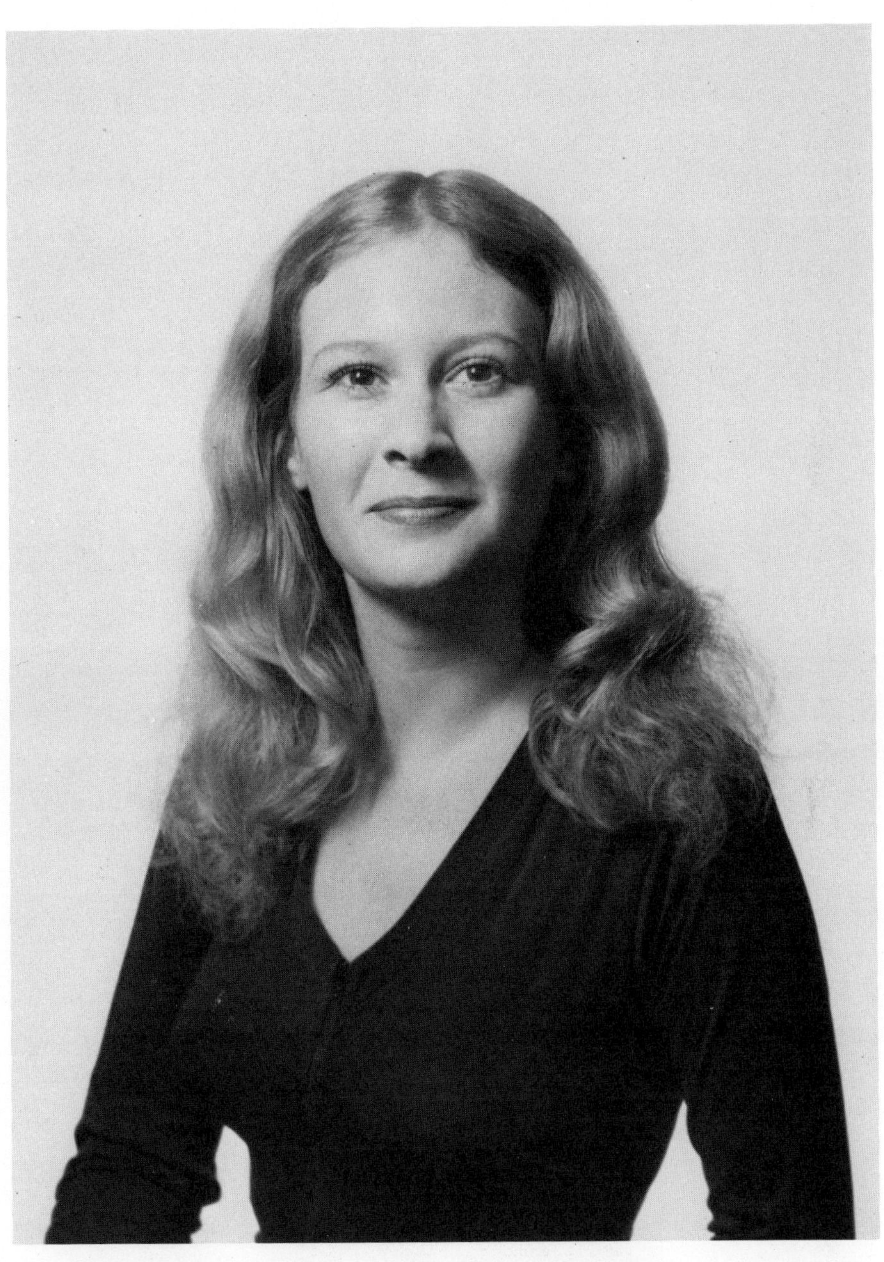

A curved spine detracts from the pose. Note how the head sinks into the shoulders, the waistline bulges, and the bust droops. Straightening the spine corrects all these problems. The photographer must be on the alert to prevent the subject from relaxing into the curved-spine position.

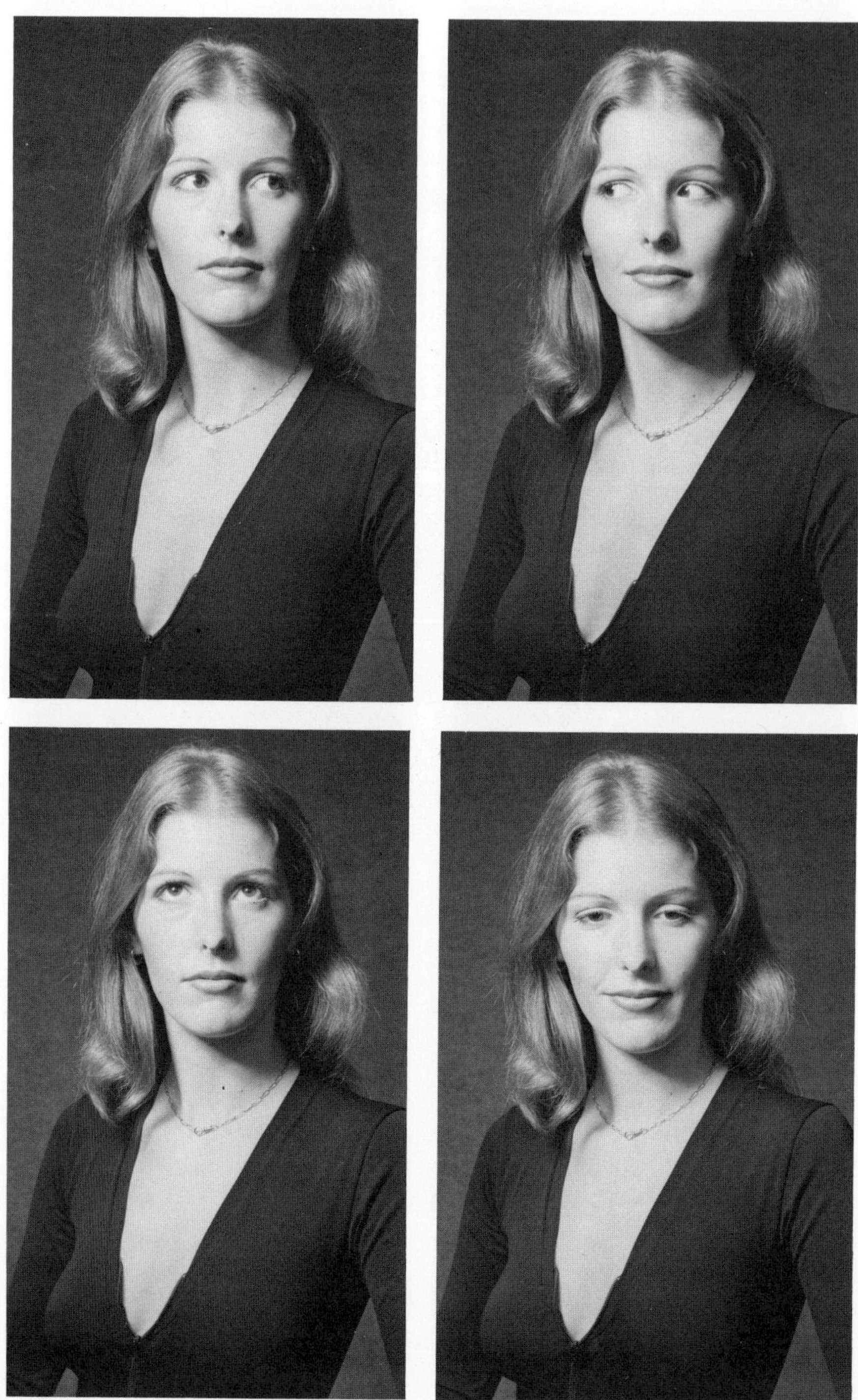

EYE POSITIONS

Eyes positioned too high, too low, or too far to the right or left, (opposite) can spoil an otherwise beautifully posed portrait. A good eye position (below) will show more of the white of the eye on one side than the other. This gives a feeling of animation and movement. Dead-center eye positions look static and expressionless.

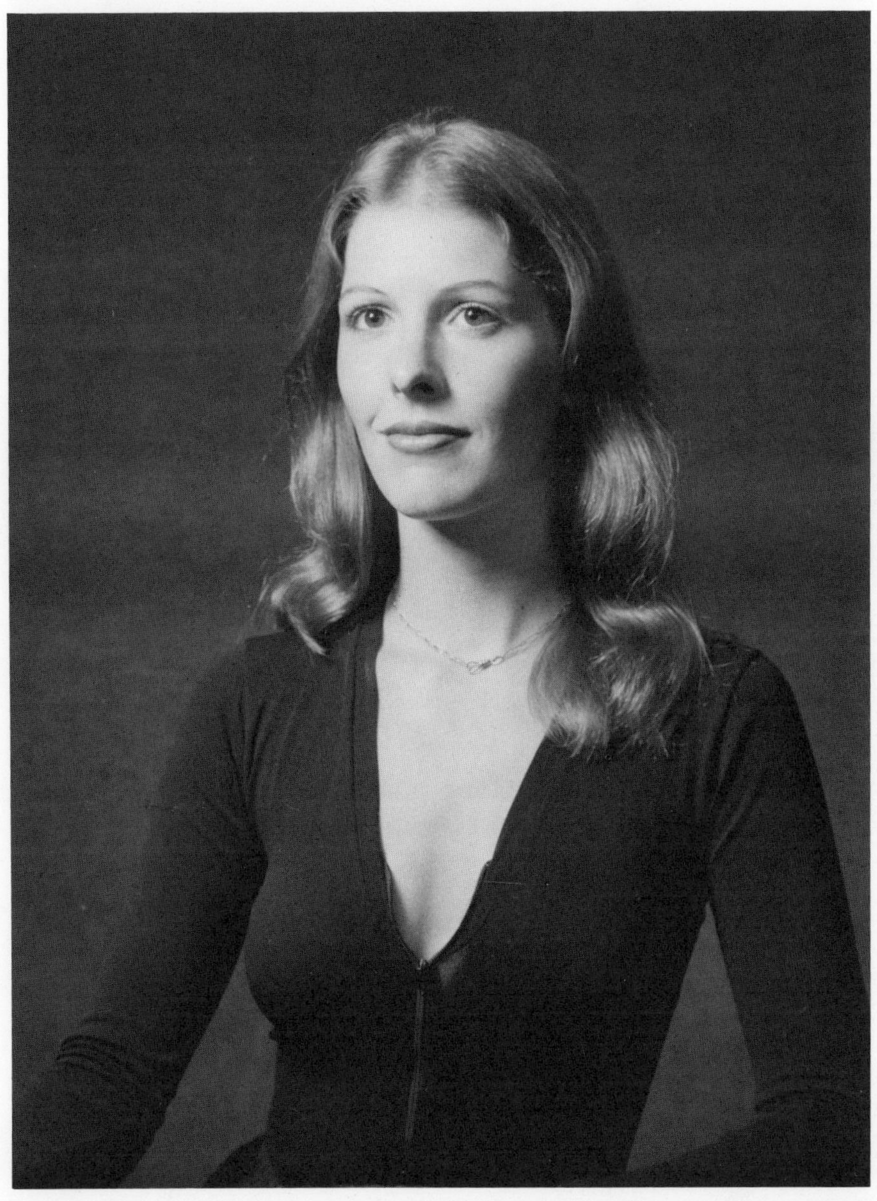

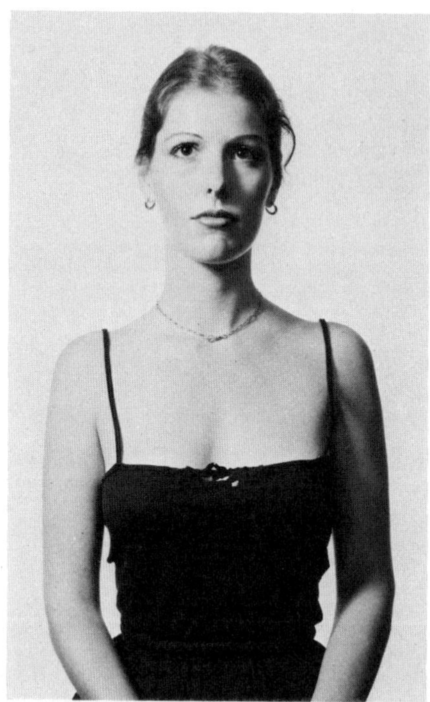

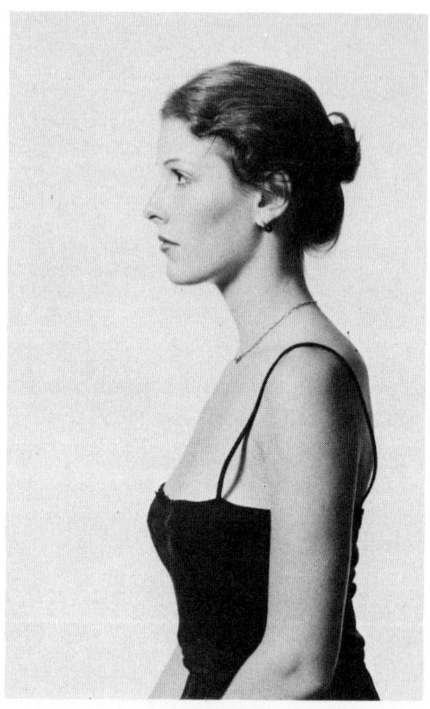

A full square-shoulder position, whether frontal or profile, is stiff. A swing of the shoulders presents a better perspective and feeling of movement. The former poses are referred to as static, the latter as nonstatic.

Posing and Lighting Tips Keep a handy file of portraits clipped from the professional trade magazines. When a picture impresses you with its particular grace and beauty, clip it. An ideal way to develop a collection is to tear out and store the poses in a folder. Keep these nearby to refresh your memory before you do a sitting of an engagement portrait, a bride, a child, family group, a couple, or whatever. This way you can walk into the camera room with a positive approach.

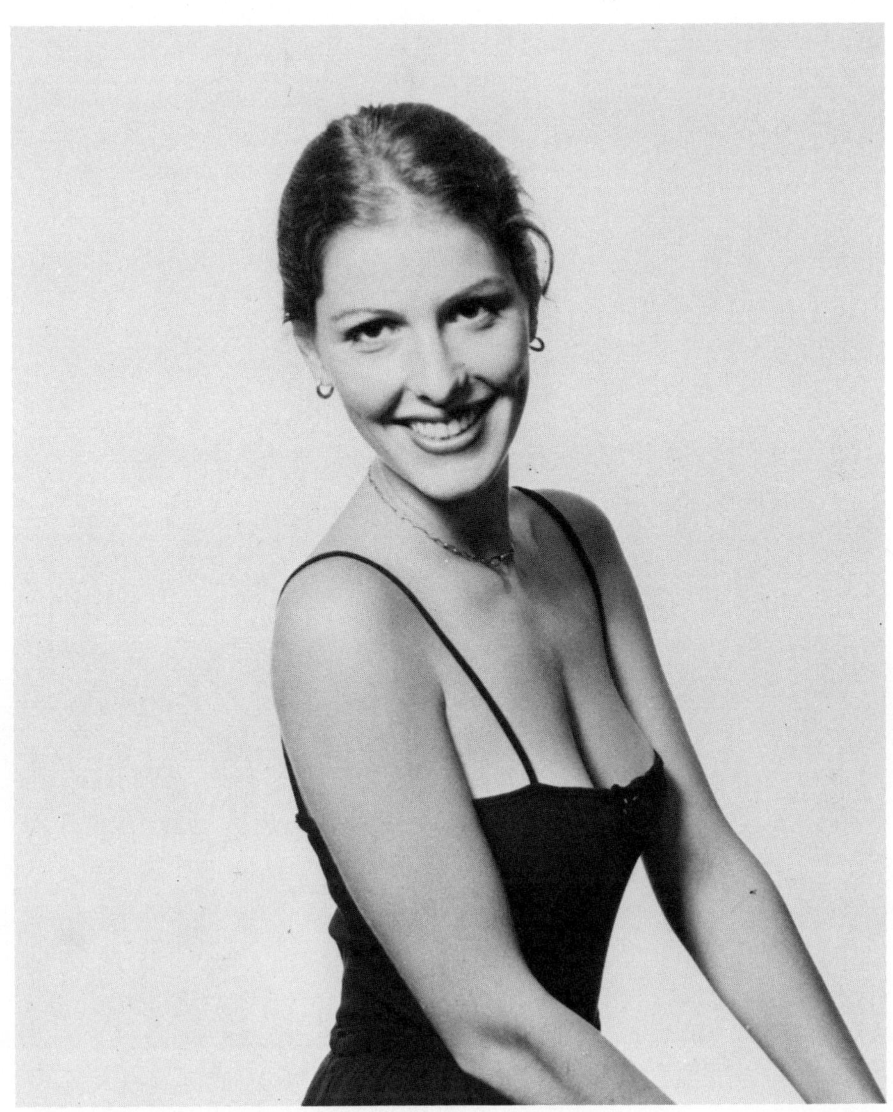

You can also get posing and lighting ideas by studying art books and visiting museums. Painters had thousands of years of head start in producing portraits and photographers should learn from their work. Often the mood of a painting can be translated, interpreted, and developed to add to your collection of poses, lightings, and groupings. Developing an understanding and appreciation for fine art can be a useful and valuable tool to the photographer practicing his craft.

SEATED POSES

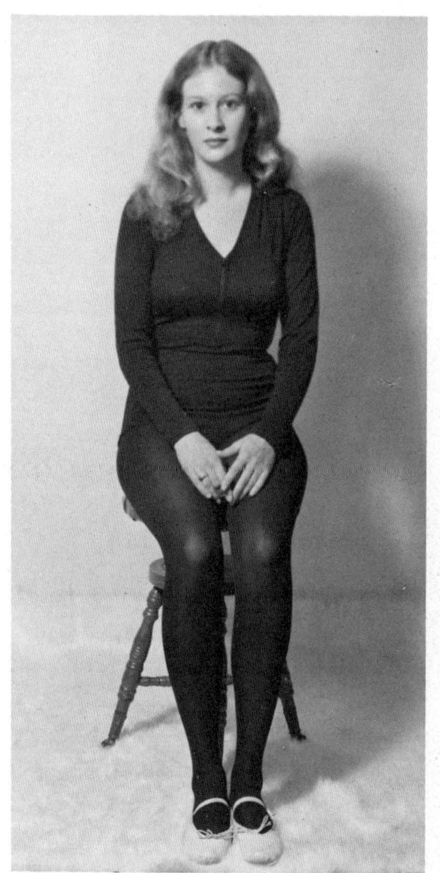

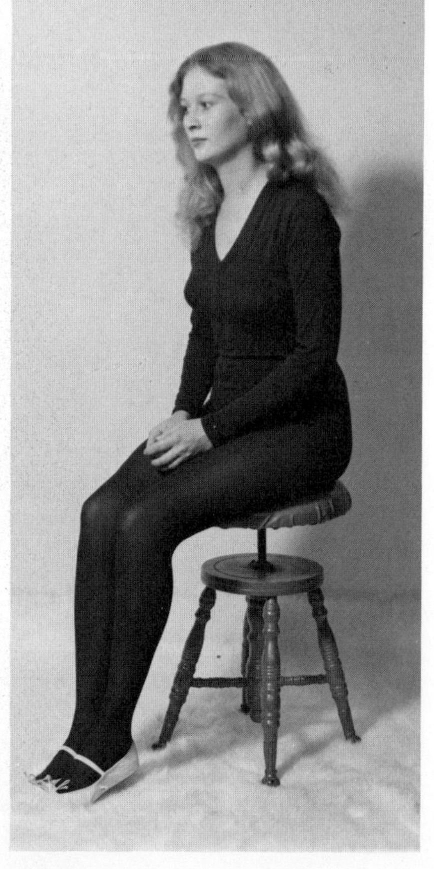

The photos on this page and on the facing page bottom show incorrect seating for good body posture in the front, side, and profile positions.

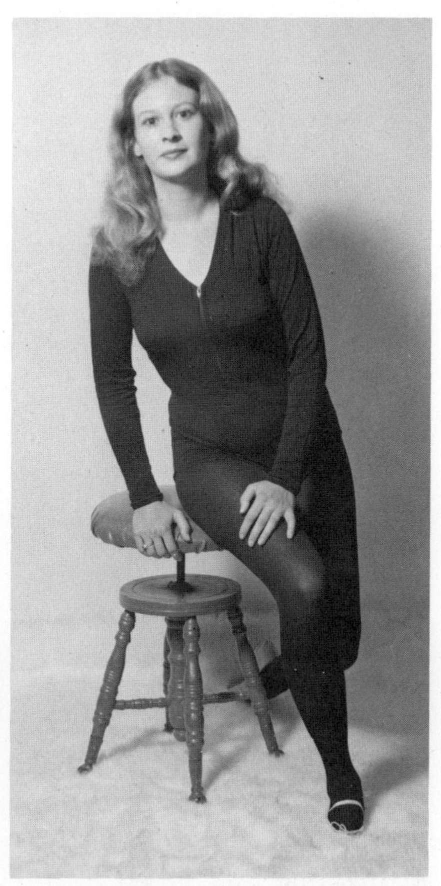

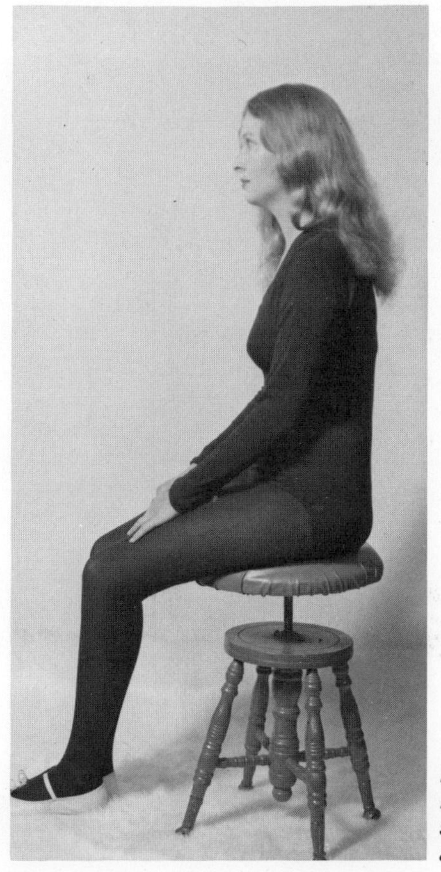

By half-seating the subject, (above) as illustrated, the body is extended, the spine is straightened, and the shoulders and bust are more gracefully posed.

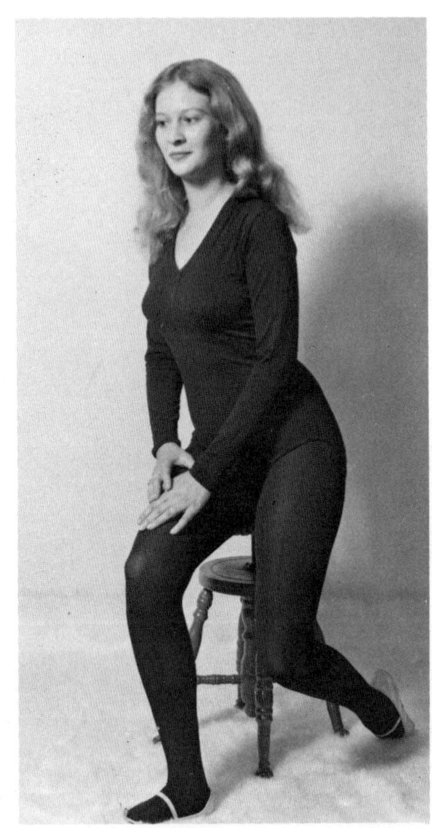

Further examples of the half-seated poses for a graceful look.

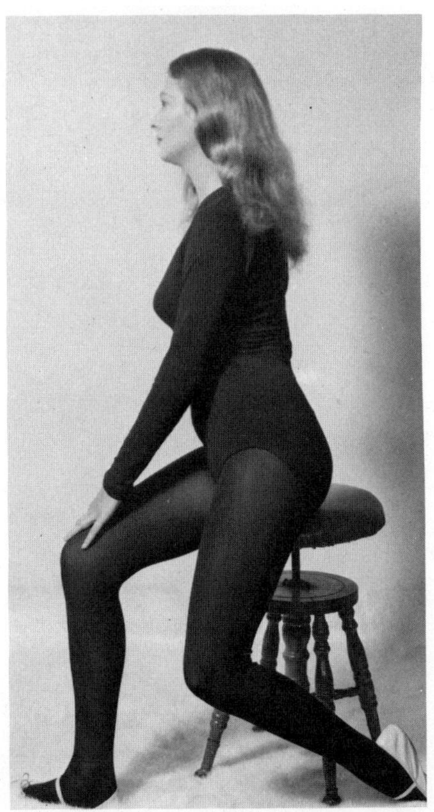

PYRAMID POSE

The basic pyramid pose (or triangular composition) supports the body and supplies a solid base upon which the head can rest. If the model's arms are permitted to relax at her sides, the support of the pyramid is removed.

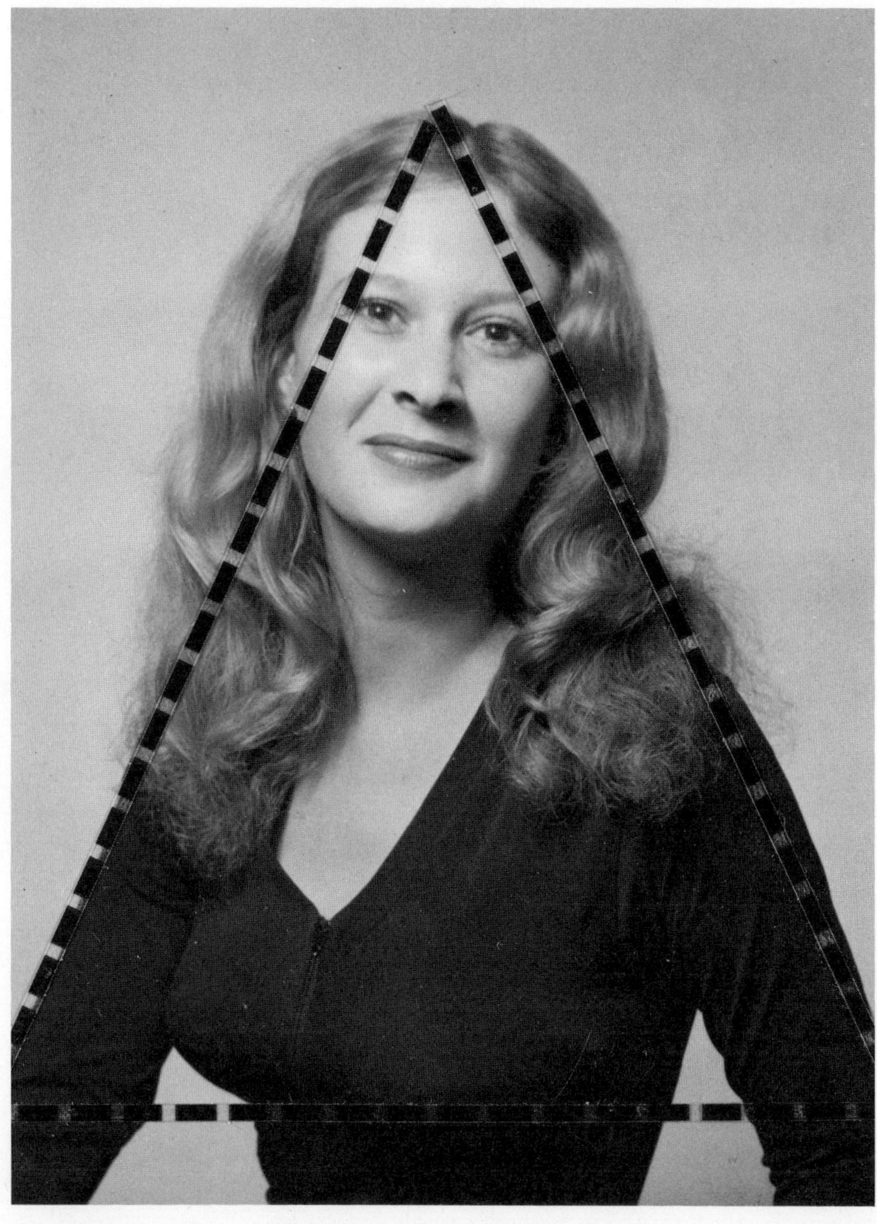

HEAD POSITION

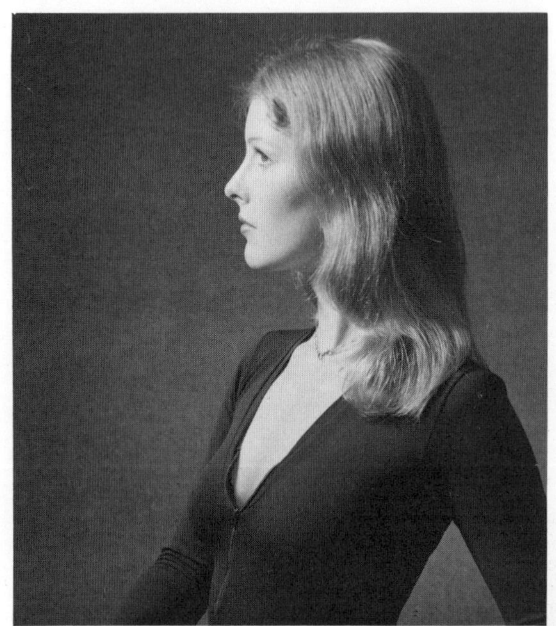

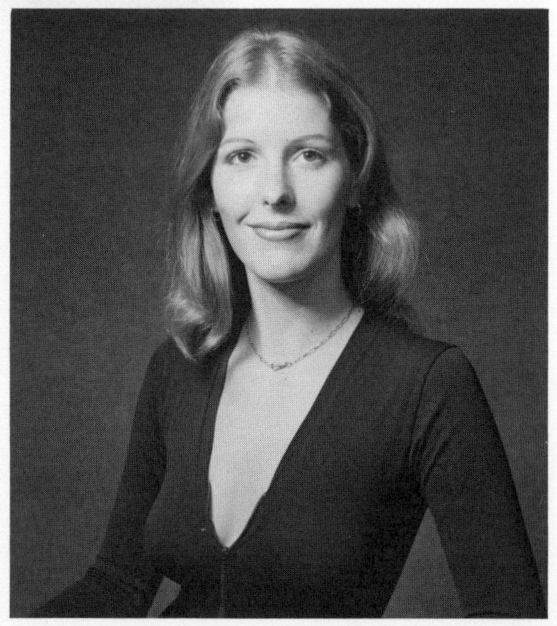

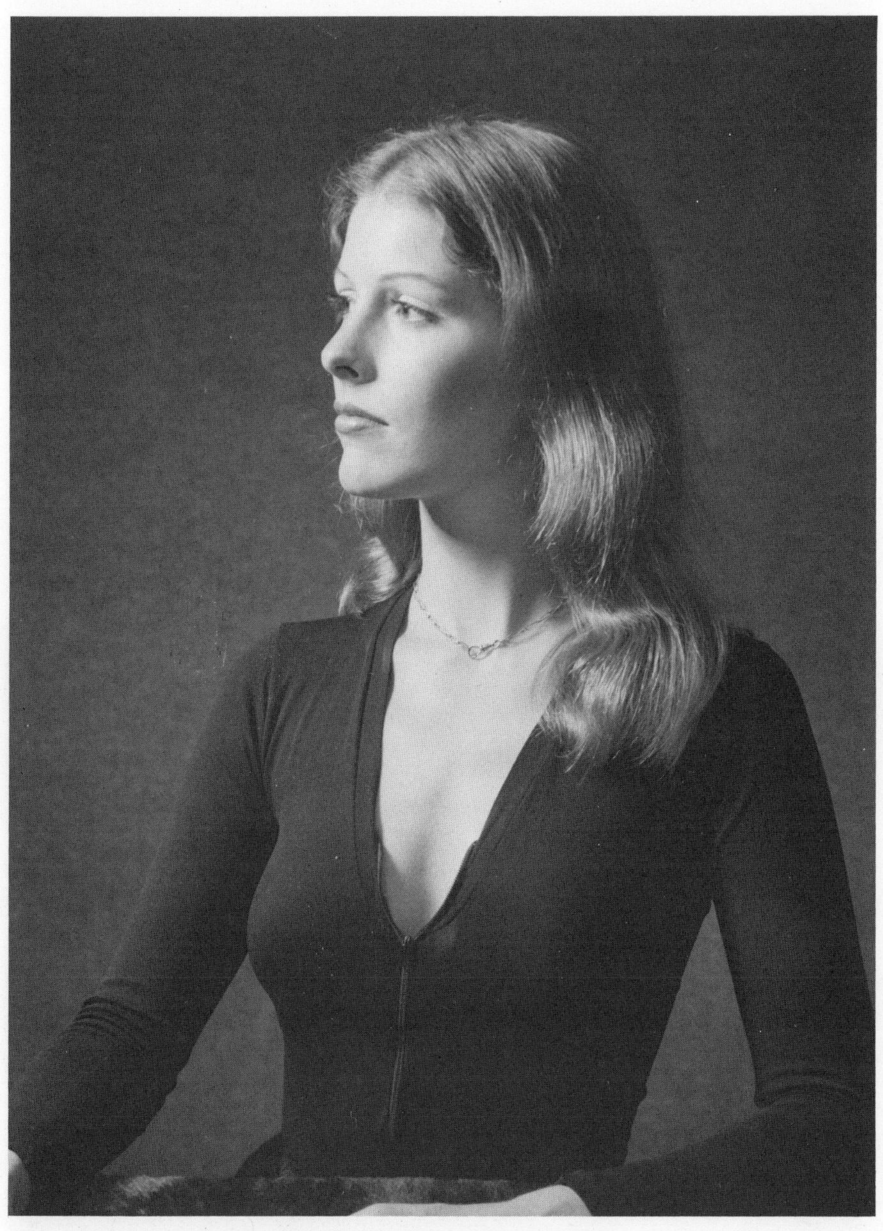

In the head positions, it is quite acceptable to do a profile (opposite top) showing one eye, or an almost full face (opposite bottom) showing both eyes. During the rotation from one of these positions to the other, only one eye shows and only part of the second eye is visible at various times. This is commonly referred to as a "split eye" (above) and should be avoided.

HANDS

Hands, when properly posed and lit, can add much to any portrait.

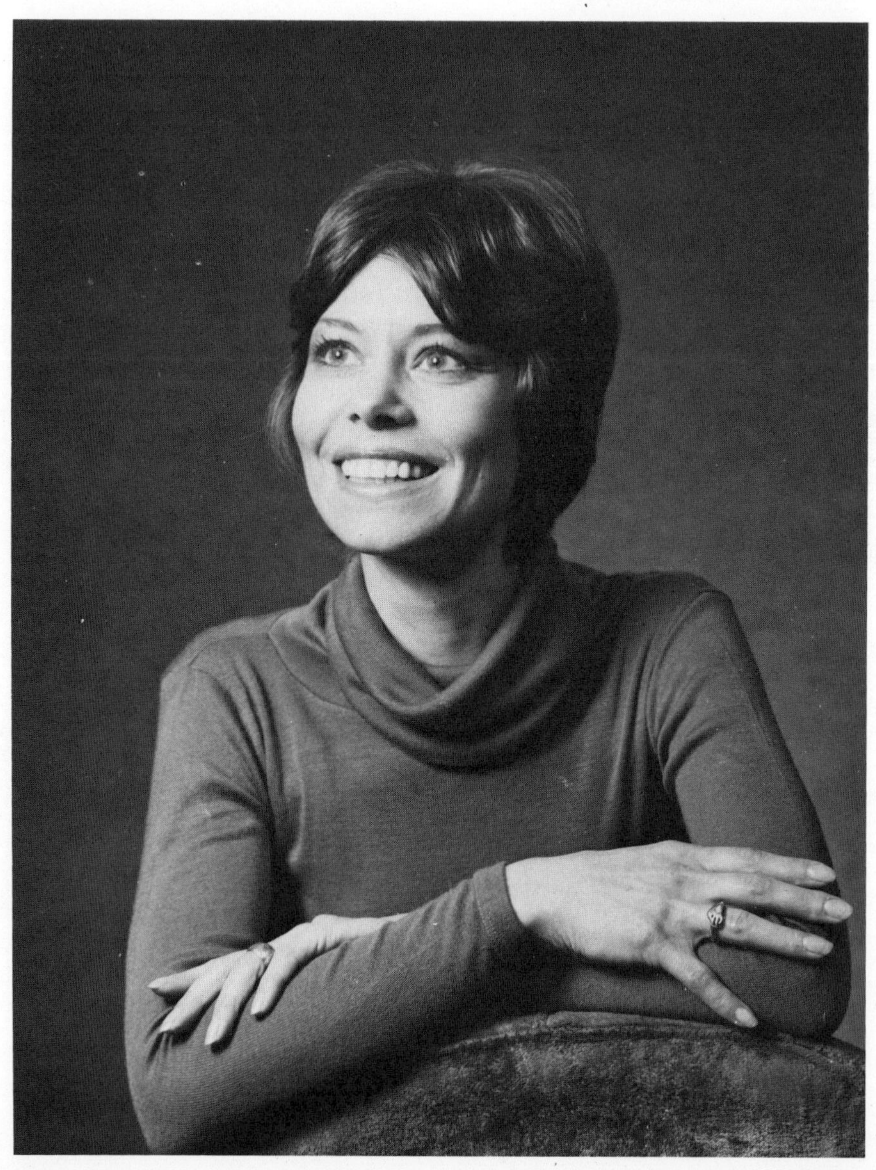

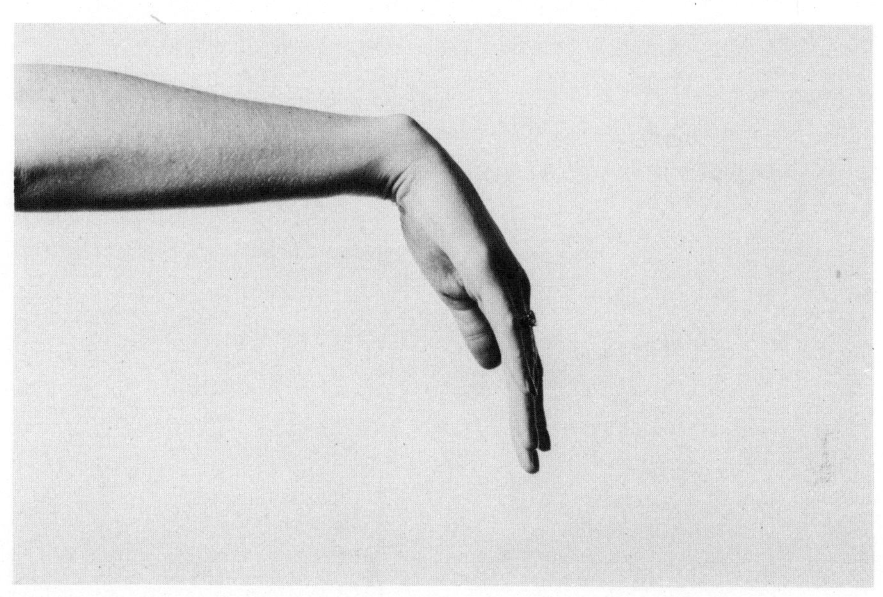

Breaking the wrist sharply (above), or using the hand in a stiff pose (below), is not very graceful.

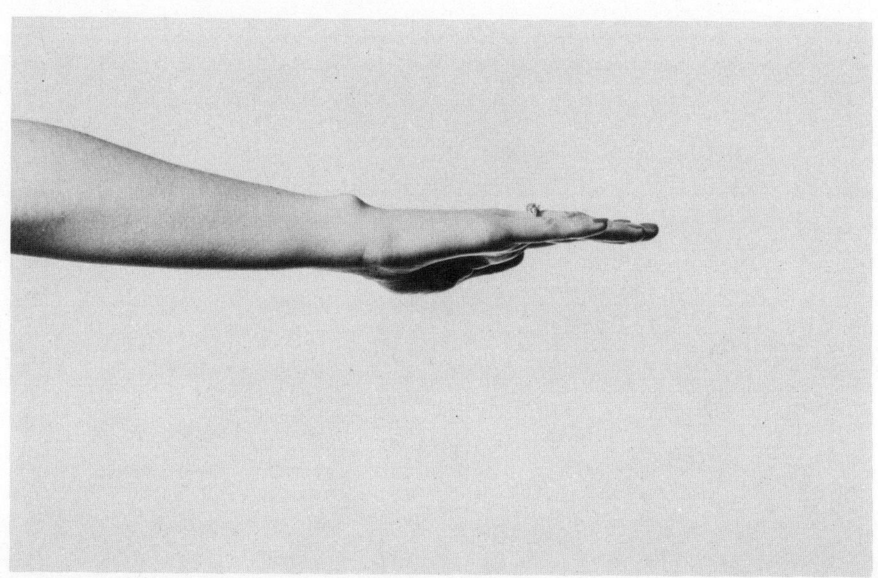

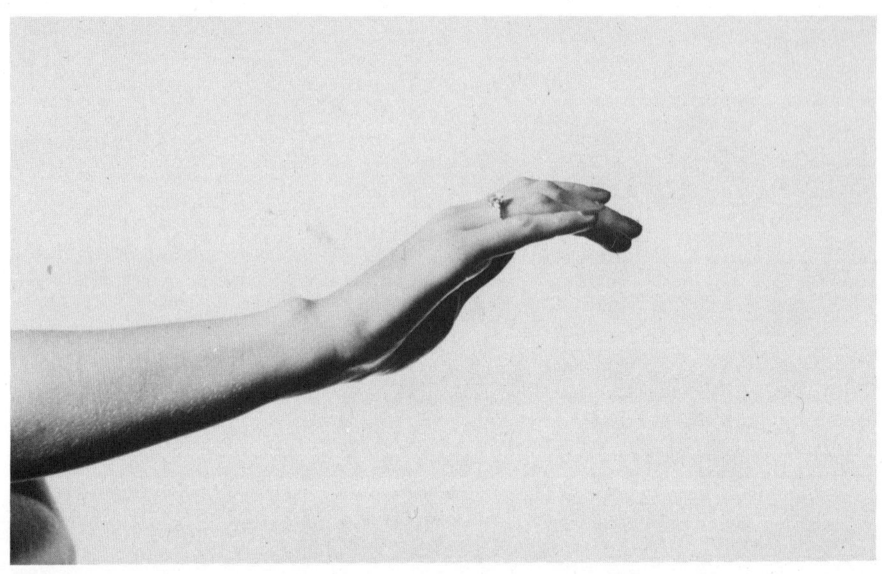

The soft curve produced by pushing the wrist down (above) is far more graceful than the two poses on the preceding page. The thumb of the hand (below) is not as graceful as the pinkie side (opposite above).

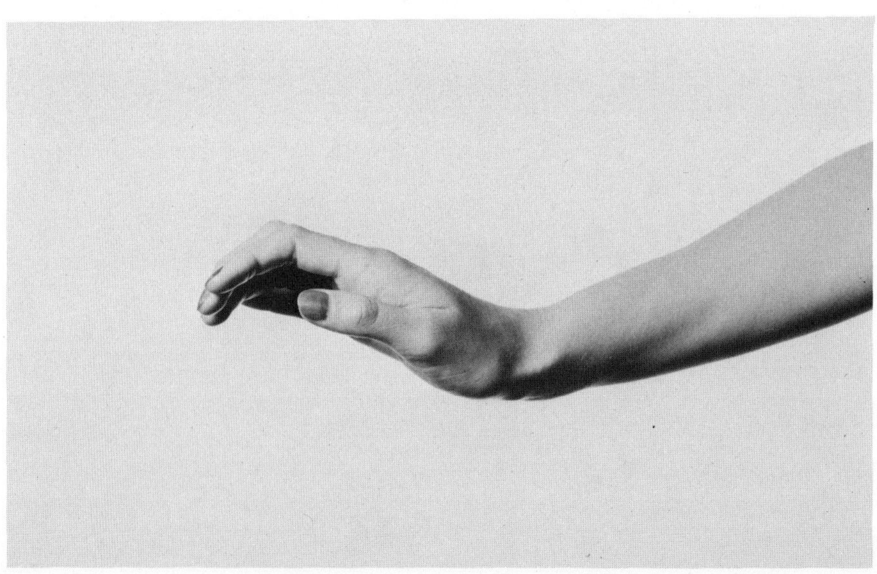

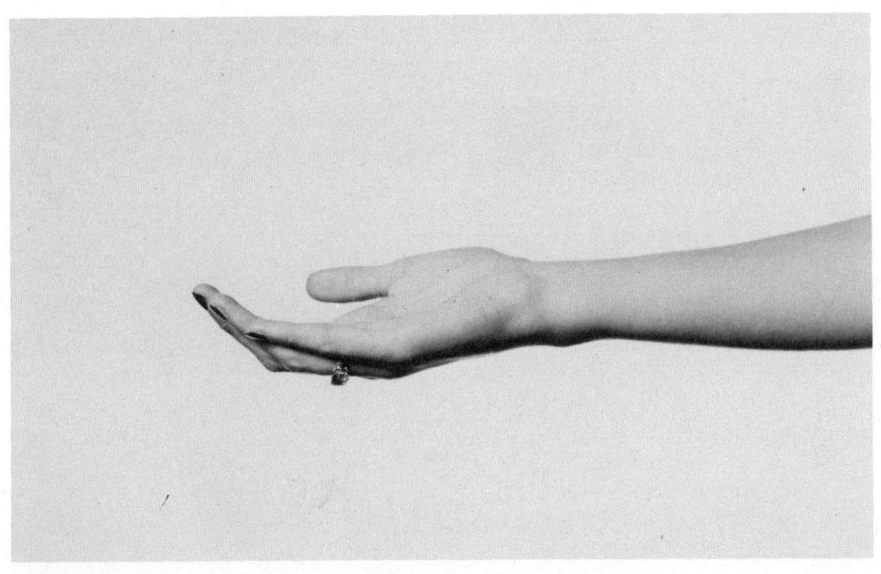

Closed fingers facing the camera (below) look short and stubby.

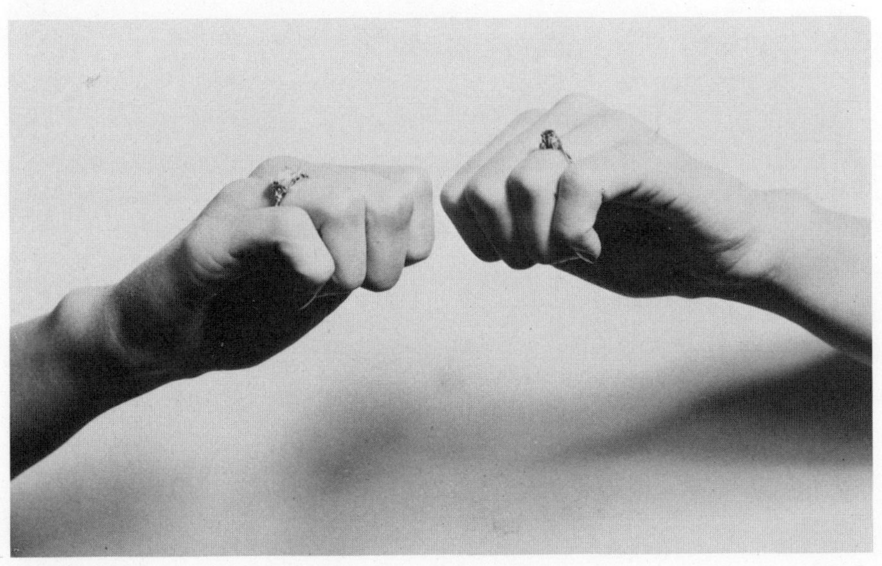

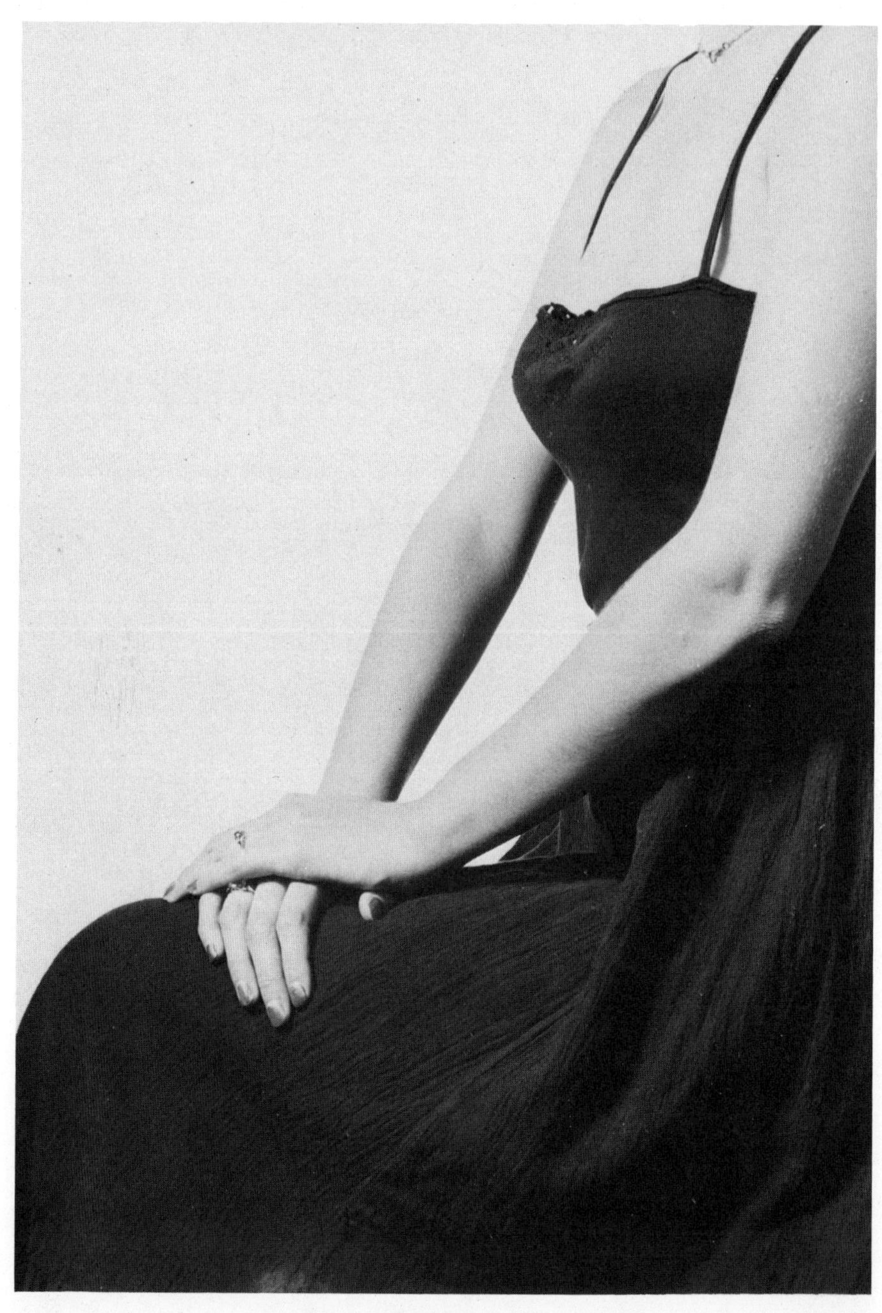

Incorrectly posed hands for a three-quarter or full-length pose amputate the fingertips of the model's right hand (above). A more natural pose with better lines is the picture opposite.

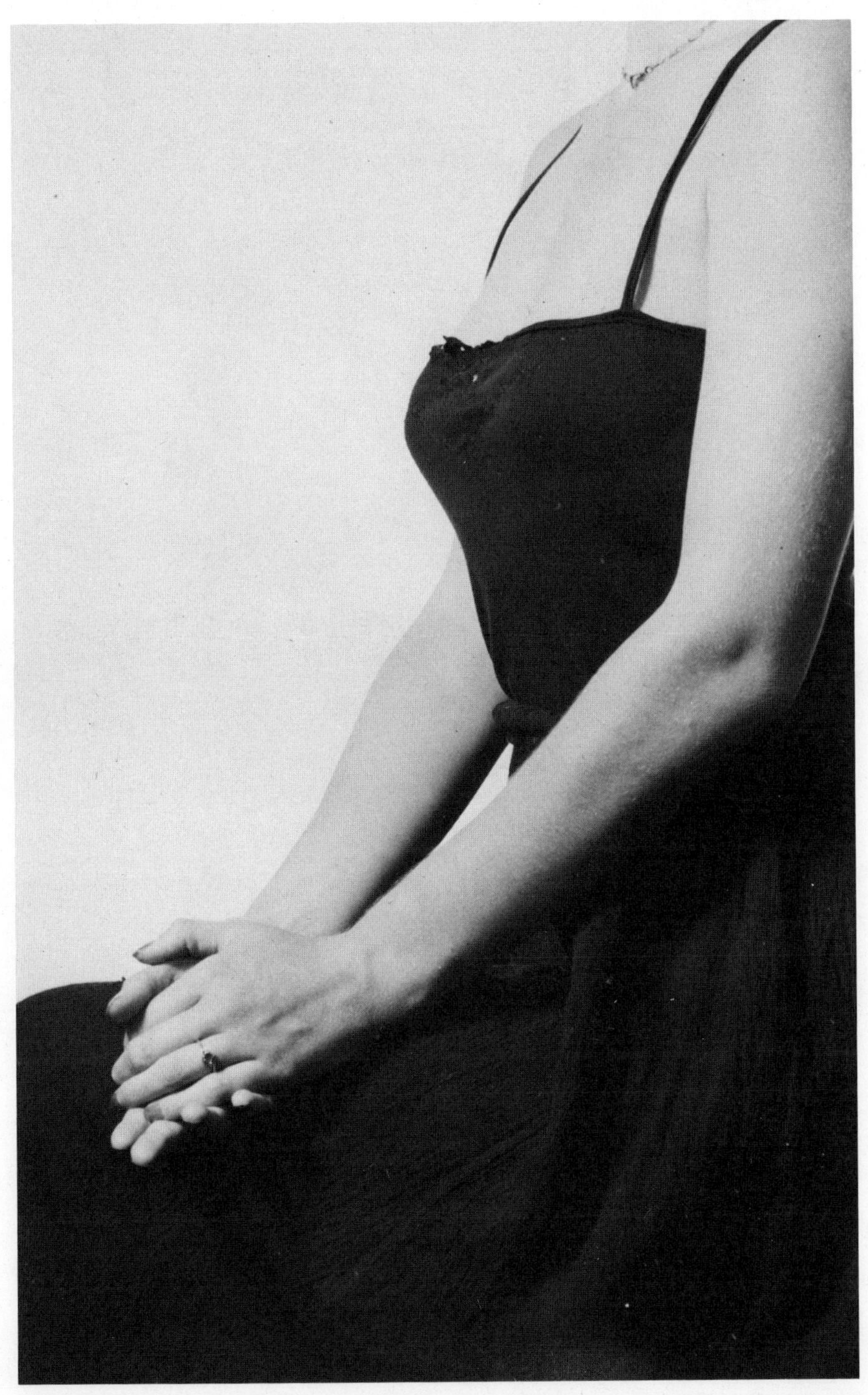

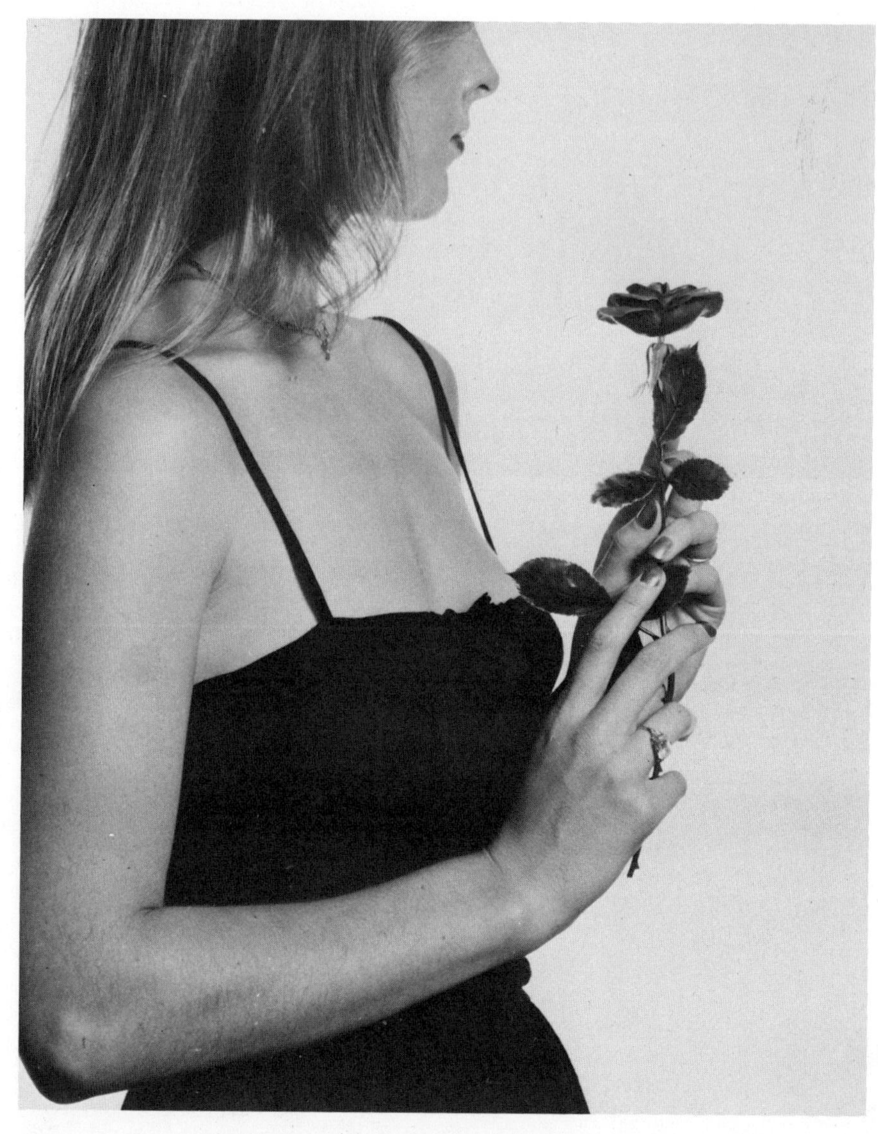

A graceful series of hand poses illustrates the basic rules. When hands are posed above the waist, the fingers are extended in an upward direction (above). Hands below the waist are more graceful with the fingers pointing downward (opposite).

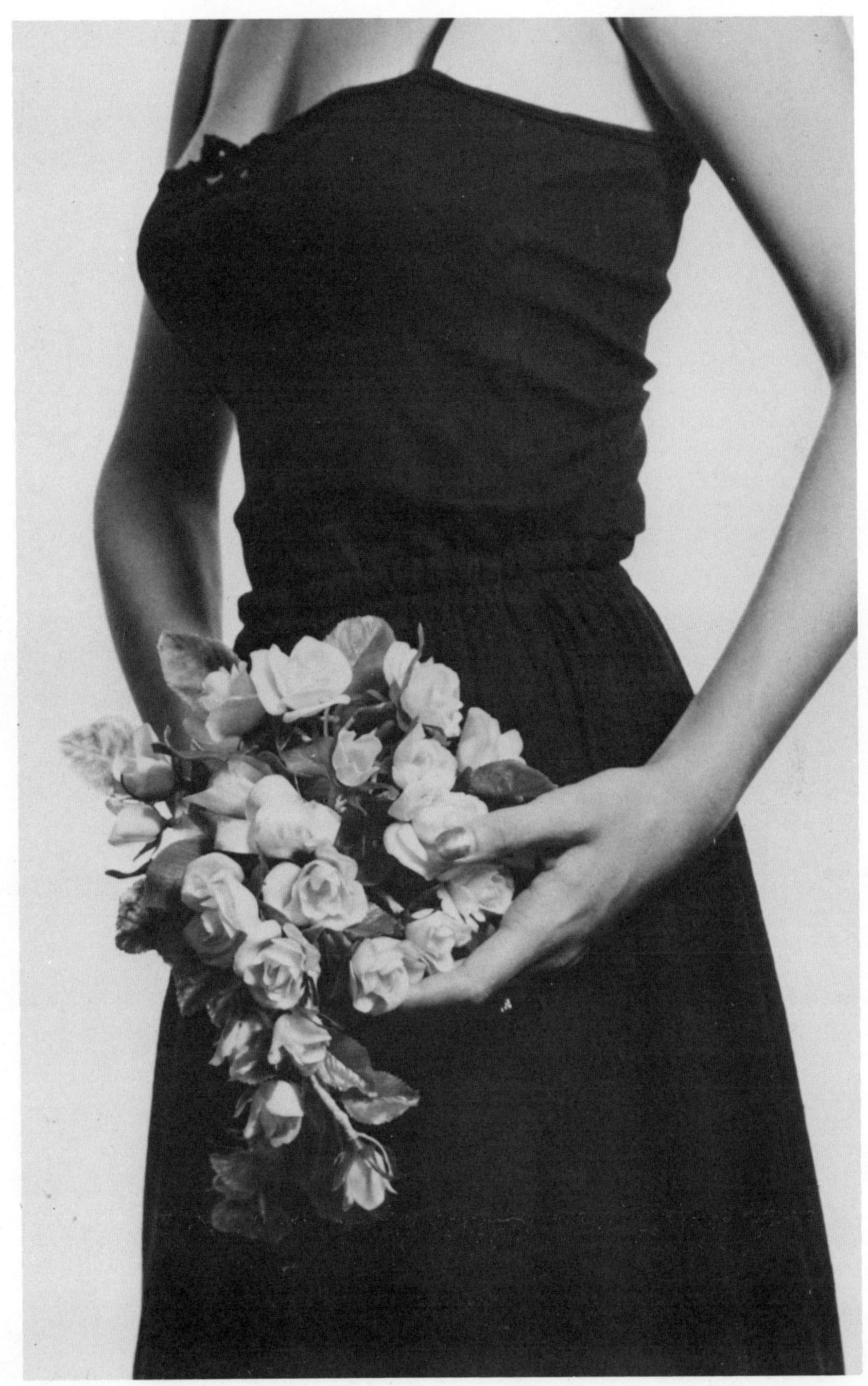

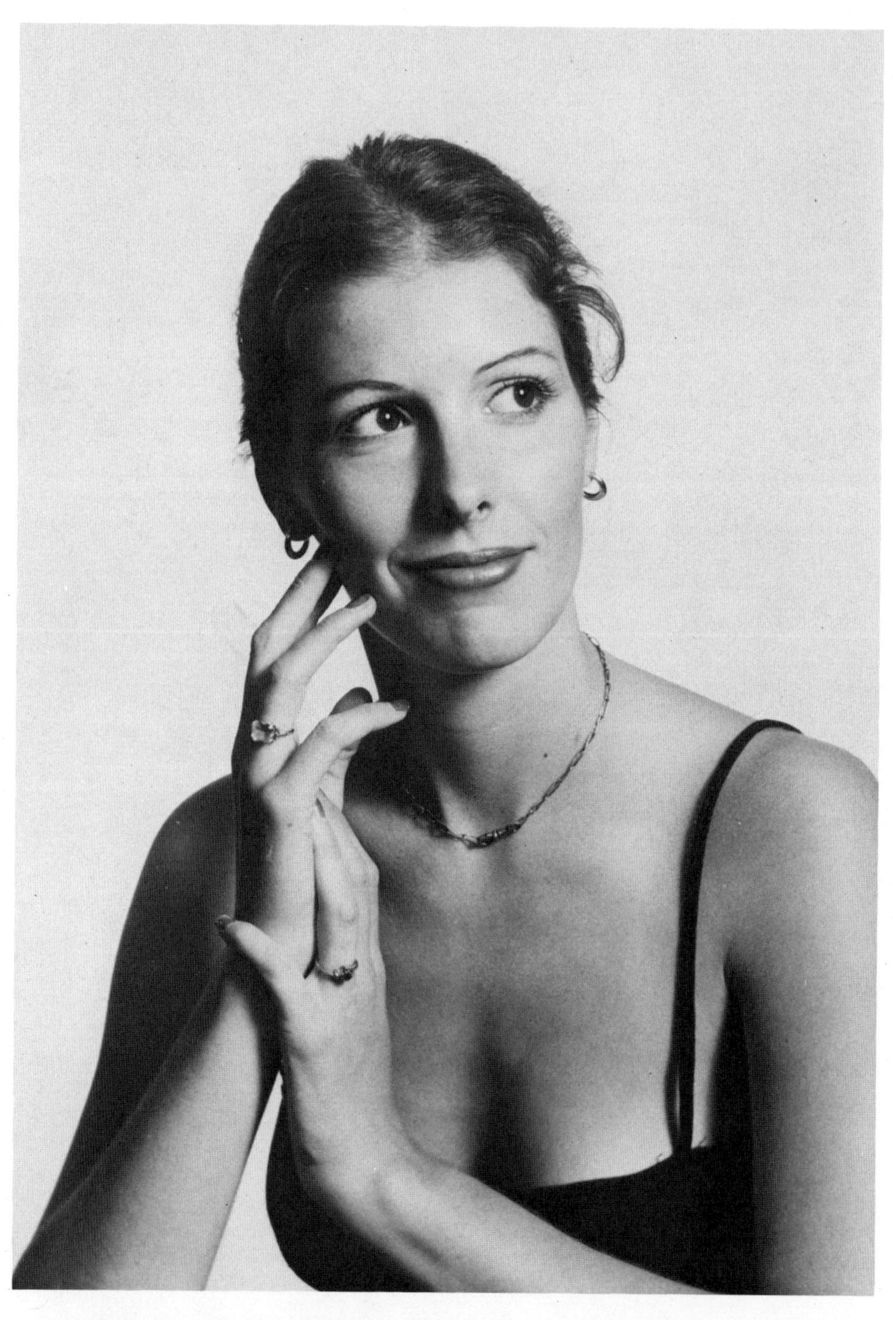

When both hands are posed together, placing one above the other gives the feeling of length to the fingers and wrists.

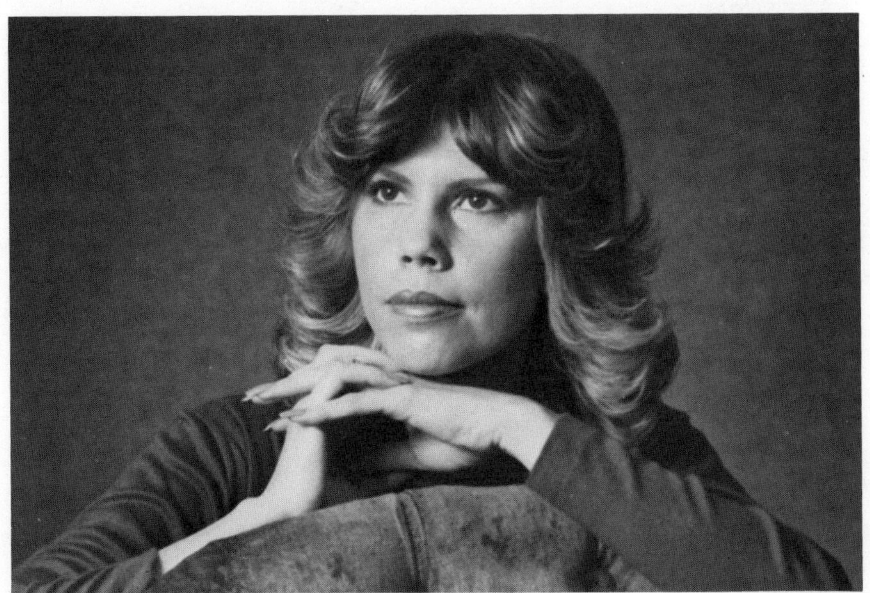

The delicate grace of the model's hands enhance the picture.

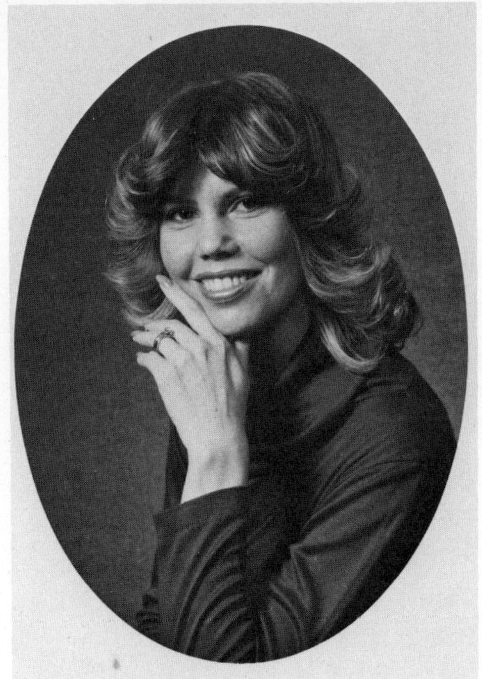

This pose is useful for engagements and weddings as a means of displaying rings.

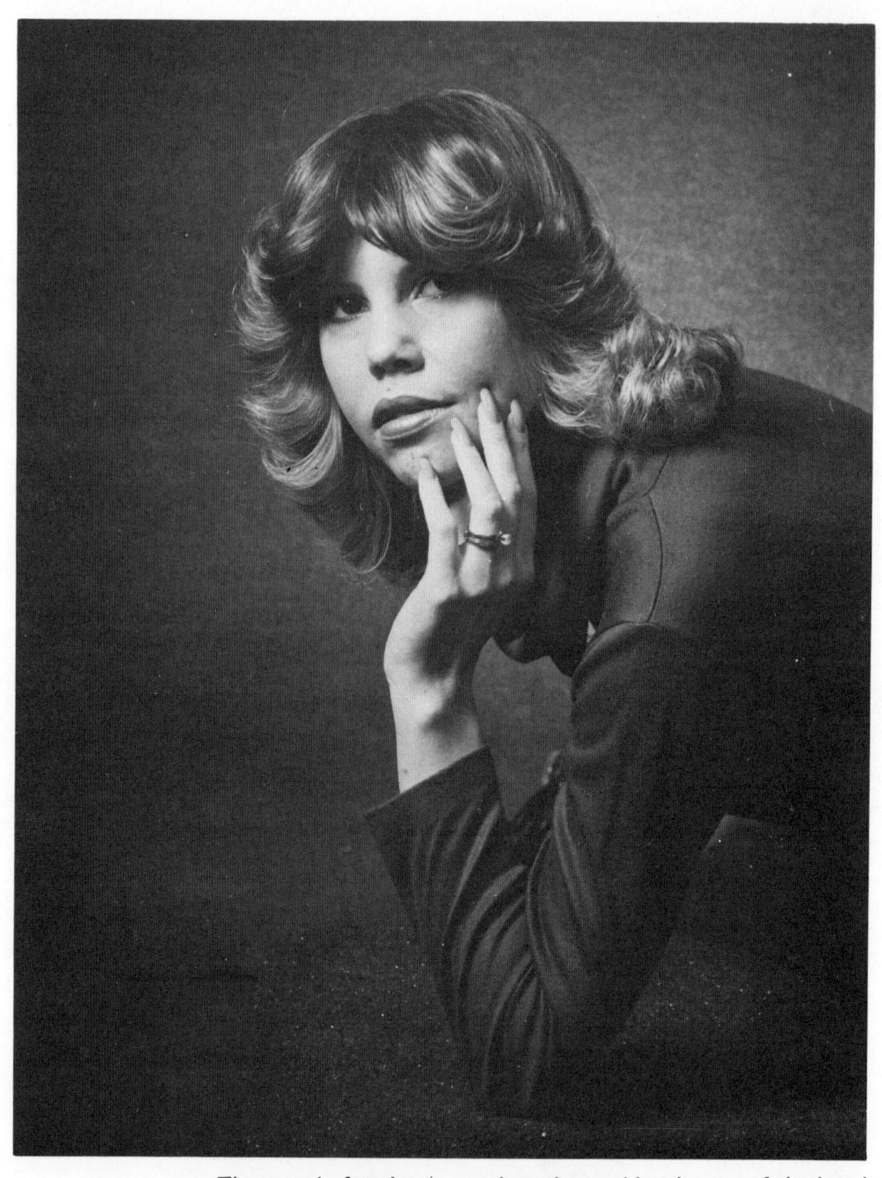

The mood of a picture can be enhanced by the use of the hands.

Chapter 19

Basic Posing

Suppose you were presented with an extremely glamorous, professional model and assigned to photograph her, and you placed her parallel to a wall, stood her flat-footed with hands hanging down at her sides, with her shoulders and head facing the camera. The result would probably be a horrendous photograph. Just as you must be completely familiar with the tools of your craft (cameras, lights, and processes), as a portrait photographer you must also develop an understanding of the human form and the way the body is connected so that you can position it in the most attractive manner to make presentable and salable pictures of people. Failure to understand the basics of posing and anatomy can only interfere with the production of exciting and beautiful portraits.

When making a closeup or three-quarter photograph of a subject in a standing position, start by proper positioning of the feet. If these are not correctly posed, the entire body will assume a clumsy stance. Posing the feet so that the body weight is predominantly on one foot while the other foot is used as a balance. In posing a young lady or a bride, a good starting point for a foot pose is the first ballet position. If the portrait is to be made with the subject seated, avoid very soft cushions into which the subject can sink, or chairs with backs, which permit the sitter to slump, resulting in a drooped or round-shouldered pose.

HEAD AND TORSO

In studying posing, recognize that the torso can be moved in three basic directions, which are also applicable to the head position: The body rotated right or left is the turning position, very much like a phonograph record on a spindle; the movement of the axis to the right or the left is the tilting position; and leaning forward or backward is the tipping up or down position. Tip, tilt, and turn are three short words you can use to direct the subject. Using specific language and demonstrating what you mean can simplify the process.

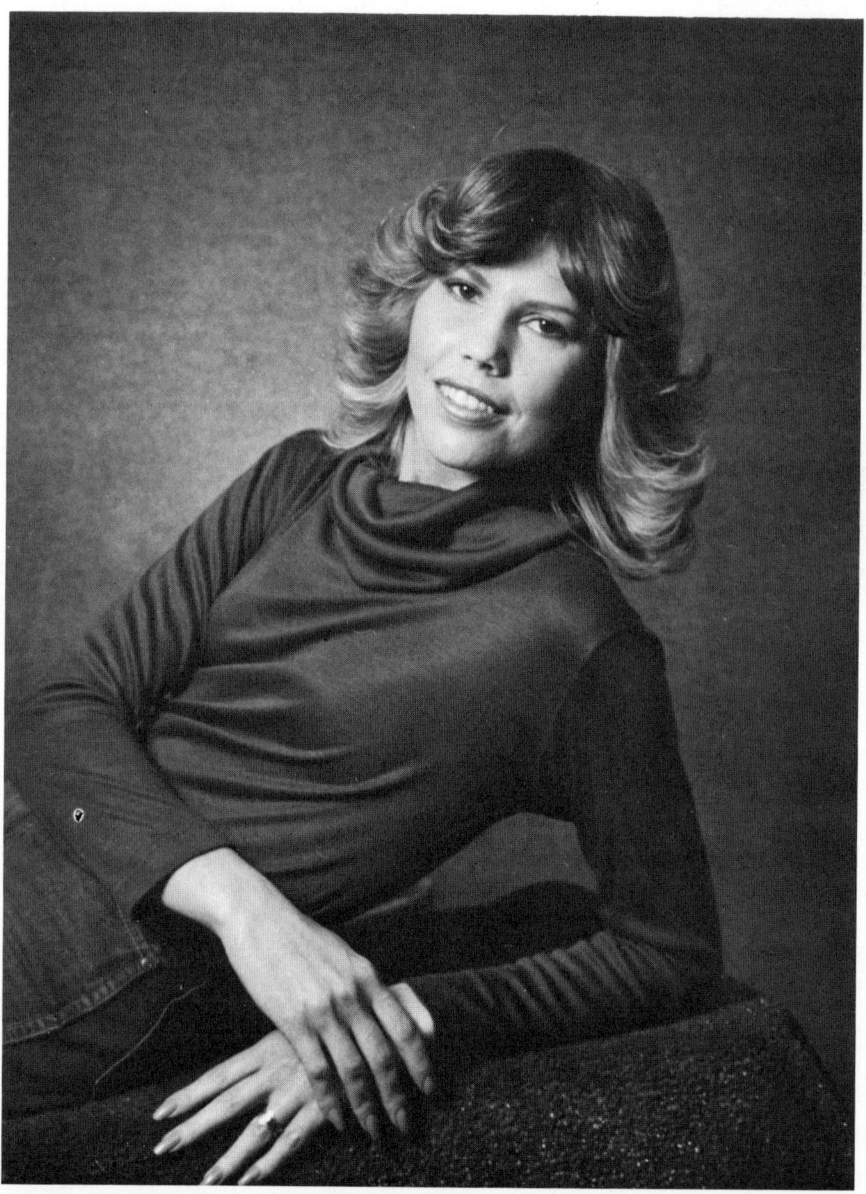

THE SPINE

The way the body is positioned reveals what you want to communicate in a photograph. In portraiture, therefore, you certainly do not want to convey the idea of weariness, defeat, fatigue, or depression. A curved spine and head sunken into the shoulders in its lowest position would convey this. But this is not what the customer wants, so in almost all portraits, the head should be erect and lifted away from the shoulders, and the spine, a critical part of the basic pose, must be straight. Sometimes the photographer will pose a subject, move back to the camera to make the exposures only to discover later that the photographs are unacceptable because the subject had slumped into a more relaxed seating or standing position. Being aware of the subject's spinal position at the instant of exposure is therefore critical. An upright position depicts youth, alertness, an active and aggressive person. Dynamic poses of younger people can be modified and used for older subjects, none of whom wants to give the appearance in their portrait of being over the hill. So *watch that spine*!

VANTAGE POINT

In addition to body angle and the position of the head, another factor to consider is the subject's vantage point, or where the subject is looking. Earlier you learned that cross-eyed subjects should be given a distant vantage point to help straighten the eyes, and wall-eyed subjects a closer vantage point for the same reason. With normal eyes, where you tell the subject to look is very important. Eyes that are turned to an extreme, so that you see the white on one side of the eye and almost none on the other, might be adorable if you were photographing a small child, but such a position is not really attractive in an adult. The eyes should be almost centered. Moreover, the extremes of looking up or down are rarely used in conventional portraiture.

The position of the body and the direction of the head and eyes should be moderately turned off the direct camera optical axis. Extreme twisting or turning of the body rarely makes a good portrait and distorts the individual. A good portrait rarely uses a centered position. A natural, slightly off-center, relaxed position is far more attractive. By thinking of the head as a ball sitting on a pyramid and being supported by it, you can attractively pose the body and head. An extreme tilt of the head, without support underneath, gives the impression that the subject is falling over and, along with an extreme leaning position, can be disconcerting.

Glamour can be added to a portrait by simply having the subject lean back on a posing box rather than sitting.

AVOID STATIC POSES

A static pose means that the turn of the body, head, and eyes are *identical.* This type of posing creates a stiffness that is difficult to overcome. Only an individual with exceptional beauty, charm, or a particularly interesting face can be photographed successfully in a static pose, although he or she would look far more attractive if this were avoided. This pose is generally used when a subject is being booked after an arrest or is being photographed for identification, say, for a passport. The only time when you should pose a subject looking directly into the camera is for campaign photographs of politicians. This is done to create the illusion of honesty. In all other photographs, avoid having the subject look directly into the camera.

Possibly the only other exception where this type of direct gaze is used is in the girly-type magazines. In most such picture layouts, there are a number of photos with the model looking directly into the camera. What creates the excitement and intimacy of the picture is the direct eye contact, not the draped or undraped parts of the girl's body. The direct look gives the provocative, sexy feeling about these pictures. If a portrait is intended to show an intimate glimpse of a person, the direct stare into the camera with a sparkling eye expression will certainly accomplish this.

In portraiture, the rotation of the body, head, and eye positions are moderate adjustments. Don't overdo them. The eyes should rest approximately in the center of the socket, the head should be turned, only moderately, in one direction or the other. Avoid an extreme turn of the head where only part of one eye shows. This split-eye effect can be most distracting. Turn the head so that either one eye shows, such as in a profile with the appropriate lighting, or so that both eyes show. Having the bridge of the nose dissect an eye is unattractive.

COMPOSITION

In making portraits, always remember that you are responsible for building a composition that is balanced in tone, highlights, shadows, and form. The incorrect placement of a head in a portrait can create bizarre effects. Placing it too high or too low or too far to the right or left can destroy the effect of a well-balanced portrait. There are occasions when unusual composition or placement is required, but in most portraits, such poses are out of place. Pose a head that is looking in a certain direction (to the right or left) so the eyes have more

The circular format is "different" and can lend variety to a portfolio. Beware of using it too often, however.

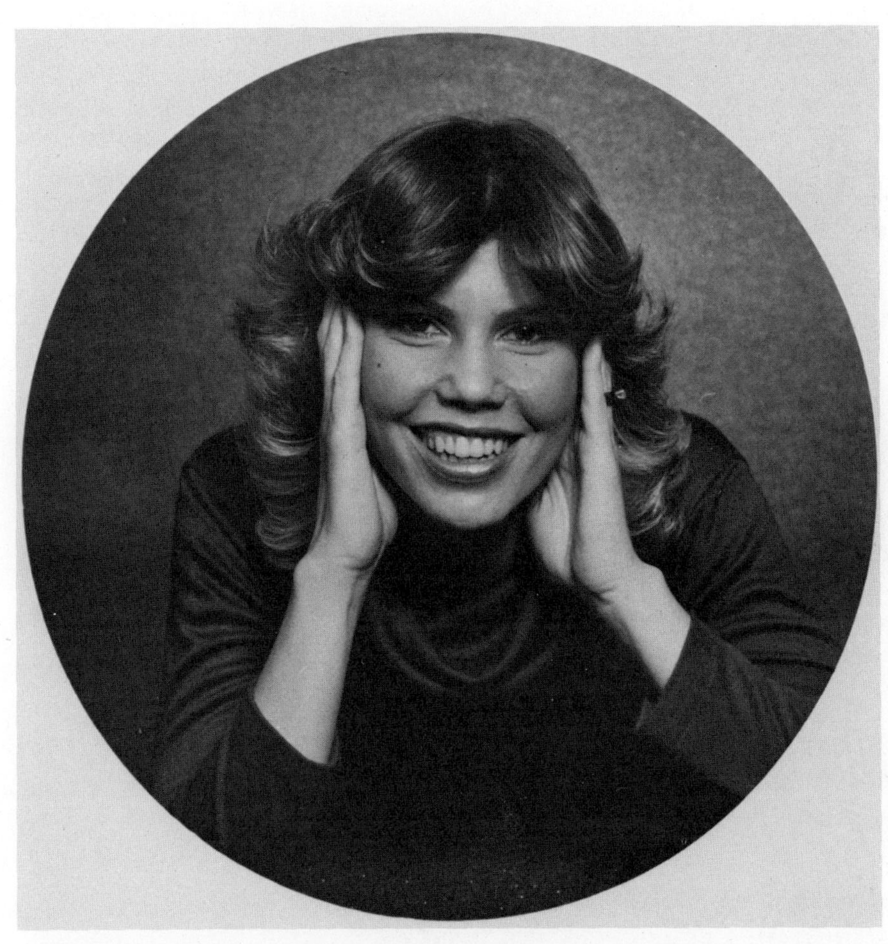

space in the direction in which they are looking than behind the subject, otherwise it appears as if the subject is looking out of the picture.

The basic rules of composition that apply to other forms of photography are equally apt in portraiture. The direction, or line, of the subject can be used to create a mood or a feeling. Vertical, upright lines depict power and strength and fall into the category of "monumental" poses. A leaning forward, or diagonal line, depicts motion, action, youth, aggressiveness, and forcefulness. A leaning back, or horizontal position, which in composition depicts defeat, death, rest, and tranquillity, is rarely used in portraiture.

Hands akimbo provide variety and is a useful pose when the model's hands are well formed.

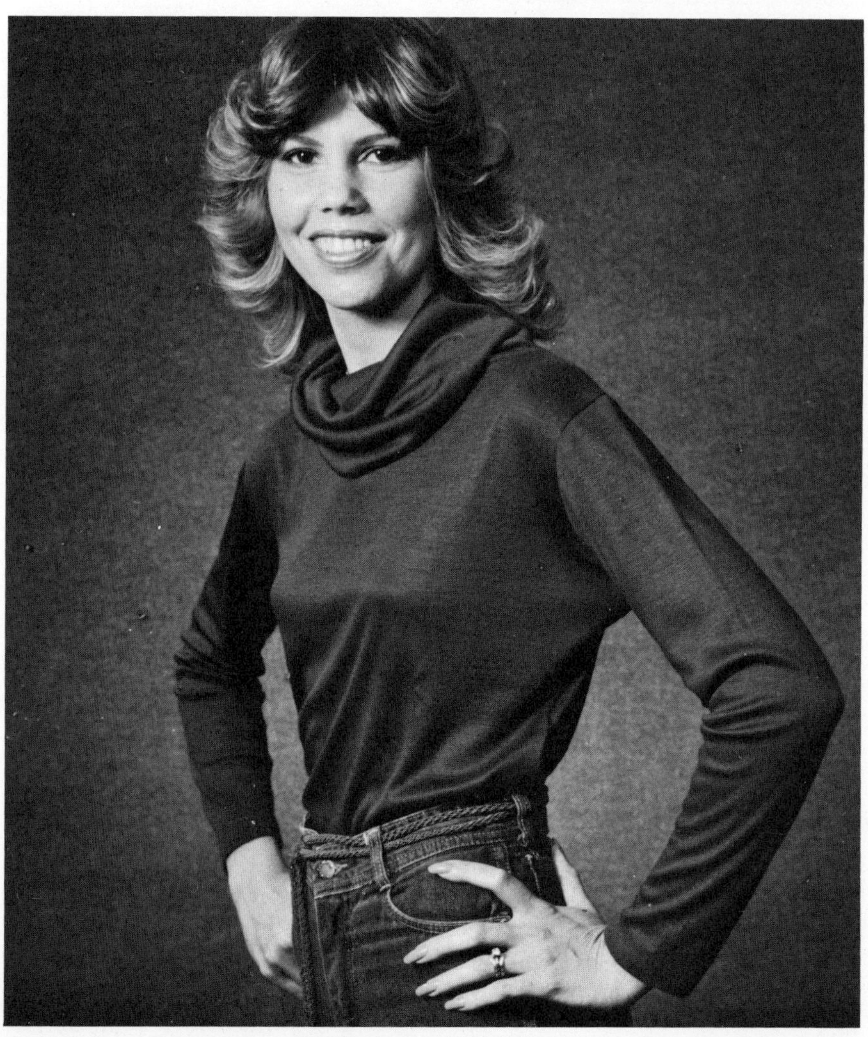

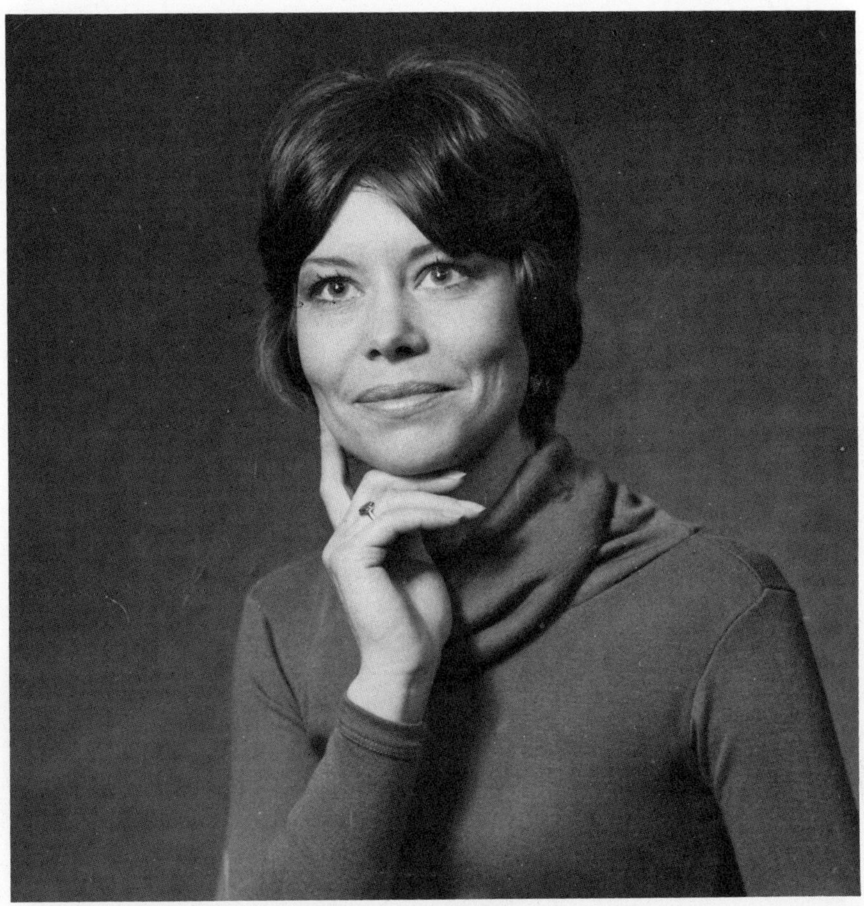

Beautiful eyes can become the center of attraction in a portrait by having the subject look up.

THE EYES HAVE IT

If you were to pose a subject, taking the foregoing factors into consideration, but failed to capture the correct eye expression, the portrait would suffer. Were you to tell someone to look here, or look there, or look over my shoulder, the subject could get very confused about directions. The best way to eliminate this confusion is this way: Tell the person to imagine that you are drawing an X in the air in a given spot, and tell her to watch where you place the X (as you draw the imaginary X in midair). When her eyes are in the right position, there will be little difficulty in keeping her eyes fixed in that position. If you want to alter the pose, "erase" the X and draw another in the new position.

People often associate a smile with the mouth. This common misconception seems to suggest that, if you photograph someone displaying a full set of pearly white teeth, the result will be a pleasant or happy picture. In truth, a smile exists more in the eyes than the mouth, and an animated or lively eye expression better represents a smile than a display of teeth. After all the posing, lighting and camera preparation are completed, it is your job to build the mood and obtain from the subject an expression that is suitable for the type of picture being made. And the key to an exceptional portrait is in the eyes.

Chapter 20

How Many Poses

Oftentimes a customer will ask how many poses or proofs you take. This type of inquiry has come about because some photographers feel that taking more poses than a competitor is an added sales feature. The confident photographer, however, thinks only of making sufficient poses to satisfy his customers and some additional poses that are unique enough to induce them to buy something above and beyond the run-of-the-mill portrait. Your intent should be to make *one* great photograph that the client will love, and if it requires more exposures to accomplish this feat, be willing to expend the film and your time.

An average sitting should consist of 10–12 poses. If you have a nervous or difficult subject, expect to take more poses and use more film. Start each sitting with basic poses and lighting setups. During this time, watch the subject carefully and try to discover interesting poses he or she adopts naturally when relaxed. After the basic poses, experiment a little. The few minutes spent in this exercise frequently pays off in the sale of additional photographs which the customer had not anticipated. Such poses are also useful for exhibitions and competition.

Screen each set of slide proofs and eliminate those with poor expressions or other flaws before showing them to the customer. It is better to show fewer yet better-quality proofs rather than a bunch of mediocre ones. Always remember that the sole objective in doing the sitting is to produce one or two exceptional photographs that will please your client.

PROOFS AND PREVIEWS

Some people in the portrait business maintain that selling proofs enhances an order by $10 or $15. Others contend that selling proofs can be costly in that it reduces the sale of additional prints. In this matter, each photographer must decide which approach is the most practical for him. One compromise in this regard is to enhance the proofs is such a way that you can sell them at a better price and still not eliminate the need for additional prints. Do so by combining the proofs into a single unit, for example, die-cut composites or the sale of "bragging books"—small albums that accommodate a number of proofs. The "bragging" books are not a new idea but they solve the problem of selling proofs as a total unit rather than as individual pictures that can be distributed. With either method, the photographs are mounted together and cannot be separated. If the price of bragging books is about $45, you can reduce the cost with a $50 minimum order. And for an order over $100, you can present the book as a gift.

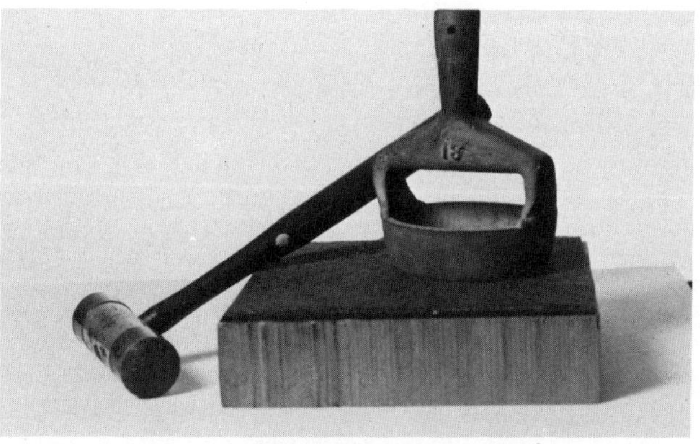

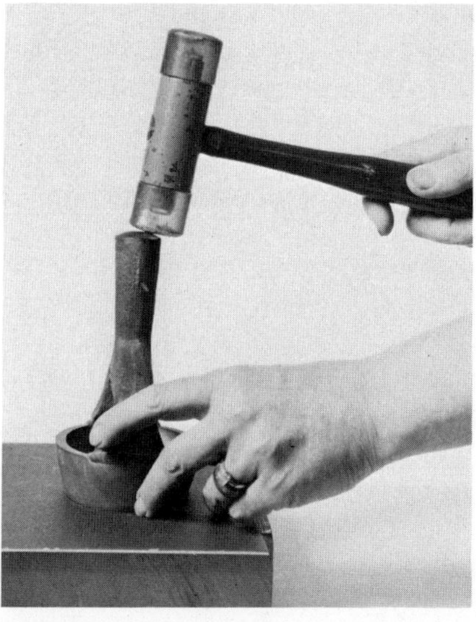

The simple tools required for die cutting custom mats include a block of rubberlike material, an oval die, and a plastic hammer. Place the matte board on the block and position the die. A half dozen sharp raps with the hammer will cut a perfect oval.

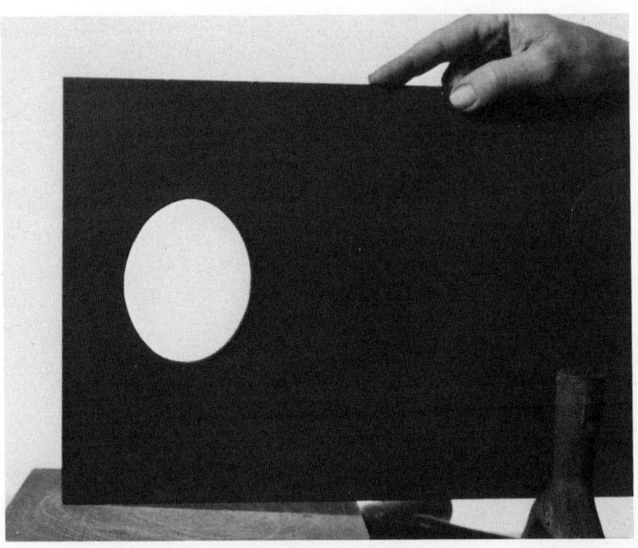

The die-cut oval completes the process begun on the facing page.

A third concept is a bragging panel. The photographer mounts trimmed and finished proofs on an 11″ × 14″ matte board which is die-cut to accommodate a specific number of pictures. Or the customer could select three or more of the previews which you then die-cut with oval dies. Several sharp blows with a special hammer and heavy, rubber like block, produce a cleanly cut oval ready to mount. Tack dry-mount tissue to each print *before* cutting it. Dry-mount the prints on tinted matte boards, available in many sizes and designs. To dress up the prints, cut underlays, with an identical die, ⅛-inch larger, in the same manner. If you want to experiment with this idea before investing in dies, you can print a set of previews using an oval mask and carefully cut them out with a pair of scissors.

Some mass producers simply do not present proofs. They select the pose that, in their opinion, is the best and go ahead and print economical, multi-print packages which are then presented to the parents in such a manner as to induce the sale of all the photographs. With their capability to mass produce photographs and standardize procedure, they find that the average sale more than makes up for any prints that are not sold.

Proof Presentation The practice of taking proofs home for selection did not exist in the early photo galleries. There was no choice of proofs and the customer purchased the tintype, ambrotype, or callotype which was exposed in the camera. Shortly after the glass plate was introduced, some photographers devised the idea of selling from a selection of proofs. It was not long before someone decided that it would be advantageous to let the customer take proofs

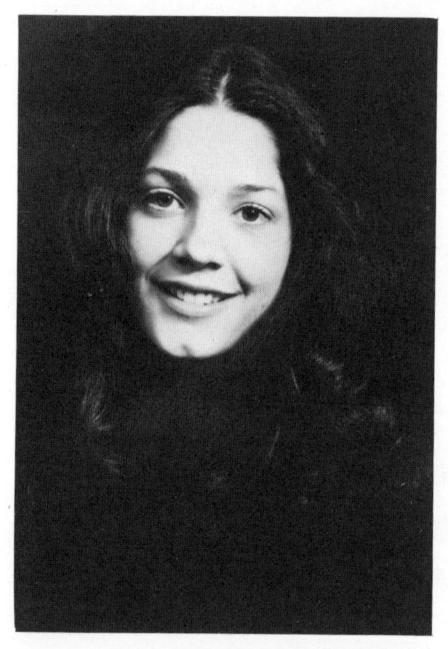
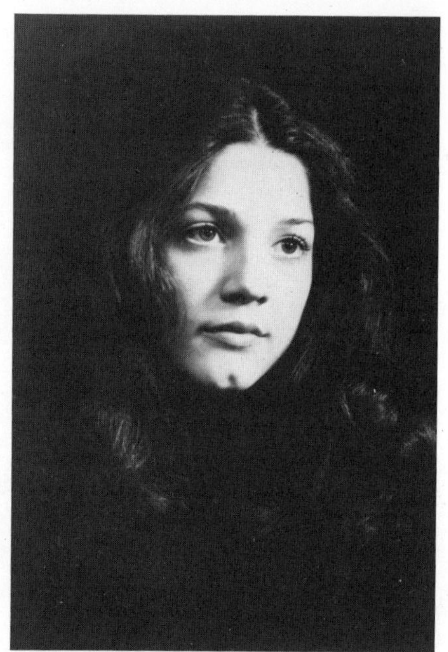
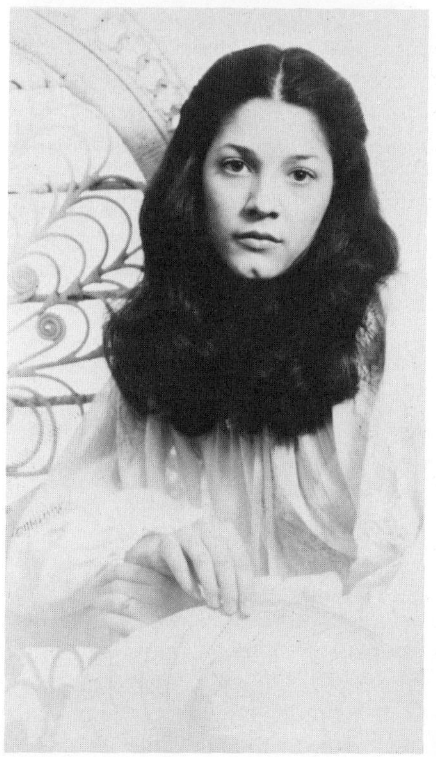
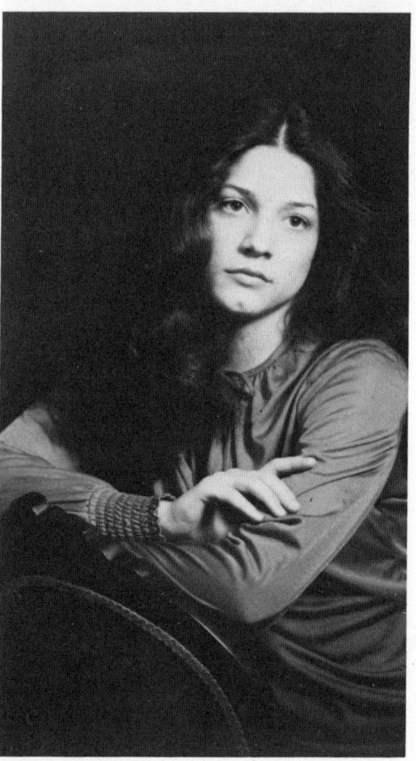

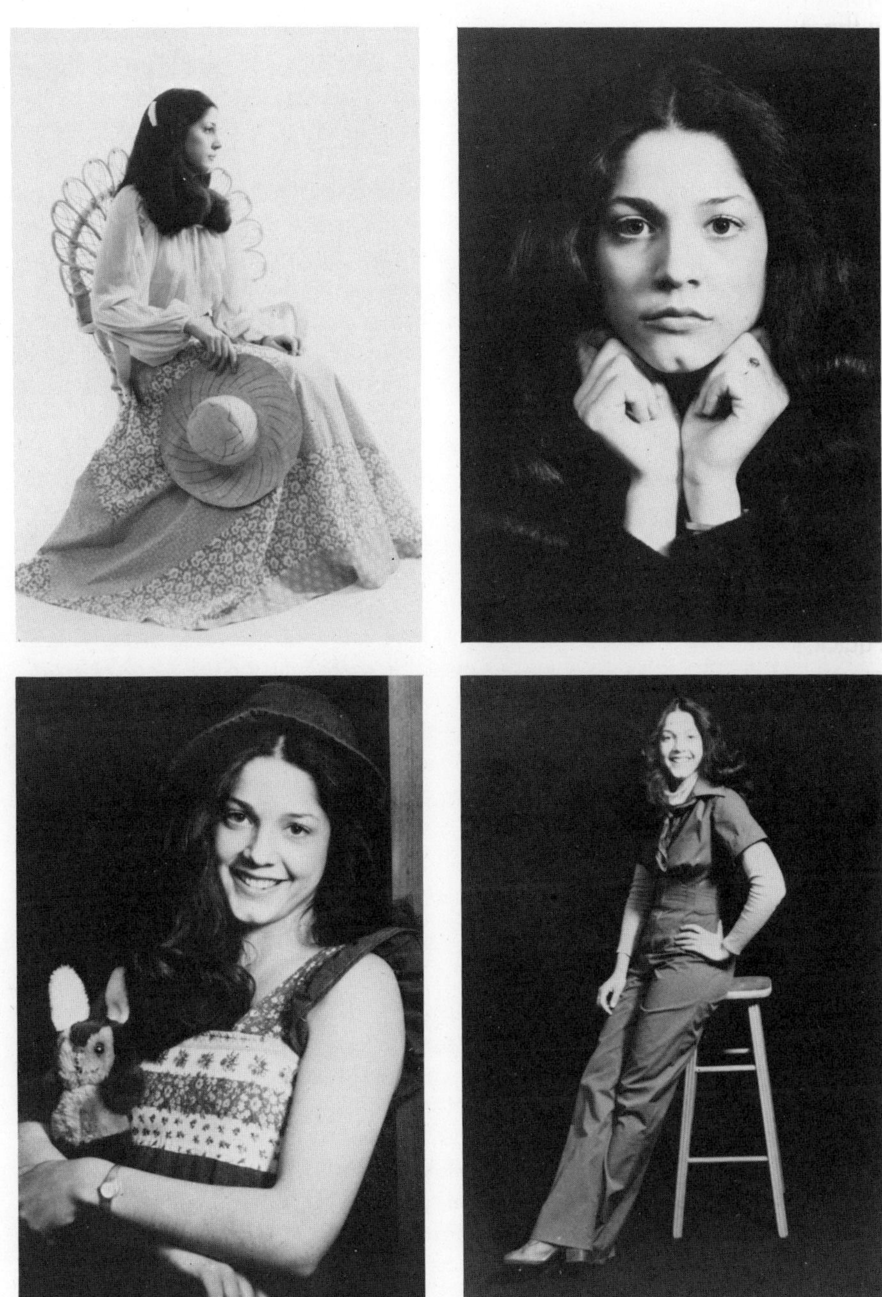

A portfolio of pictures by one young model exemplifies the variety of props, clothing and moods a portrait photographer can capture. Photos by Monteith's Countryhouse Studios.

home for perusal. Since then, the photo industry has been plagued by the problems created by this idea. The solution is to have a slide proof presentation in the studio and establish a strict policy that all proofs must be selected in the studio. There are exceptions, of course, such as when a client moves out of state.

In the studio, the client can take advantage of your advice and experience. Clients are also grateful in that they can make their selections without sales pressures. During the presitting interview or immediately following the sitting, explain that your previews are in the form of color slides which are projected for viewing. This enables the customers to see the portraits in any size they desire. Project the slides in a Kodak Carousel Projector, or equivalent, onto a screen material mounted in a 20″ × 24″ frame. Draw outlines on the screen indicating 16″ × 20″ and 11″ × 14″ sizes. By using a zoom lens, you can adjust the projector to fit the image into anyone of the aforementioned sizes. If you use 3″ × 5″ or 4″ × 5″ proofs, you can accomplish the same effect with an Astroscope or similar opaque projector.

If you don't want to move directly into the use of slides, there are a number of opaque projectors available. However, these machines must be operated in a darkened room, which interferes with direct communication. To solve this problem, make 35 mm color slides from your color negatives. This is a quick, simple procedure that utilizes available materials and the same chemistry you use for processing your film material. Once this system is set up, it becomes routine to run the negatives of the sitting through a negative carrier and produce a slide from each pose. Photographers across this country and abroad report a considerable increase in portrait sales and higher profits with the use of projected proofs.

Here are some reasons for showing proofs only by appointment and in the studio:

1. You have total control at the point of sale.

2. You can entice customers to purchase larger prints by displaying a complete set of samples in the sizes you wish to sell. The idea of using a large frame, with the smallest size being 11″ × 14″, makes the 11″ × 14″ print look tiny. To the customer, an 11″ × 14″ is considered very large as compared to snapshots and the small pictures promoted by mass-production outfits.

3. You can discuss composition so that your customer can better understand what the finished product will look like.

4. Since the order is made on the spot, you cut two to four weeks off the waiting time for collecting the final balance for your work. Although many photographers are ignorant of the economic concept of cash flow, getting the final balance from the customer quickly can have much to do with the success or failure of your business.

5. You never have the problem of lost or unreturned proofs.

The usual complaints that slide proofs take more effort, time, and cost more indicate the photographer's fear at trying something different. In a fair test with several dozen sittings, you will find that the use of projection proofs is an extremely profitable and practical approach. But you will never find out if you don't give it a try. You can also use the same system in selling wedding photographs and should find it just as successful in increasing sales and building orders as with portraiture.

Building a Slide-Making Unit You can spend from $400– $600 on slide-making units, or you can build your own. Here's how: Use an old enlarger base and post and rig it with a quick release to attach the camera. Take an old electronic flash which still recycles rapidly and works on 110 volts AC. Remove the unit from its plastic case and rebuild it into an empty cigar box. Add two small 7½-watt tungsten bulbs and sockets, and an opal glass diffuser. If you don't have a spare flash unit, you can use your present portable flash unit for both slide making and conventional photography if it is removable from its box structure. This is true of the camera as well. Thus the actual investment required to produce quality slides from color negatives is minimal.Use the tungsten light on the constructed unit for viewing, composing, and focusing, and the electronic flash for exposing the film. You may vary the construction to suit your individual needs, but if you use electronic flash, be sure to align the flashtube with the lens axis so there is no falloff of light in the corners of the opal glass diffuser. You can place filters between the opal glass and the clear glass which is positioned on top of the box. Outlets and switches for AC and the strobe are optional details.

A 35 mm camera with a macro lens and a right-angle finder was mounted on an old enlarger standby using a quick release to simplify loading and unloading the camera.

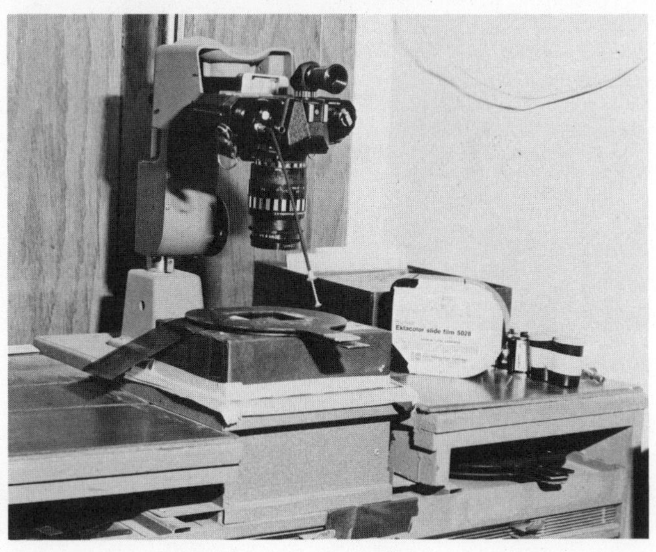

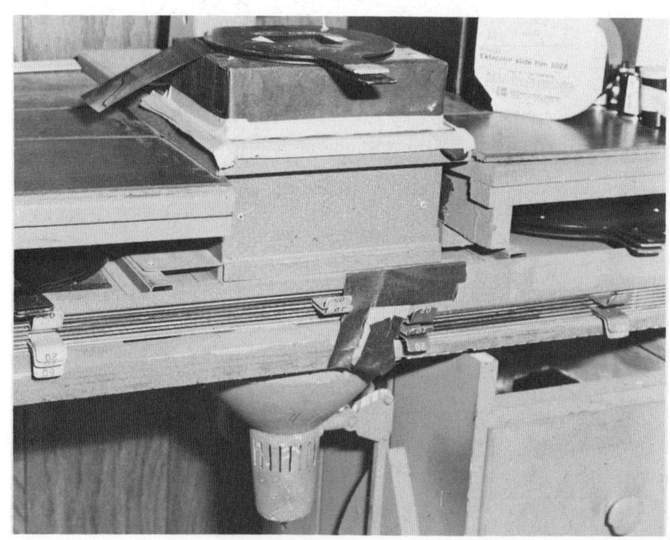

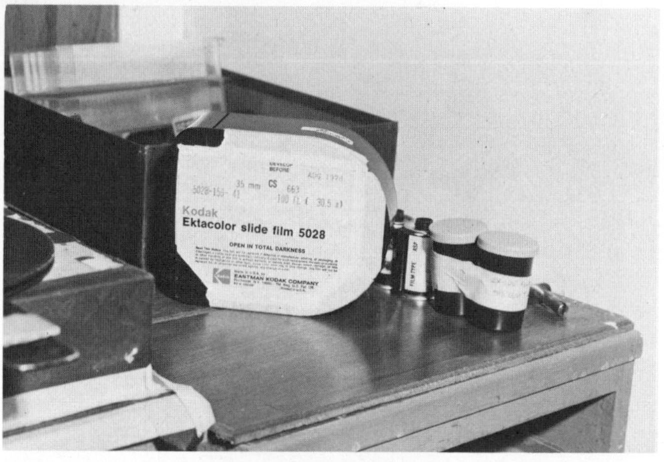

A 100-watt tungsten lamp (top) was mounted under a Lectra flip-top filter head and illuminated the negative in a standard negative carrier.

The basic tools required to produce color transparencies from color negatives include 35 mm Ektacolor Slide Film 5028 and reusable cassettes.

If you try using a bellows on your 35 mm camera, you may find that it has some limitations in producing the image sizes you require. With a conventional 50 mm camera lens and a set of nonautomatic extension tubes, you can produce high-quality slides from 2¼″ × 1⅞″, 2¼″ × 2¼″, 2¼″ × 2¾″, or 4″ × 5″ negatives. With a macro lens, which is designed to function at its highest quality in a 1:1 ratio, together with the extension rings (available for virtually every 35 mm camera with interchangeable lenses), everything from extreme magnification to photographing almost the full frame of the film can be accomplished with ease. If you use electronic flash as the exposing light source, remember that the films for producing slides from color negatives are balanced for tungsten light. Consequently, you will need to use heavy yellow filtration to overcome the blue daylight coloration of the flash.

Producing Slide Proofs You will need some Kodak Ektacolor Slide Film (sold in 100-foot rolls), plus a bulk loader and cassettes to spool your own cartridges. The reloadable metal cartridges, such as the Kodak Snap-Caps, work best. The film is processed in a standard color negative developer according to manufacturer's recommendations. The exposing light source is housed in a simple cardboard, wooden, or metal container, such as those available from an electrical supply house. The light source itself is any 75- or 100-watt lamp of the household type, for example, Sylvania Soft light bulbs. Use standard color-printing filters to correct for the individual emulsions. You need a negative carrier to hold the negatives in a flat position during exposures and to properly position the film to compose the image on the slide, plus a stand to hold the camera in a rigid position directly over the negative.

For mounting slides, you can use either the standard cardboard mounts that require a heat seal and a small mounting press or household iron. Or you may prefer Pakon plastic mounts. The slide can be cut and slipped into the mount in a matter of seconds. These plastic mounts are reusable and slides can be removed and stored in the same envelope with the color negatives when an order is completed.

Making these slides requires considerably less skill than color printing itself. The filtration is not critical because of the stability and latitude of the material. Your intent is to make a color proof; you are not necessarily interested in perfect color, as in the finished photographs. It is advantageous to have the slides just a touch off-color, as the finished photographs are then more attractive than the proofs.

When loading Kodak Ektacolor Slide Film, use a series 10 or series 13 safelight, which is designed for use with Ektacolor paper. Unopened film should be refrigerated or frozen. You can load 100 feet of film into cassettes and seal them in double plastic bags or the plastic containers in which film is originally sold. You can obtain these containers free from any photofinisher since they are discarded before the film goes to a processing plant. Once the film is placed into these containers, which have a vapor lock, they can be refrigerated without problems. Each container should be clearly marked with its contents.

Once you determine the proper exposure and filtration for your film, you will be amazed to find that there will be only the slightest changes in filtration and exposures over many months. The only time you need to resort to additional testing is when you start using a new emulsion. Use one basic filter pack for all studio exposures and a second, which varies slightly, for weddings, candids and flash photographs. Then each time you make slides, note the filters used and the exposure for future reference.

The photographer who doesn't wish to do his own processing, and refuses to look at the advantages of a self-contained operation, can take advantage of the slide proof presentation system by having his slides made by Kodak, which, in quantity, are as inexpensive as conventional machine-made proofs.

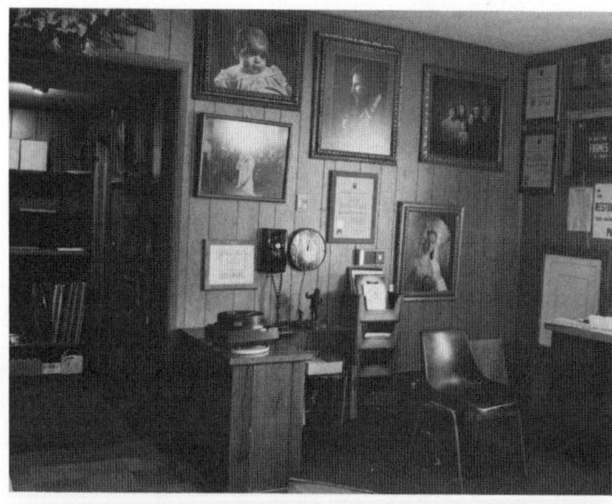

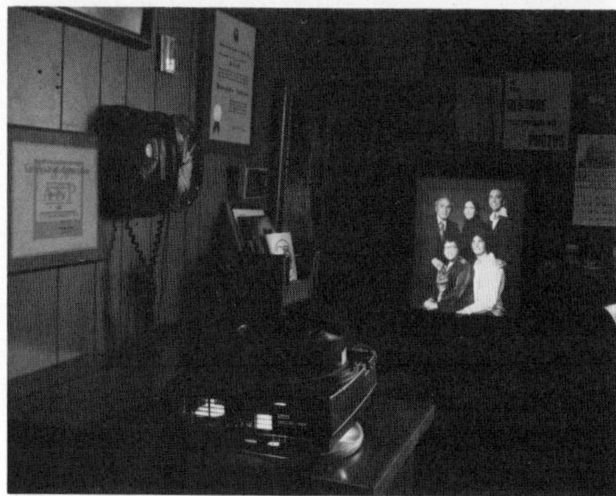

(Top) Be prepared to seat as many clients—up to six—as will be expected for previews. (Bottom) Projector displays a family group of five on a 20" x 24" size. Note other size guidelines on the screen.

Chapter 21

Building a Reputation

Many people assume that when they do business with someone and pay their money and receive the product, that this is the end of the transaction. During the course of any transaction, we leave an impression, be it good or bad, on the individual with whom we have dealt. That impression is an important part of what we call "reputation." This impression remains long after the business arrangement has been concluded and is important to the survival and growth of a business.

Each of us asks friends for advice about a service or product and where best to purchase it. Sometimes they will suggest a place if they were happy with the service. Other times they will warn you against doing business with an establishment. It is a fact that no one can satisfy each and every person with whom he deals. If the majority who do business with you are satisfied and can recommend you to others, your business will grow. Each customer becomes your sales representative when he or she exhibits your work in their home, speaks with pleasure of the way they were treated and how you responded to their needs. This is the key to building a successful business.

When a client has gone through the rigors of a sitting, he or she is usually anxious to see the previews, and, later, the finished work. Therefore, planning your production to satisfy your customer's needs is very important. If proofs and delivery of finished work are delayed for extended periods, the client will be less enthusiastic about having her portrait made in the future. You must determine how quickly the consumer needs a job and, above all, never fail to keep your promise to deliver work by a specific deadline. Prepare your proofs as quickly as possible, and establish a schedule and stick to it. If there is no deadline for the pictures, still give an approximate time and promise to call when the work is ready. Failure to keep promises concerning delivery can destroy a business that has everything else in its favor.

THE UNHAPPY CUSTOMER

There will be times when, no matter how skilled, a photographer will fail to live up to the mental expectations of the sitter. Often this is because he or she is seeing a preview—unfinished work. It is therefore up to the photographer to explain how the finished product will look—about final composition, skilled retouching and print finishing, and color correction and modification. If the customer hates all the proofs, the worst thing a photographer can do at this point is to defend his position or argue with the client. The result is often a disaster for the photographer both in loss of reputation and revenue. The proper way to handle a situation like this is to tell the customer that you would be delighted to make additional poses from which he or she can select. Also advise the customer that everything you do is unconditionally guaranteed and you will refund the deposit if you cannot make them happy. This bit of information usually settles the person.

Do not simply accept a customer's flat rejection of a pose or photograph. Have the person verbalize and explain the objections so that you do not make the same mistake when you do additional poses. Let the customer talk as long as it takes to run out of steam. By the time this is over, 70 percent of the time he or she will come to realize that there is really nothing wrong with the proofs. In a few instances, it may be that you failed to observe something that was important to the customer, and this you can correct during a second appointment and some additional poses. By offering to make additional poses, you are simply giving the client a larger choice from which to select. There is no implication of failure on your part. Interestingly enough, in a majority of cases, when the customer views the second set of poses, he or she most often will order from the original photographs. When this happens, you will have invested more time and possibly another roll of film, but you will have assured the client of your sincerity in giving complete satisfaction. Usually this results in a customer that will return again and again and will recommend new customers as well.

Occasionally you will meet someone whom you just cannot satisfy. In this case, it is wise to recognize this as early as possible and refund the deposit and suggest that the client tries someone else in the area. By following a generous refund policy if the customer is not satisfied, your reasonable approach will elicit similar response in the customer and very few people will ask to be refunded. You are within your legal rights in insisting that you be paid for a job even when the customer is dissatisfied. However, this individual could cost you a considerable amount of business over the years if you did, by advising others to avoid you. Being hospitable, on the other hand, helps build your reputation for reliability. This concept or a generous and open-handed refund policy is good business, one which department stores, catalog houses, and business firms use with success year after year.

TAKING ORDERS

Write up your transactions on one of several forms, amending each to suit your needs. The reason for writing down what the customer orders, the style, finish, matting, or framing, is to eliminate any misunderstanding or ill feeling all around. Even on telephone orders for additional photographs or on the acceptance of assignments, write down the client's instructions and carefully read them back for verification.

If the assignment is for location photography, suggest that the client or a representative be present and show you precisely how and where they wish the pictures to be made. In cases where you are dealing with one individual in a business or social organization, request that somebody be assigned to accompany you so that you clearly understand exactly what they want. Usually, people are happy to oblige and it makes life simple for the photographer when he arrives to have someone there who is part of the organization so that arrangements can be made easily and with minimum delay.

DEPOSITS AND REFUNDS

At the time of a portrait sitting, request a deposit. If the customer is a long-term valued customer of the studio, you may dispense with the deposit. In dealing with large business organizations, where responsibility sometimes shifts from day to day, request a purchase order when accepting the job and before delivery of any work. This insures and proves your claim for payment, and it is rare that a problem will arise once you have a written purchase order. For legal photographs, insist on payment on delivery, as this is the most difficult profession from which to collect money.

ANSWERING YOUR PHONE

Too few photographers comprehend the importance of the image they present to the public. In this age of electronics, your telephone personality can play a major role in the success of your business. Moreover, so much business is conducted over the phone, with calls from customers asking such questions as: "How much is an 8″ × 10″?" or, "How much do you charge for wedding pictures?" The photographer who refuses to quote prices over the telephone costs himself a good deal of business. Most people will call a photographer on maybe six or eight occasions in their lives, and very few know what to ask for except the price. They know they need pictures of an occasion but have no idea of whether such service costs $5 or $500. Primarily they seek reassurance that they can afford to buy your product and won't be embarrassed by your fee.

While this is not to advise that you make a policy of quoting many prices on the telephone, you can tell a potential client that he or she can purchase a portrait for as little as X dollars (based on your minimum cost). If the minimum price is within the customer's reach, you can immediately eliminate the price barrier and can then lead the conversation onto clothing, makeup, and appointments.

Begin a telephone conversation by first determining the client's needs, how she came to call your studio, and establish rapport. Most folks appreciate your interest in them. Never start by quoting a price. One top studio receptionist advises: "Keep a pencil and pad handy, get the caller's name and keep referring to them by name. Tell them your name, and you will soon find yourselves in a one-to-one relationship." If you develop a "voice with a smile," you will never lose a customer who can afford your services. Get your customers talking by asking questions, then let them do most of the talking. They will rapidly conclude that you are very intelligent.

One of the best ways to discover your shortcomings is to tape one or more of your conversations and then replay them. This will make you aware of your telephone personality and faults. You may discover that your voice is dull, aggressive, defensive, harsh, or expressionless. Once you discover the flaws, they are easily corrected. Remember that nobody likes to buy anything from someone they don't like, and improving your telephone personality can mean an improvement in your bank balance.

Although many people hate talking to machines, a phone-answering device is better than having a call go unanswered. Although half the callers will hang up without leaving a message on the machine, you still derive some benefits, and your investment in an answering machine will pay for itself many times.

Thus, in a typical phone conversation, never hesitate or refuse to respond to a customer's price inquiry, but first talk about his or her needs and your service. Make each caller welcome and let the person know you are sincerely interested. At no time should you permit the conversation to become a review of your entire price list. If the customer asks about other sizes and finishes, suggest that it would be better for her to come to the studio for complete information.

Chapter 22

Exhibiting Your Work

In order to successfully market any product, you must be able to demonstrate capability to your prospective marketplace. If the only information people have about you is that you are a photographer who may be able to serve their needs, you will reach only a small segment of the market. Showing your work to the world opens a vast new area of potential clients and may well make the difference between a marginal and a successful portrait operation. There are the usual methods of advertising: local newspapers, radio and TV commercials, and printed brochures delivered via the mail—all successful means of telling the public about your services. With these, you have to invest considerable amounts of money, and sustain the advertising campaign long enough to get any meaningful return on your investment. Most photographers, particularly in the early years of their operation, find this type of advertising extremely costly and beyond their means. Yet there are many ways to promote yourself without investing large sums of money; all it takes is planning and preparation.

It is good practice to incorporate a simple model release on each sales slip or receipt you use. The signature means that your customer permits you to use his or her photographs to advertise your skills. In most cases, customers are delighted to have you use their portraits. As the photographer, you have a quasi-legal right to ownership of the negatives you make, so you could prepare samples of pictures you have taken without releases. However, should anyone object to the use of their picture, you must immediately remove it from display. Avoid complications and protect your rights by obtaining this consent immediately and directly on your receipt or sales order. (More on photography and the law later in this chapter.)

An easy way to accumulate prints for use in shows and exhibits, is to make one or two extras each time you print a photograph for a customer, particularly if you feel the picture has special merit that might encourage others to seek your services. If the client orders a smaller print than you would normally make for display, make a larger print for your own use. This practice sometimes sways the customer into buying the larger picture, but primarily these photographs should be used around the studio to promote your work.

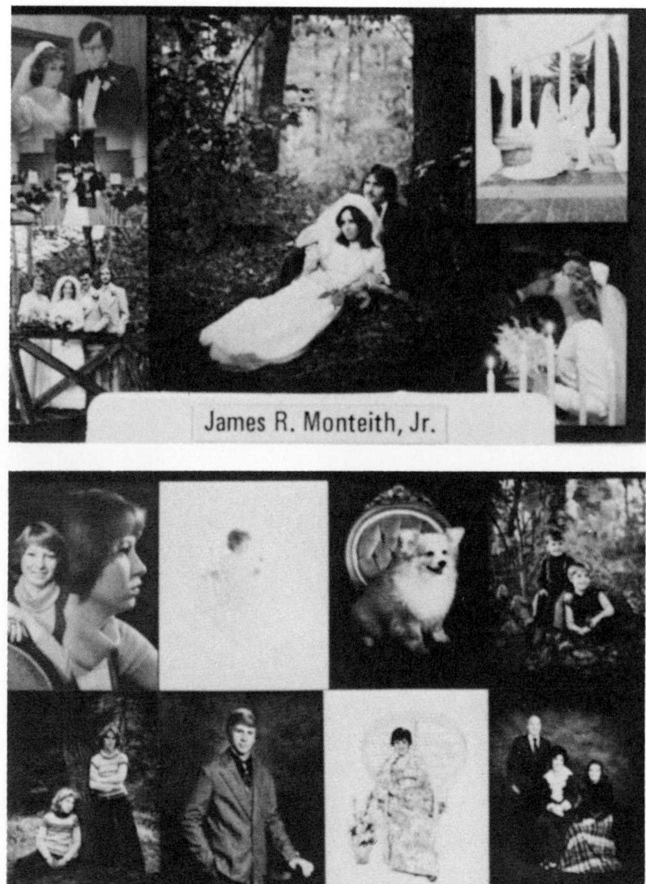

A unique business card helps people to remember you and the services you offer.

SHOWCASES

A little imagination can do wonders in getting people to show your work on their premises. Try exhibiting photographs of children in the window of a local department store or children's clothing shop, for instance. These merchants are frequently hard-pressed for ideas to decorate their windows attractively and, if offered the opportunity of showing some exciting pictures of children, will be delighted to use your prints. This gives you a showplace located in the heavily traveled area of your community which otherwise would be very expensive if you tried to rent it. Or approach your local bank. Not all banks are amenable to setting up exhibitions, but high-quality work can frequently persuade them to show your work at a location where prospective customers come to do their banking. If you have a good mixture of pictorial photographs and special effects along with the portraits, you can arrange for an exhibition of your work at the local library. Many libraries have programs where they exhibit works of art, including paintings, sculptures, and ceramics. Photography can and should be included among these artistic endeavors.

If you can combine a special theme in a series of pictures, this in itself will act as an inducement for people to exhibit your photographs. Some of the themes might be historic sites in your area that would be of interest to the community, picturesque, old, covered bridges, rivers, lakes, and recreation areas. Coverage of civic activities, such as scouting groups, service clubs, and volunteer workers who serve the community, make wonderful themes for picture material. A very successful theme was entitled National Brotherhood Week, a photographic display of all the ministers, priests, and rabbis who served a particular area. Preparing and photographing the subjects or events can be done by the photographer or with the cooperation and assistance of the bank or institution where the pictures will be exhibited.

Many photographers use popular dining areas and restaurants to show their samples. Any place where people congregate and where prospective customers meet is appropriate for exhibiting your work. The exhibition should incorporate photographs and a newspaper story for release by the media. Many papers are very happy to publish stories like this and this gives you the opportunity to "steal" space which otherwise would cost you. Building your reputation in the community and indicating your involvement in community projects and themes helps your business grow. It also benefits your community, where you are providing a valuable service.

A unique show was done by a photographer who gathered old glass plates of landmarks in the community. These were cleaned up and carefully printed and each landmark was then rephotographed fifty years after the original picture was made. Each pair of photographs was exhibited side by side and was of great interest to all who had lived in the area for any length of time.

Getting publicity and promoting your business is simply a matter of finding an area or concept and then convincing others that it has validity. Once this is done, a reasonable amount of effort on your part will produce something that will excite and interest people and will also help build your status as a photographer in the community. You make many new contacts and acquire new customers when you exhibit photographs. Frequently sales of photographs from exhibits will more than cover the initial cost of your investment and help immeasurably in building your reputation.

COMMUNITY WORK

Participating in community events can be gratifying personally as well as from a business standpoint. Offering to present programs dealing with local activities, special historical events, or special fund-raising drives can also be very beneficial to the photographer. If you wish to build a business that deals primarily with family groups and portraiture, you can offer local service clubs a show on decorating with photographs that can be useful in building this type of business. Some prepared shows are available through manufacturers such as Eastman Kodak and the Professional Photographers of America. You need only arrange the time and book the show well in advance to obtain the material. These shows are usually slide presentations and often include a synchronized tape showing how photographs can be used to enhance the home. In addition to the professional-packaged presentation, display large framed pictures of your own around the room and discuss them afterward.

Another way to endear yourself to the buying public is by presenting programs for garden clubs and women's groups. The people who handle the programs for such groups are constantly looking for new and interesting programs to entertain their membership. Contacting them can give you a wonderful opportunity to present your work to prospective customers. Pictures of Boy Scout or Cub Scout activities and their special projects can also be used for this type of show. If your area has a service club that supports a particular hospital, charity, or children's activity, these are opportunities for you to make a professional picture story which you can show again and again to promote your prestige in the community.

SELLING BY SUGGESTION

Perhaps half the customers entering a studio have a fairly good idea of the size and type of photograph they wish to purchase. If they have been to your studio previously, they are fully aware of the services you offer. Sometimes the customer knows there is an occasion that requires pictures but has no fixed idea of what she wants to buy. In such cases, try not to take a specific order at the beginning of the transaction unless the customer is absolutely sure of her needs. Suggest that a decision be made after she sees the proofs. One of the subtle ways of selling by suggestion is by your display of samples. Often the customer will remark that she likes a specific sample. This is a clue to the type of product the customer may consider purchasing. If the photograph is a gift for a special person, your response should be, "What a lovely idea! What a thoughtful gift this will make!" This reinforces in the person's mind that she is doing the right thing. If the customer is unsure, recommend a style or finish and point out the advantages of a special matting or frame to make the photograph look more elegant and impressive. Make it a point never to present these concepts on the basis of price alone. First point out the advantages and desirability and then casually mention that it will only cost so many dollars additional. The soft sell by suggestion is something the customer appreciates, and if you are helpful, you reinforce the fact that this is a pleasant, friendly transaction and the person will be more apt to return in the future.

Usually by inquiring where they plan to use the picture will enable customers to think and plan ahead. More often the response is, "I don't know."

From the initial telephone contact, at the end of the sitting, and several times during the slide proof showing, casually mention the words "wall portrait." Often the customer's plans do not include a wall portrait. But the continual use of this term will, if the client is exceptionally pleased with the proofs, often sell that wall portrait for you. Once the pose has been selected, the size determined, and all other details settled, next ask how the client plans to frame the picture. At this point, indicate a display of moulding corners and suggest that the customer try and find one suitable for her decor. If the client selects a specific moulding, next determine the price of the frame. Provided the price is right, you will have sold a framed portrait. Most people prefer not to go to a separate shop to purchase a frame, and you make it easy for them to have the completed photographic work ready to hang on their wall without additional travel or effort.

Suggestive selling can build a sizable framing business for you. Not every picture you sell will go out in a frame, but a large percentage will and again you will have found an additional source of revenue for the studio that is both convenient for the customer and profitable for you. Occasionally the customer will mention that she has a frame, perhaps an antique, that she would like to use. In that case, offer to do the framing free of charge in order to protect the photograph before it leaves the studio. Such service is appreciated and the result is a firm basis for good future relationship.

WALL PORTRAITS

You should display prominently what you wish to sell. If you want to sell wall portraits, for instance, don't display 8″ × 10″ in your studio. Many patrons who start with the idea that they prefer small prints can be persuaded otherwise through excellent personal service, attractive displays, and the belief that they are buying home decor rather than just a photograph. On every portrait job, make a maximum effort to please the customer with a variety of proofs and sell prestige wall prints. Although the 8″ × 10″ print is easy to make and profitable, yet the difference between an 8″ × 10″, 11″ × 14″, or 16″ × 20″ insofar as your production cost or lab fees is small and the profit on the larger size is considerably greater.

Another valid reason for attempting to sell large prints is in their use and display. Scarcely anyone will brag about having purchased a small portrait as they would of a large portrait, elegantly framed and displayed is a prominent place in the home. If photographs are taken home and then placed in a drawer, album, or tucked away in a personal room, they do little good in promoting your service to the visitors to that home. Each wall portrait can become a salesman for your studio, and people will point to a portrait with pride when it represents a considerable investment on their part. Those who come to you because they have been impressed with your craftsmanship will usually purchase a portrait as large or larger than the one they saw.

MAKING SAMPLES

Each photographer must recognize that in order to sell his product, the work he shows must conform to very high standards. If you fail in presenting samples that inspire the customer to want beautiful wall portraits, you certainly won't be able to sell them. Usually the excuse given by photographers who have poor displays is that they're too busy to make proper samples. This is tantamount to saying that they have no interest in selling larger, more beautiful wall portraits to their customers. Selling larger pictures is the name of the game, and it is virtually impossible to sell large pictures unless the customer sees them displayed. Fine photographs, well framed and displayed in the home, are treasured assets. Well-displayed samples of family group and bride portraits not only advertise the photographer's work, it also promotes their sale, particularly in large sizes. For suggestions on how to improve your sales and increase orders, a very rich and well-organized source is the handbook *Selling the Name of the Game,* a sales manual for studio owners, managers, and receptionists written by Betty Lensmith and published by the Photographers Specialized Services.

Most photographers find that they will usually sell a portrait one size smaller than the largest size they show to the majority of their customers. If you display a large number of 20″ × 24″, some 16″ × 20″, and a few 11″ × 14″ prints, most customers will buy the 16″ × 20″ size. By going continually to larger and larger prints, you can help insure that each sitting is producing the maximum sales potential for you.

Carefully balance the subject matter in your display area. Show photographs that will promote the type of business you wish to develop. If you are interested in child photography, for instance, displaying several large pictures of children with unusual costumes or expressions is always effective in developing new customers. When someone visits your studio, allow ample time for viewing your samples. Often these portraits are silent salesmen. Frequently a customer will come in for a commercial service, passport, or other type of photography and will comment upon the display of a child or animal portrait. Encourage such conversation because it can plant in the customer's mind the desire for a similar photograph of their child or pet.

Your display area is a constant, permanent place to develop your business and sell ideas for photographs without your having to discuss these possibilities. If you don't have a permanent display area, put together a portfolio and include in it the type and size of product you wish to sell. By using large, attractively matted photographs, you are utilizing a tool that will function for you in a more eloquent manner than if you tried verbally to describe the product. The walls in your camera room can also display a number of framed prints. These act as silent salesmen, and often during a sitting, a customer will comment about one or more of them because of their desire to have something similar for themselves or their loved ones. And don't neglect to use some of your work in your own home.

THE LAW ON SAMPLE PHOTOGRAPHS

Although the law regarding the use of photographs varies to some degree in every state, the rules are basically as follows:

Although pictures purchased by a client are his or her exclusive property and the client retains the right to repurchase additional photographs from the negatives at any future date, the photographer retains a quasi-legal ownership of the films.

It is generally accepted that photographers have the right to make samples of these photographs in order to show the quality and type of work they do to promote their business. This does not mean that the photographer has the right to sell these pictures to a commercial company or business for advertising purposes. The latter is considered a separate use and requires a written model release.

To protect yourself from controversy, it is wise to get a release in the first place. This need be nothing more than a signature on the purchase agreement or contract of sale which the photographer uses. The person signing such a release is fully aware that you may use the photographs for promotional purposes. Without the release, you should not contemplate using a picture for anything more than a studio sample on your own premises. Even then, it is wise to obtain a written release from the subject, parent, or guardian. If the subject refuses to sign the release or is hesitant, the wisest thing to do is never to use that photograph.

In making photographs for a commercial or industrial client, the law states that each recognizable individual *must* sign a model release. If you fail to obtain one at the time of the picture-taking, you could place your client in a compromising situation. Even if the client is the employer of a model, the situation can always change, and upon leaving that job the model could conceivably cause problems for the employer.

It is the photographer's job to obtain all releases unless there is an advertising agency that handles it. Obtain a signed release from each person photographed in a job or work situation, which specifically states that the picture may be used for any and all commercial sales and promotional purposes by the photographer and/or his heirs and/or assignees. So rather than put yourself or a client in jeopardy, having a signed release, even if you don't intend to use a specific picture, can be of great value should the situation change. You can print or reproduce the standard model-release consent form. If there is a special legal problem due to the kind of pictures you make in a unique situation, it is always best to consult a local attorney and have him draft the proper forms for you.

Chapter 23

Special Sales Promotions

The promotion techniques described in this chapter should help introduce you to the buying public.

Tying in with a quality children's shop to run an annual "Beautiful Child" contest can be profitable for the shop and the photographer. The shop can promote the contest in newspaper ads and encourage its customers to come in and have their children's portraits made as a gift of the shop. You then make the photographs of children in a certain age group and attractively frame and display them in the shop window. Keep the judging fair. After all ballots are cast, the photographs of the three top winners can again be displayed. Finally the large portraits can be presented to the winners with additional prizes supplied by the shop. This type of promotion generates activity and exposes you to potential clients whom you might not reach otherwise, and requires only a modest investment by the photographer and shopkeeper.

A number of studios have built very healthy operations using coupons to promote their services. Offering one picture at a special introductory price, with the rest available at the regular studio prices is another way to gain new customers.

Some photographers restrict their efforts to one type of subject matter with great success, for example those who operate at race tracks, dog shows, horse shows, and special athletic events. However, it may be difficult to gain access to these places if they are under contract. Making pictures of teams at bowling alleys, of pilots and their planes at airports, and of ladies and their prize-winning plants at garden clubs are just a few of the approaches you can use to develop a business. Photographing little league teams in baseball, soccer, football, and hockey can also be a profitable addition to your business. The opportunities are limitless. The people who are involved in these various activities are always grateful to the photographer who will come out and take pictures of their events, and this can lead to other assignments. Once people get a chance to see what you can do and are happy with your performance, they will seek your services again. This type of work should be carefully planned with the organizers of the event so that there is minimum photography time. Also arrange and announce the prices in advance.

MAKING THE MOST OF THE MILESTONES

Many people place a strong value upon there being "something special" about their date of birth. As children, an impending birthday evoked exciting dreams of ice cream, cake, and gifts. Many commercial establishments also have special sale days honoring their founding. Far too few photographers take advantage of this natural approach to good public relations, although they can profit from our birthday- or anniversary-oriented society. The newly established studio could use a birthday sale approach even for a first or second anniversary, claiming, "It's our birthday, but you get the gifts!" or "Serving your community for ______ years." After the tenth anniversary, using the line, "Established in 19_____," is the practice of many firms. From that point on, at five-year intervals, you could schedule additional events. One studio used to send a complimentary calendar to its customers each year at Christmas. Its mailing list was compiled from active customer files and the owners found this to be a successful way of keeping their name before the public. For those fortunate enough to survive 25 years in business, a silver anniversary certainly holds the promise of a public relations opportunity. Taking advantage of all these promotional opportunities requires a certain amount of advanced planning, but the result can be of immense value to your studio and you.

DIRECTORY ADVERTISING

If you decide on telephone directory advertising, it must fit your business needs, the size of your studio, volume, price range, and location. The advice of directory sales personnel is sometimes tied to their commission rather than your specific needs, so don't let some representative talk you into buying space by showing you what your competitor is buying.

Certainly, if you run a commercial or mixed operation in a small box ad, it can be of considerable value. A business firm will often call someone who has expertise in a specialized area, such as aerial or high-speed photography. Most portrait and wedding appointments are made by women, and studios indicate that they will run their fingers down the listings and call the nearest studio; they will usually ignore a half-page display ad if it requires a toll call. In that case, there is very little need for display advertising. Remember that when the sales person tells you that it costs only $30 per month, you must multiply that by 12 and add taxes to determine your actual cost per year. If display advertising has proven successful for you, then by all means keep it up. If you're not sure, determine whether the amount of business it brings you makes it worthwhile to continue.

Chapter 24

Pricing

There are two basic prerequisites for operating a photographic studio successfully so that it offers a reasonable return for you, your time, efforts, and training. Your knowledge of photography and your skills and capabilities have to be as good as, or better than, the other people in your area who operate the same type of business. Along with this, you must also have a good working knowledge of business practices. Over the years, many talented, young photographers have failed in the business solely because they lacked good business sense. Rarely does a week go by without a visit or phone call from someone who has recently started a business, asking how much to charge for a certain type of job. Unfortunately, each situation is unique and it is up to each photographer to determine the prices he will charge.

Far too often the beginning photographer will accept a job at a lower fee because of promises of future work. To the wide-eyed novice, this type of offer smacks of opportunity. However, experience shows that all the work generated by reducing one's fee usually brings more offers of work at lower fees. Once a client knows that he can dicker and cut your prices, there is little chance for you to increase your rates. Each future offer will be based on the fact that your price can be reduced by a bit of bargaining. Your objective should be to examine each transaction from every angle and determine if you have covered all your costs and earned a reasonable profit for your efforts. If not, you must realize that no business can operate successfully without profit. Handling large sums of money which subsequently go to suppliers, labs, and employees and include little or no profit for you is a dangerous business practice.

Even if your pricing is profitable, there are other factors that can destroy a photographer's operation, for example, failure to institute a proper deposit system so that your costs are continually covered as the transaction proceeds.

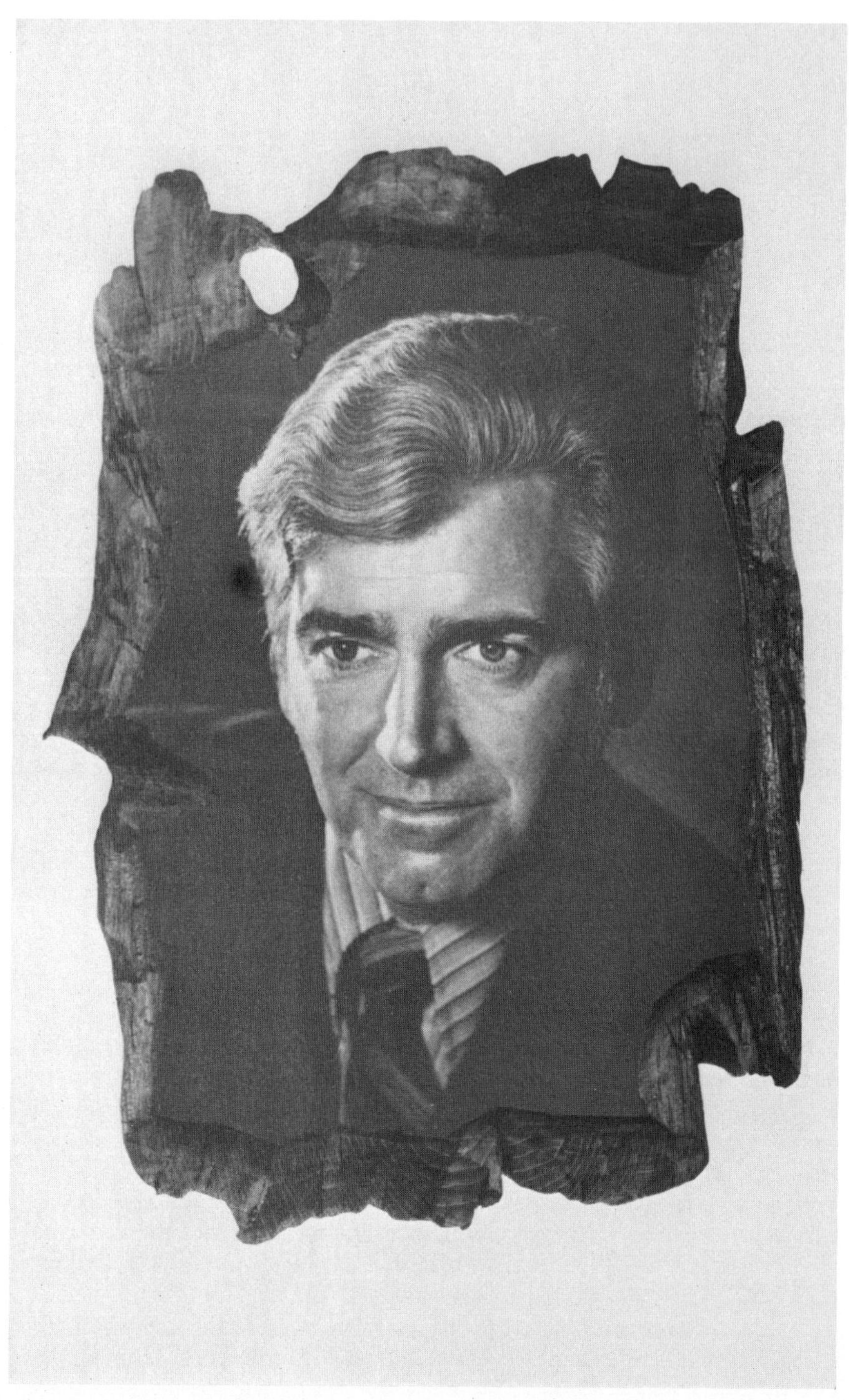

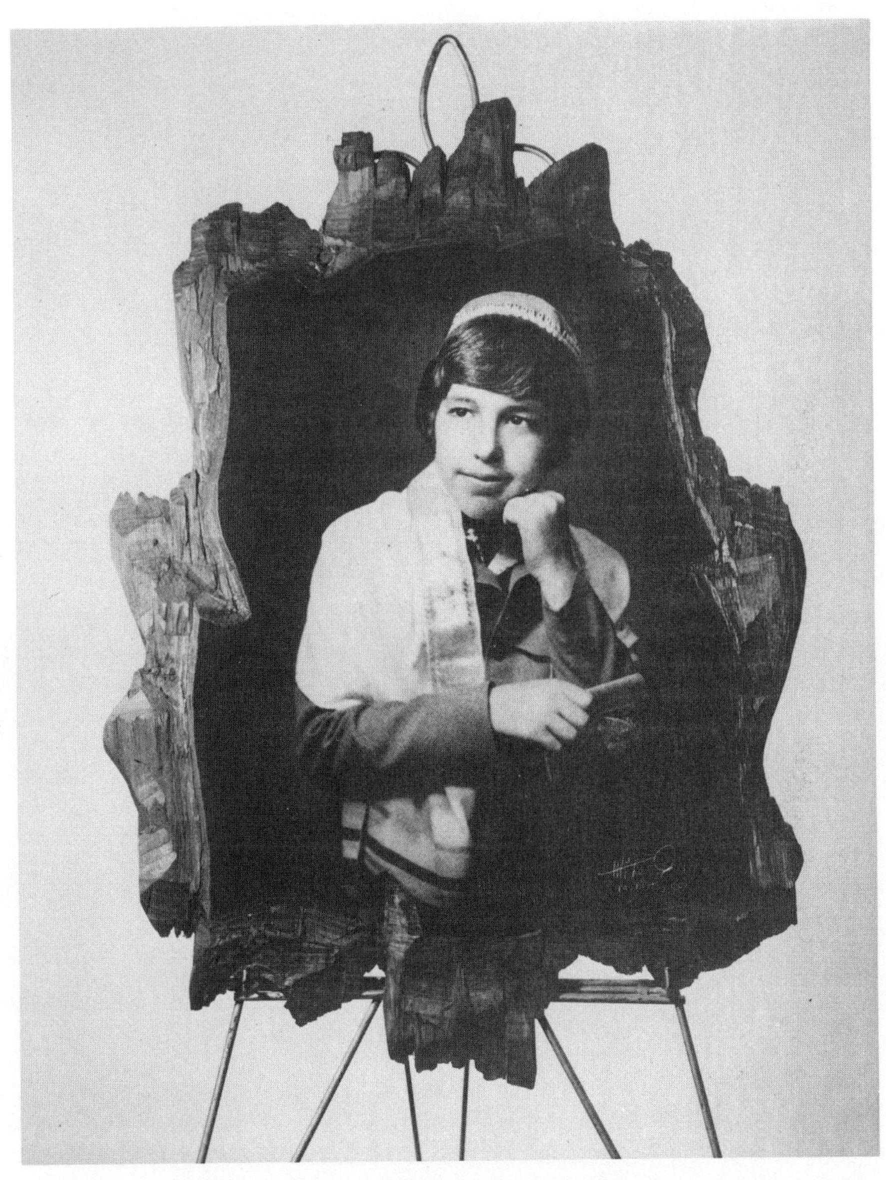

Individually hand-carved plaques, each sculptured to suit the photographic composition, can make your portraits a decorator conversation piece. These plaques were made for Hand Krafts by Erica.

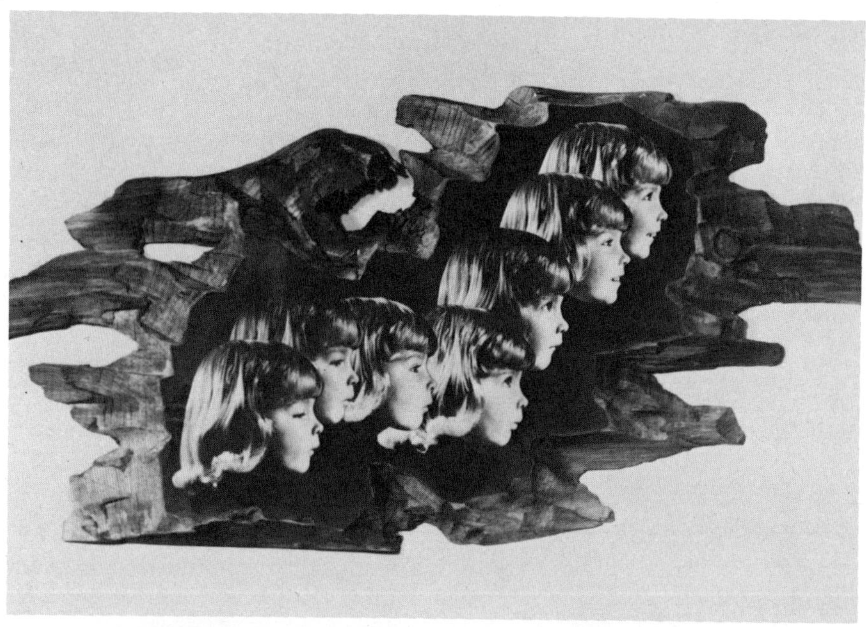

Adequate deposits guarantee that you will not be left with shelves of undelivered work should the customer change his or her mind. These losses can be substantial and, if permitted to exist, can create all sorts of problems. The approach of continually writing or calling the customer may, in some of the cases, get you your money, but will have created a very bad feeling and you will have lost one customer and perhaps others whom the customer might have recommended. You can avoid much of this in advance if you have a very visible written or printed policy on deposits that guarantees that only a small balance remains to be paid when the finished work is delivered.

It is good business practice to have a printed price list which you can show a customer who asks about prices. This establishes in the customer's mind the fact that yours is a one-price studio and your rates do not vary for the same service. The casual, off-the-top-of-the-head quotation of a price can later raise questions in the customer's mind. Using a printed price list does not take much effort, and it can be a very valuable tool in showing customers a range of prices that sometimes induces them to buy larger photographs. The one exception to a specific printed price list should be for restorations. Unless you see the original photograph, you cannot give estimates over the phone. Moreover, this can be a dangerous practice and costly to you because the client cannot evaluate the picture in a technically correct manner or understand how many hours of work go into restoring a portrait.

Periodically survey the work that you have done and the income for each type of work you have produced. If you discover that one or more of your services is not producing a proper level of income and profit, decide whether to discontinue it or raise your prices so that the proper margin of profit can be obtained. No segment of a business should be operated at a loss. If you have serious doubts about any part of your business, consult an accountant. The money thus spent can help you prevent weak spots in your business structure.

OFFER A VARIETY OF PRODUCTS

Take a simple product, such as an 8″ × 10″ photograph. This should never be offered in a single finish or style at a specific price. Ignoring the possibility that some customers wish to spend less and others more can often hurt you. By offering that 8″ × 10″ (from a color negative) in black-and-white, sepia, or blue tone in addition to natural color, you can sell the same basic product in many ways, permitting the customer to seek his or her price level. As a rule, people will select a product somewhere in the middle price range rather than the cheapest or the most expensive offered. Catering to this habit is good business and can be profitable once you understand the concept.

A successful "old-timer" once suggested that if you want a free lesson in salesmanship you should visit an automobile dealer. By watching how a seasoned salesman works to determine the amount a person is willing to spend, and how he offers additional services, accessories, and goodies, you can develop your own approach.

The soft sell approach also works. By making your clients aware of the services, styles, and products you offer, they make their own choices and decide when they have had enough. Avoid overselling a customer. If you sell them everything but the kitchen sink, leaving them with the feeling that they've been had, rest assured that they won't return. Fulfilling the client's needs without overselling is just as important as failing to let the customer know about the products and services you have available, or underselling.

PLAN NOW FOR SURVIVAL

The world economy is currently experiencing great instability. There probably won't be a depression, such as in the early 1930's, but the economy is suffering and many will feel the squeeze. In a situation of impending disaster or emergency, a well-prepared plan of action represents the difference between those who survive and those who merely get by or fail. The police officer, fire fighter, physician, or pilot can respond in emergencies and react efficiently only because he has been trained to a course of action before the need arises. In the same way, the photographer must recognize the direction of the future and plan ahead rather than wait until the emergency gets out of hand. In all likelihood, those in the top 10 percent of the industry will need to make a few minor adjustments to weather the economic storm, while the mechanized, low-priced

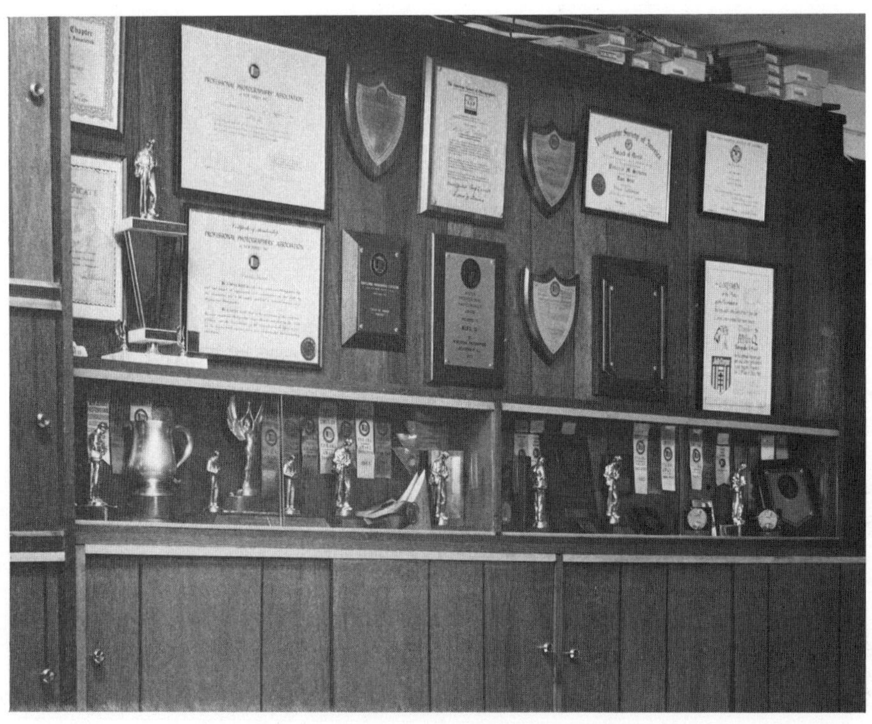

Don't hide your light under a bushel! Special photographic awards, trophies, and honors should be displayed prominently. They have as much impact on a customer as your photographs.

photographer will have little difficulty surviving provided he can develop the merchandizing tools and promotion and keep his machines rolling. Past experience indicates that the most vulnerable victim is the man in the middle. The individual serving the middle class will lose many of his patrons to the low-priced photographer.

If you have already developed a plan of action, there is an excellent chance that you can buffer drastic changes in the economy. If not, now is the time to develop one. If the situation improves, you will have lost nothing; if it deteriorates, you will not have to flounder in desperation. Because each operation is different, there can be no single plan of action that will act as a panacea. Your adapting might entail a change of location, the number of your employees, price structure, or an entirely different field or photography which is more immune to a changing economic structure. Developing a new market is one way of coping with the problem. Remember that there are markets that prosper during the worst of times.

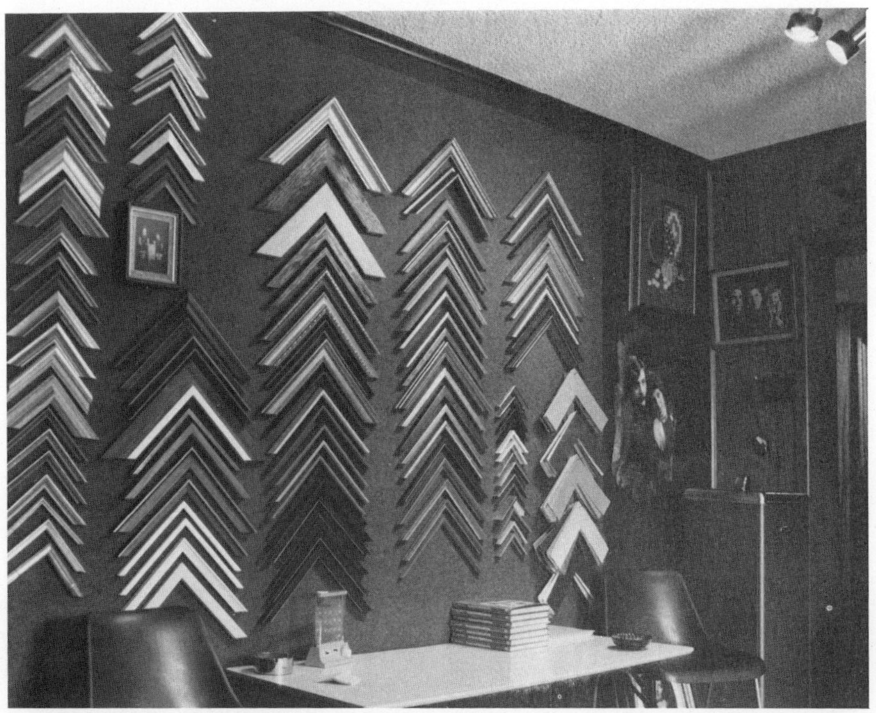

A framing wall is a silent advertiser, making customers aware of new and unusual services available.

During the Depression, there was a young photographer who was faced with supporting a wife and two children. His bleak prospects caused him to rent a pony and walk it through neighborhoods offering to photograph children seated on its back. In those days, the pictures sold for 25¢, 50¢, or $1, depending on the size and number ordered. At a time when the average factory worker earned $12–$15 a week and a house painter received $3 a day and rarely got more than two or three days work per week, this enterprising, unemployed photographer was earning $35–$50 weekly. He was able to save enough money to open a camera store when the economy improved. This is not to suggest that you run right out and buy a pony; it is mentioned simply to point out that for every problem, including recession or inflation, there is a practical solution.

On the other side of the financial coin, there was a woman photographer who had developed a great reputation photographing children. Her business supported her and two youngsters during the Depression. Circumstances and a second marriage made it unnecessary for her to remain in business, and she wanted to reduce her volume of work but not retire entirely. Since most photographers were cutting prices, she felt that a radical increase in her prices would reduce the number of sittings. Rather than decrease, in less than a year her workload had doubled. She had accidentally hit upon the fact that high-quality work was in demand even though the country was suffering a vicious depression, and that there were people who had money and would spend it if they considered the product worthwhile.

Only you can decide how best to cope in a difficult time. What you can do is to look over your financial picture and develop one or more contingency plans. And if the economy does not improve, you will be prepared and can make the best of a difficult time.

Chapter 25

Start Small and Build

Anyone wanting to make professional photography their life's work should be told that their chances of succeeding are small. National statistics show that nine out of ten people who enter the field fail within the first 18 months and suffer financial losses from $5,000–$15,000. These are not very encouraging figures. However, it is possible to make it in the field if you do so in an intelligent and planned manner. By developing one's skills to a sufficient level and understanding the basics and prerequisites for operating a business, the odds can be materially improved.

One very practical advice to the would-be photographer is that he should find work that will sustain him for one or two years. During that time, he should spend his spare time learning and practicing photography. When he has developed a fairly substantial clientele and his photographic efforts are bringing financial remuneration equal to the amount he earns in his other job, then he can practice photography full time. If the person still lives with his family and has little financial responsibility, this is an ideal opportunity to work with a studio as a trainee. In exchange for his services, the trainee is able to learn all aspects of the business. This arrangement involves more than technical knowledge and can teach the intern how to operate a business better than most schools. Not only that, but the student learns how to deal with customer situations and develops work and planning attitudes. Although few studios are willing to take the time and effort to train young people, the trend is growing and is certainly an excellent way to move into professional photography with a minimum of risk and investment of time.

Anyone attempting either of these approaches should look carefully at his personal life. If married, his mate must have a sincere interest in seeing him grow and must be willing to make sacrifices to enable him to develop into a

full-time professional. Many talented young people fail simply because of lack of support from a spouse.

PRACTICE MAKES PERFECT

Practice is the key to success in this profession, and one of the least expensive commodities used in making photographs is film. By making many pictures and many mistakes, you learn to eliminate the serious errors and not repeat them. Once you have made enough mistakes and corrected them, your work will improve. You must be able to evaluate, discuss, and take criticism. Constructive criticism can be very useful to you, while defending your position when someone suggests you are doing something wrong can be costly to you. You may win the argument but lose an opportunity to learn from your mistakes. Learn to utilize failures to help you succeed. If you don't try, you can't fail, nor can you succeed. Be adventurous. Experiment and look for new and exciting approaches. At the same time, be intelligent enough to know when you have goofed, and evaluate what has happened and why. This is the most valuable part of the learning process and can help you to develop your personal photographic approach.

THE COMPETITION

The term "competitor" has been used throughout to refer to a fellow photographer, but in many instances the term is misused and misunderstood. The mass producer of inexpensive children's photographs in department stores and malls handles a large volume of portraits but cannot really be considered as competitors. Their clientele includes couples with young children and modest incomes—people who make purchases out of need rather than out of pride of ownership. You may cater to people in a higher income bracket.

The large-volume wedding photography studios cannot deliver the same kind of product or personal attention that you deliver to a customer. Interestingly enough, in the wedding field, your competitors are the other services that compete for the dollar for that particular social event—caterers, florists, musicians, dress shops, and printers. By convincing the bride and groom that your product offers lasting sentiments and memories as compared to the other services, you will get a fairer share of the consumer dollar. If you justify the benefits a client receives from the services you render, this reduces sales resistance.

In fact, you should not consider any photographer as a competitor. Your efforts to promote your products should be directed at the consumer, not against another photographer. If you want to sell your services and products, do it by enhancing what you have to sell. Don't do it by putting down the products of others.

THE SECRET IS OUT

There are photographers who still delude themselves in believing that they are the possessors of some secret specialized knowledge shielded from the eyes of others. They also believe that transmitting this knowledge to anyone else would enable the latter to steal their business. They dissociate themselves from other photographers and feel as safe as a child clutching a security blanket. Yet such individuals are only cheating themselves. Any teacher will attest that a wealth of ideas comes from students. By communicating and exchanging ideas, each is the richer.

Photography, like any other graphic medium, is a process of constant evolution and growth. If a person can look with satisfaction at photographs he produced one or two years ago, it is obvious that he has neither grown nor advanced since that time. In order to compete today, there must be constant improvement and change in your product.

Very few fields flourish and grow without the benefits of a community of interested people who have the same goals. For this reason, you should utilize every opportunity to exchange ideas and techniques with other photographers. Whether it be in an amateur camera club or a professional association, you individually will grow and benefit in the long run from what you learn from others.

There are professionals who remark derogatorily about "amateurs," yet some of the most respected teachers of photography are people who have no particular interest in making a livelihood from photography but still retain a deep love for the craft. The word "professional" only connotes that you do photography for money. There are many amateur photographers whose craftsmanship is far superior to the average professional photographer, and many a professional stands to benefit from them.

Never stop learning about photography. The field is so vast and so full of technical and artistic information that no one person could learn it all. For this reason, constant change and growth are important. Confidence in what you produce photographically is important, but so is the inner knowledge that there is always a better, easier, more practical way, and we should all be constant seekers in the direction of self-improvement.

Appendix

LIST OF MANUFACTURERS

Diversion Dynamic Inc.
P.O. Box 5055
Santa Barbara, Calif. 93018

Eastman Kodak Company
343 State St.
Rochester, N.Y. 14650

Edmund Scientific Co.
555 Edscorp Bldg.
Barrington, N.J. 08007

Hand Krafts by Erica
24 Westbury Rd.
Iselin, N.J. 08830

Larson Enterprises Inc.
Fountain Valley, Calif. 92708

Photogenic Machine Co.
Youngstown, Ohio 44512

Photographers Specialized Services
612 Summit Ave.
Oconomowoc, Wis. 53066

Pierce Co.
9801 Nicolet
Minneapolis, Minn. 55420

Polaroid Corporation
Cambridge, Mass. 02139

Spiratone Inc.
135-06 Northern Blvd.
Flushing, N.Y. 11354

Testrite Instrument Co.
135 Monroe St.
Newark, N.J. 07105

Index